Dangerous Speech

Dangerous Speech

A Social History of Blasphemy

in Colonial Mexico

Javier Villa-Flores

The University of Arizona Press

Tucson

The University of Arizona Press
© 2006 The Arizona Board of Regents
This book is printed on acid-free, archival-quality paper.
Manufactured in the United States of America

11 10 09 08 07 06   6 5 4 3 2 1

Library of Congress Cataloging-in-Publication Data
Villa-Flores, Javier, 1966–
   Dangerous speech : a social history of blasphemy in
colonial Mexico / Javier Villa-Flores.
      p. cm.
   Includes bibliographical references (p.) and index.
   ISBN-13: 978-0-8165-2556-0 (hardcover : alk. paper)
   ISBN-10: 0-8165-2556-0 (hardcover : alk. paper)
   ISBN-13: 978-0-8165-2563-8 (pbk. : alk. paper)
   ISBN-10: 0-8165-2563-3 (pbk. : alk. paper)
      1. Blasphemy—Mexico—History. 2. Language and
languages—Religious aspects—Catholic Church—
History of doctrines. 3. Mexico—History—Spanish
colony, 1540–1810. I. Title.
BX1428.3.V55 2006
364.1'88–dc22
                                        2006009138

Publication of this book is made possible in part by
the Program for Cultural Cooperation between Spain's
Ministry of Culture and United States Universities.

To Marv and Olivia

Contents

Figures

Acknowledgments

With their support and encouragement, many people and institutions made possible the completion of this book. For their courteous aid, I am greatly indebted to the directors and staffs of the following institutions in Mexico City: the Archivo General de la Nación, the Archivo Histórico del Museo Nacional de Antropología e Historia, the Biblioteca Nacional, and the Archivo Histórico del Arzobispado de México. I also thank the personnel of the Archivo Histórico Nacional (Madrid), the Biblioteca Nacional (Madrid), the Archivo de Indias (Seville), the Newberry Library, the John Carter Brown Library, and the Huntington Library.

Several friends and scholars read or commented on portions of the manuscript over the years. I would like to thank Carlos Aguirre, Dain Borges, Nicholas Brown, Sherwin Bryant, Connie Dickinson, R. Douglas Cope, Linda Curcio-Nagy, Martha Few, Susan Fitzpatrick, Leo Garofalo, Pedro Guibovich, Katherine Hoffman, Cristina Jiménez, John Kicza, Emilio Kourí, James Krippner-Martínez, Claudio Lomnitz, Laura Matthews, Jeremy Mumford, Martin Nesvig, Frederick D. Opie, Rachel O'Toole, Robert Patch, Stafford Poole, Cristián Roa-de-la-Carrera, James Saeger, Susan Schroeder, and Bruce Tyler. I am most grateful to Christopher R. Boyer, Susan Deeds, Sonya Lipsett-Rivera, Eric Van Young, and Paul Vanderwood for their extensive comments on previous drafts. Kris Lane and another, anonymous, referee for the University of Arizona Press read the manuscript and offered valuable criticism and wise advice. Thanks also to my editor, Patti Hartmann, for believing in this project, and to Patricia Rosas, for carefully copyediting this work.

I would also like to thank the members of my dissertation committee—John A. Marino, Dain Borges, Charles L. Briggs, Eric Van Young, and Paul Vanderwood—for their encouragement and advice. I am particularly indebted to my adviser, Eric Van Young, for his guidance, constant support, and intellectual generosity. At the University of California, San Diego (UCSD), several of my fellow graduate students—María Butler,

Carlos Sánchez, Andrew Fisher, Susan Fitzpatrick, Kevin Ingram, Christina Jiménez, Alberto Loza, Curtis Martin, Kenneth Maffit, Luis Murillo, Tanalís Padilla, Gabriela Soto-Laveaga, and Ángela Vergara—offered not only their friendship and good advice over the years but also their moral support.

Initial research for this book was undertaken during the summer of 1996 with financial assistance of the Mexican Consejo Nacional de Ciencia y Tecnología (National Council for Science and Technology) and the UCSD Department of History, both of which also supported my research in Mexican archives and libraries in 1997–1998. A grant from UC–Mexus enabled me to do archival and library research in Madrid and Seville in 1998. Short-term research grants from the John Carter Brown Library, the Newberry Library, and the Huntington Library gave me the opportunity to do research in their wonderful manuscript and rare-book collections during several months in 1999 and 2000.

In 2002, a grant from the Office of the Vice Chancellor at the University of Illinois at Chicago (UIC) enabled further research in Spanish and Mexican archives. Special thanks go to the UIC Institute for the Humanities and its director, Mary Beth Rose, for the luxury of spending the whole 2002–2003 academic year revising the manuscript.

For their permission to reprint a shorter version of chapter 5, I gratefully acknowledge Duke University Press ("To Lose One's Soul: Blasphemy and Slavery in New Spain, 1596–1660" in *Hispanic American Historical Review* 82:3 [2002]: 435–468).

For their kindness, friendship, and collegiality, I also thank my colleagues in Latin American and Latino Studies at UIC: Frances Aparicio, Ralph Cintrón, Nilda Flores, Elena González, Suzanne Oboler, Joel Palka, Amalia Pallares, Cristián Roa-de-la-Carrera, and María de los Angeles Torres. Thanks also to Astrida Tantillo and Leon Fink for their mentorship and to Victor Espinosa, Fernando Leal, and Hugo Velázquez for their friendship.

Finally, I wish to thank my mother, Carmen Lucía Flores, and my numerous brothers, sisters, and nephews for their love and persistent support. My deepest gratitude goes to my wife and outstanding intellectual companion, María Eugenia de la Torre, who has encouraged and patiently endured my research. I dedicate this book to her and to my daughter, Olivia, with the hope of becoming a better historian.

Dangerous Speech

Introduction

Blasphemous Speech, Colonialism, and Danger in New Spain

> . . . in a new land, among people new to the Christian faith, and in
> such dangerous times . . .
> —A group of theologians in New Spain, 1560

On July 12, 1560, a group of theologians, appointed by the Mexican Holy Office as *calificadores* (theological consultants), were gathered at the convent of Santo Domingo in Antequera (Oaxaca) on an important mission. Dominican Fray Pedro de la Peña, Bishop Bernardo de Albuquerque, and Dominican and theology professor Alonso de Sotomayor had been asked to determine if the Inquisition should prosecute Bernardo de Biamonte, a Spanish mason and resident of Oaxaca, on blasphemy charges. The group weighed the available evidence. According to several witnesses, Biamonte had claimed that a man would not go hell for fornicating with an unmarried woman because in those circumstances, sexual intercourse was only a venial sin, which could be forgiven with holy water. He had also declared that Saint Peter had been a "great fornicator" himself, and the saint would deny entrance into heaven to anyone who had not fornicated during their life. In an even more grievous offense, Biamonte had enjoyed repeating a popular story in which Christ surprised Saint Peter having sex with a woman. "What are you doing, Peter?" asked Christ. "Multiplying [the human race], my Lord." "Good," answered Christ approvingly. "Finish as soon as possible, and come with me (*vente luego*)." In the town of Guajolotitlán, Oaxaca, Biamonte once asked an Indian to pluck a hen for him so he could cook it, but when the Indian refused, Biamonte threw the animal to the ground while exclaiming angrily, *"Pese a Dios!"* (may God regret it). The theologians found all these statements profoundly "scandalous" and recommended that Biamonte, a man with an "obvious penchant" for the sins of the flesh, be punished. They added that a harsh sentence was especially merited, since the sinful remarks had been uttered "in a new land, among people new to the Christian faith, and in such dangerous times."[1]

Written in a colonial setting, the theologians' report to the Mexican Inquisition clearly voiced the widespread conviction that blasphemous speech constituted not only a derogatory verbal assault on the Christian god, but also a profanation that could endanger the entire colonial enterprise. Although, juridically, blasphemy was a victimless crime—for who could possibly harm God?—theologians and Christian writers believed in the necessity of punishing blasphemers both to uphold society's moral standards and to deter others, as well as to assuage God's wrath, which could otherwise manifest in the form of plagues, earthquakes, and famine.[2] Such forms of divine punishment were visited not only on the offenders but also on society as a whole. Thus, understandably, defending "God's honor" was a constant concern for both the political and religious authorities and the wider Spanish population of New Spain. Secular and ecclesiastical authorities punished this crime severely, arguing that it not only dishonored God but also jeopardized Spanish colonial interests. By exposing the Indians and other subjects to examples of bad Christian behavior, blasphemy undermined the colonial enterprise's primary justification, that of Christianizing the heathens in New Spain.

Indeed, from the very outset of the wars of conquest, nationalism and providentialism were powerfully intertwined in the minds of the Spanish colonizers. Most saw the quest in the New World as one more episode in Spain's long struggle against the enemies and offenders of God's honor. "Conquest among the Indians," wrote López de Gómara in his famous dedication to Charles V in the *Historia general* (1552), "began when conquests among the Moors had finished, so that there might always be Spaniards at war with infidels."[3] Spanish providentialism was never stronger than after Charles was crowned Holy Roman Emperor (1519), reigning thenceforth over a conglomerate of lands comparable in extension only to that ruled by Charlemagne seven centuries earlier. Charles's unprecedented accumulation of titles, power, and lands clearly indicated that he was on his way to becoming "monarch of the world" and chief defender of the Catholic faith against heretical Protestantism and the Muslim threat.

At a time when Spain seemed entrusted with the providential tasks of reuniting Christendom, defeating the Turks, and even reconquering Jerusalem, it was easy to consider the wars of conquest in America as one more front in the expansion of the holy faith at the expense of the infidels. The possibility of finally converting the whole world to Christianity never seemed closer.[4] Accordingly, in 1525, Charles V ratified the harsh laws issued by Ferdinand and Isabella in 1492, which dictated that blasphemers be sentenced to imprisonment, monetary fines, piercing of the tongue, and banishment. In 1566, Philip II decreed that blasphemers be sentenced to ten years as galley slaves, thereby helping to offset the acute shortage of oarsmen brought on by the sixteenth century's many wars.[5] The Spanish decrees applied to America, but in 1516 in the Antilles and in 1526 in New Spain, the Council of the Indies issued its own rigorous laws against blasphemy, perjury, and taking God's name in vain. For his part, Hernán Cortés issued a decree against blasphemy in 1520. A few years later, fearing that players would blaspheme, Viceroy Antonio de Mendoza and Luis de Velasco forbade gambling as well.[6]

The Crown's interest in repressing blasphemous speech persisted. As the Spanish empire faced increasing challenges, its king tried to secure the favor of a god who seemed to have deserted his chosen people. With the English fleet's defeat of the Invincible Armada in 1588, the Spanish empire entered into outright decline. The Iberian kings explained this as a divine punishment for the nation's sins. In New Spain, the devastating epidemics of 1545–1546 and 1576–1579 inaugurated a century of economic contraction characterized by a sharp decrease in mining production and commercial trade with Spain. Then, in 1629, Mexico City experienced a catastrophic flood that paralyzed the city. On the European front, the trials sent by the Almighty to the Habsburgs multiplied as France declared war against Spain (1635), the Netherlands defeated the Spanish army at the Battle of the Downs (1639), Portugal became independent (1640), and Catalonia rebelled (1640–1652). In an attempt to placate God's anger and stop the empire's decline, in 1594, 1633, 1646, and 1667, the Spanish kings instructed the viceroys of colonial Mexico to severely punish *juramentos* (a type of blasphemy where the speaker swears on God's name) and other kinds of public and scandalous sins.[7]

As a strategy to promote religious conformity in the colonies from the beginning of the wars of conquest, the Spanish Crown bestowed inquisitorial powers on the clergy so that it could punish blasphemers and other transgressors. The tribunal of the Holy Office was to be manned by bishops, but because of the scarcity of clergy of this rank, in the 1522 bull, *Exponi nobis,* also known as *Omnímoda,* the pope also granted inquisitorial powers to missionaries. Thus, from 1524 to 1534, Franciscan and Dominican friars acted as ecclesiastical judges, in what is now known as the Monastic Inquisition. Starting in 1535, bishops and archbishops assumed the authority to punish religious crimes, but this lasted only until 1569, when King Philip II replaced this Apostolic Inquisition with an independent tribunal of the Holy Office. The first chief inquisitor, Pedro Moya de Contreras, did not arrive for two years, however. As in Spain, the Inquisition worked as a privileged instrument of royal control but with an important difference. In contrast to its counterpart in Spain, the Mexican Inquisition did not have jurisdiction over most of the population. Indeed, the Inquisition regularly tried Spaniards, Africans, and mixed-bloods, but following the infamous execution of the cacique, Don Carlos Ometochzin, in 1539, it was stripped of its authority to punish Indians.[8]

Despite the Inquisition's early establishment, blasphemy became one of the most recurrent crimes in Mexico. Between 1522 and 1700, the Holy Office initiated proceedings against approximately 489 individuals for blasphemy and 246 for *reniegos* (literally, "denials [of God]"; the form of blasphemy generally used by black slaves), or 6 percent of inquisitorial proceedings (which included both denunciations that never reached trial and those that were actually tried). However, between 1526 and 1530, blasphemy constituted nearly 70 percent of all inquisitorial proceedings, and during the colony's first fifty years, it accounted for almost 22 percent of all religious crimes.[9]

Why did people blaspheme? What made individuals from different social backgrounds risk human and divine punishment? What was the social force attributed to blasphemous speech and its ensuing dangers? Historians of the Holy Office in New Spain[10] have given these questions some attention, but with a few notable exceptions,[11] no one has offered a systematic treatment of blasphemous speech as a transgression, of its representation as a sin and crime, and of its repression in this Spanish colony.

This situation contrasts with the European context, where following the seminal works by Johan Huizinga and Jean Delumeau, an increasing number of historians have been debating the subject. Huizinga and Delumeau formulated divergent hypotheses for understanding the paradoxical relationship between blasphemy and Christian belief in early modern Europe.[12] Christian writers often asked: How could an individual of faith dare commit blasphemy? And why would an individual without faith bother to blaspheme? Huizinga and others have argued that blasphemous speech must be regarded as a clear sign of faith, albeit a "perverted" one, whereas followers of Delumeau have wondered if blasphemy was not an incipient but steady rebellion against the authoritarianism of the Catholic and Protestant reformers.[13]

Beyond the important issue of unbelief, legal and social historians have often studied the delimitation and repression of blasphemous speech as one more example of the perpetual battle between freedom of speech and censorship.[14] In doing so, they often cross cultural and chronological boundaries to establish unwarranted and anachronistic parallels. These range from the episode described in Leviticus 24:11, in which the son of Shelomith is sentenced to death by stoning for blaspheming the name of God, to the commotion Salman Rushdie's *Satanic Verses* (1988) created among faithful Muslims and his resulting death sentence, pronounced by Ayatollah Khomeini. Obviously, blasphemy has meant different things at different times and for different people. Think, for example, of the implications of decrying blasphemy for people who are convinced that God will punish them or their land compared to those for whom that notion of punishment is no longer a shared conviction. It is only through the study of the specific historical settings and social practices to which blasphemy responded that we can begin to unravel the complicated relationship between blasphemy, censorship, and unbelief.

This book explores the paradoxical connection between blasphemy and religious belief by analyzing the social uses of blasphemous speech among different social groups in colonial Mexico between 1520 and 1700. The Spanish colony provides a privileged window through which to explore the social tensions and the complex relationships colonizers and members of subaltern groups established with the Christian divinity in "such dangerous times." In contrast to the existing literature on blasphemy, this work contends that blasphemous speech can be not only a manifestation of deep belief and rebellion but also a powerful verbal device for multiple social purposes. Stemming from a rich religious imagination, blasphemy constituted an assault on the Catholic pantheon, one that was usually staged for others to hear. Only through the involvement of an audience does blasphemous speech becomes a forceful verbal resource "to do things with words," such as self-fashioning, resisting, and rebelling.[15]

Following the work of sociolinguists, a new generation of social historians has researched different kinds of linguistic behavior to analyze social differentiation based on race and ethnicity, gender, and social class. The

basic premise of these studies is that those parameters socially and his-
torically condition language use, and that speakers not only acquire cog-
nitive-linguistic competence but also a system of use regarding persons,
places, purposes, and situations that operate as specific social contexts in
which the speaker is to achieve communicative competence. Recent work
by ethnographers of speech has shown that far from merely *reflecting* the
social location of speakers and their audiences, linguistic practices are crucial to the *creation* of social identities along those social divides, and to the
transformation of the circumstances surrounding the verbal exchange.[16]
My discussions of blasphemy in colonial Mexico build upon these insights by analyzing the way speakers of various backgrounds resorted
to blasphemous speech in an attempt to establish a particular identity in
defiance of or compliance with the multiple social scripts of domination
articulated in terms of class, race, and gender. In this way, blasphemy constituted a forceful and even dramatic way of manifesting estrangement
from the Christian community. It could defy gendered morality or be a
tool for gender assertiveness. It could constitute an attack on the Divinity, provoking fear and scandal, or it could be a strategy for attempting to
"negotiate" directly with God in the presence of others.

In all these cases, the social alchemy that allowed the blasphemers "to
do things with words" rested not upon the utterers themselves but upon
their audiences, the neighbors, bystanders, and others who provoked the
intervention of the Holy Office by denouncing the sinful cursing. In this
sense, I examine blasphemous speech as a kind of deprecatory language
that was not only aimed *at* the deities of the Catholic pantheon but also
staged *for* an audience. In examining the instrumental uses of blasphemy
in the interface of class, gender, and race relations in New Spain, this work
places a strong emphasis on the analysis of the dialogic settings in which
blasphemous utterances were produced, and on the repressive institutions in which those blasphemies were later repeated and reported. My
analysis is based on archival material gathered in Mexico, Spain, and the
United States on the Inquisition's prosecution of blasphemers. In order
to contextualize those sources, I also consulted confession manuals, sermons, religious treatises, emblem books, inquisitorial manuals, and contemporary laws on blasphemy, all of which addressed the seriousness of
this crime and the pressing need to punish the transgressors. The analysis
is anchored in some basic assumptions about the meanings that theologians and moralists attached to blasphemous speech, the jurisdictional
competence of colonial authorities to punish this transgression, the pun-

ishments established by ecclesiastical and secular normative legislation, and the process of denunciation to the Holy Office.

A Sin of the Tongue

To the extent that it constituted a religious transgression, theologians and moralists generally defined blasphemy as a "sin of the tongue." In the early days of Christianity, theologians advanced two conceptions of this verbal crime: Augustine in *Contra mendacium* stressed that "in blaspheming, false things are spoken of God himself."[17] Such "falsities" can be understood as attributing to God something he is not, denying an attribute that belongs only to him, or usurping a divine prerogative. Aymon d'Auxerre defined blasphemy as a verbal offense or insult against God.[18] Seeing that these two definitions were not antithetical, later Christian writers, most notably, Thomas Aquinas, attempted to reconcile them. Aquinas defined blasphemy as an insult against God, disparaging his divine goodness. This took three forms: attributing to God any characteristic that does not conform to his nature (which later commentators deemed a crime against his mercy); denying to God attributes that belong only to him (a crime against his justice); or ascribing to a creature qualities that conformed only to God (a crime against his majesty).[19] By adding, subtracting, or misattributing God's properties, the blasphemer falsely represents God's nature, disparages him, and attacks his honor. As Edwin Craun comments on Aquinas's definition, "Since God is a being, to speak falsely of him is to defame him, especially when what is represented is his moral nature or his stature."[20] Besides falsely slandering God, blasphemous speech could defile God's honor by addressing him disrespectfully. Thus, insults and verbal assaults—such as swearing by Christ's limbs, abjuring or renouncing God, or giving oneself to the devil—were also deemed blasphemous not because of the actual meaning of these expressions but on account of the irreverent way in which God was addressed by his creatures.[21] Similarly blasphemous were expressions that attacked the Virgin, the saints, or sacred things, such as the baptismal Chrism, for they redounded to God as their creator and giver of sanctity.[22] Although there were attempts to expand the definition of blasphemy to nonverbal behavior, such as attacking holy images or worshipping idols—as was the case during the early days of the wars of conquest in Mexico—theologians and moralists generally restricted blasphemy's definition to a form of derogatory speech.[23]

As a sin, blasphemy differed significantly from heresy in theological terms. According to Aquinas and later writers, the heretic embraces an opinion contrary to Christian dogma without necessarily attempting to slander God or detract from his goodness. The heretic was often convinced that he or she was honoring God.[24] Thus, heresy was considered an intellectual error, not an attempt to disparage the Divinity. Blasphemy, on the other hand, was fundamentally a malicious effort to harm God. As theologians frequently put it, blasphemy is not a sin against the Christian faith, but against the confession of that faith, that is, against the reverence and piety expected of all professed Christians vis-à-vis their God.[25]

This distinction notwithstanding, theologians also differentiated between non-heretical blasphemy and heretical blasphemy. The first kind was merely imprecatory or contumelious, as, for example, *"Por vida de Dios!"* (by God's life). The second involved a declaration against the Christian faith, as in the utterances *"No creo en Dios!"* (I don't believe in God) or *"Reniego de Dios!"* (I renounce God). However, habitual and contumacious blasphemers could also be accused of heresy, which complicated these theological distinctions.[26]

Beyond the manner in which God was addressed and the content of the utterances, theologians and moralists were particularly concerned about blasphemers' intentions. Indeed, if intent was the most important aspect of a sin, then it was of paramount importance to establish the role of personal will in blaspheming and the blasphemer's degree of awareness of the affront to God. Although inquisitors seemed to have assumed that words were the "sonorous double"[27] of the speaker's soul, and thus reflected his or her intentions, they also paid attention to the specific circumstances in which a blasphemy occurred. Thus, blasphemy could be classified as a venial sin if produced in anger or drunkenness. Yet, theologians distinguished between legitimate and illegitimate motives of anger and degrees of drunkenness. Getting angry to defend one's religion, for instance, was considered most praiseworthy, but bursting into anger when losing money at the gaming table was always sinful.[28] Similarly, anger could never be an excuse to express heretical blasphemies, such as *"No hay Dios!"* (there is no God).[29] Although drunkenness could also be advanced as a mitigating circumstance, Christian writers believed that only those who were completely drunk could possibly ignore the magnitude of their sinful utterances.[30] Finally, if the transgressor was aware of the sense of what he or she expressed, the blasphemy would be considered a mortal sin and even be taken as evidence of a perverse will to insult

God.[31] From the perspective of Aquinas, this would constitute a "perfect" or fully accomplished blasphemy, for the blasphemer not only had a false idea about God but also verbalized it with the intention of affecting the way others perceived the Divinity.[32]

In addressing the subject's responsibility for blasphemy, Christian writers warned the faithful about the need to control their own tongues, that "flabby little organ" whose malign potential rendered it capable of endangering and defiling both the individual and the entire society. Indeed, like the remora, a tiny fish thought to be capable of stopping a ship in full sail, the wandering tongue could keep the faithful from salvation for it exerted "an influence far out of proportion for its size."[33] Reflecting common anxieties about the difficulty of controlling injurious speech, early modern moralists frequently depicted the tongue as endowed with a life of its own. In his famous *De lingua* (1525), a highly influential treatise on the sins of the tongue, Erasmus imagined a dialogue in which a man reproaches his unruly member whenever it is about to engage in sinful and contumelious speech: "Where are you going tongue? Where? . . . Are you preparing to do good or evil?"[34] The imaginary conversation evidenced the ambivalent status of the tongue as the best and worst of bodily members. As Carla Mazzio has pointed out, the tongue was imagined as being capable of "pulling in two directions at the same time."[35] Given the potential depravity of the tongue, moralists recommended containment as the only possible way of guaranteeing virtuous speech and achieving moral excellence.

Ottavio Scarlatini's *Homo et eius partes figuratus* (1680) contains a good example of this Christian ideal. An emblem portrays the tongue as detached from the body but standing still under the careful surveillance of the eye. The emblem's motto reads *dilucidus sermo* (clear speech), thus intimating that the man who controls his tongue (here represented in quasi-phallic form) has reached perfection in speech. The king, as the supreme patriarch and a representative of God on earth, was expected to resemble God's awe-inspiring *brevitas* (conciseness) not only by avoiding all effeminizing loquacity but also by being a model of self-control for his people.[36]

Following this patriarchal ideal of moral perfection through speech control, moralists in colonial Mexico encouraged men not only to "bridle" their tongues but also those of their subordinates—women, children, and slaves—who were deemed "incapable" of censoring themselves and thus in need of constant surveillance. In practice, it was free men who most commonly fell short of the patriarchal ideals of verbal self-control, and punishing

"Dilucidus Sermo" (clear speech). Although detached from the body, the tongue stands still under the surveillance of the eye. The man who controls his tongue reaches perfection in speech. From Scarlatini, *Homo et eius partes figuratus*. (Courtesy Lilly Library, Indiana University, Bloomington, IN)

them became a priority in order to avoid endangering the Spanish colonial enterprise. But, who had the jurisdictional competence to punish the transgressors?

Jurisdiction over Blasphemy

Under canon law, blasphemy was regarded as a *mixti fori* crime, that is, punishable by both spiritual and secular courts.[37] In New Spain, the Audiencias (the secular high courts), the *provisores* (ecclesiastical judges) and bishops, and the Inquisition all had the authority to punish blasphemy.[38] This entailed the possibility of a double punishment for the transgressor. If the ecclesiastical judge learned of the crime first and punished the blasphemer lightly, the secular judge could rightly try the transgressor anew and impose a harsher sentence.[39] Another area of overlapping jurisdiction related to the two categories of blasphemy, "heretical" and "non-heretical." In Mexico, secular and ecclesiastical judges had the power to forgive non-heretical blasphemy, but only the Inquisition had jurisdiction over cases of heretical blasphemy. Although confessors could forgive non-heretical blasphemy, they were expected to "forward" cases of heretical blasphemy to the Inquisition. Some confessors were learned enough to know the difference between the two kinds of blasphemy, as evidenced by cases in which a priest refused to absolve a parishioner and advised him or her to self-denounce before the Holy Office. However, the distinction between the two types of blasphemy was not always clear, and in practice, the Inquisition sometimes tried non-heretical cases. In 1534, the Cortes of Madrid requested that non-heretical blasphemy cases be tried by the secular courts exclusively. Nevertheless, the Inquisition continued to intervene in these cases for many years.[40]

The Levitical Codes prescribed death by stoning for the offense of heretical blasphemy. An example is the blasphemy by Shelomith's son: "If anyone curses his God, he will be held responsible; anyone who blasphemes the name of the LORD must be put to death. The entire assembly must stone him. Whether an alien or native-born, when he blasphemes the Name, he must be put to death" (Leviticus 24:15–16).[41] Although less harsh, canon law on blasphemy was still severe. In the *Decretals* (1236), Pope Gregory IX condemned the transgressors to stand before the door of the church during mass for seven Sundays. On the final Sunday, they were to stand shoeless with a rope about their necks. Additional punishments included fasting, monetary fines, imprisonment, and giving alms to the poor. In the Fourth Lateran Council (1214), Pope Leon X ordered confessors to impose heavy penances on those who blasphemed God and his holy mother, a mandate that was commonly repeated even in sixteenth- and seventeenth-century confession manuals.[42] During the Council of Trent (1545–1563), Counter-reformists considered it necessary to draw a clearer line between sacred and profane to undermine what was deemed to be people's excessive familiarity with holy matters. This led to a revitalization of the rigorous punishment for crimes, as dictated by the ancient laws. In his constitution *Cum Primum*

Apostolatus (1566), Pius V launched a harsh campaign against all blasphemy by establishing that those found guilty of this crime were to be fined, ordered to stand before the church-door with their hands tied behind them, flogged, imprisoned, or sentenced to work on the galley ships.[43]

Starting with the Justinian Code (535–540), which punished blasphemy with death, secular authorities had also exhibited a keen interest in castigating this crime. A famous decree by Louis IX (1263) ordered contumacious blasphemers to be branded on the forehead and recidivists to have their lips and tongues pierced. On the urging of Clement IV, the French king reduced the severity of corporal punishment, but punitive mutilation of blasphemers was reinstated by his successors: Philip the Bold (1271), Philip VI of France (1347), Charles VI (1397), Charles VII (1437 and 1460), Charles VIII (1486 and 1487), and Louis XII (1510).[44] In early modern Italy, punishing this crime was a matter of state concern. In Venice, for instance, the infamous committee of the "Executors against Blasphemy" was particularly active arresting individuals who were denounced by their neighbors through the lion-shaped letterboxes, known as the "mouths of truth."[45]

Spain also had a long punitive tradition against blasphemy. In 1245, King Alphonse IX decreed monetary fines for noblemen and burghers and flogging for the destitute. He established fifty lashes for the first offense, branding the lips with the letter "B" for the second offense, and cutting out the tongue for three-time offenders. Clearly, equality before the law was an unknown concept at the time, and the Iberian tribunals distributed sentences according to the race, social status, occupation, and even gender of the defendants, a practice that was later extended to the Spanish colonies. In Bribiesca in 1387, King Juan I decreed one hundred lashes and cutting out the tongue as punishment for blaspheming God or the Virgin Mary in the royal court or within a five-league radius of the palace. King Ferdinand and Queen Isabella confirmed this law in 1476, and they also authorized any person overhearing a blasphemer to take that transgressor to the public prison. Almost twenty years later, in 1492, the Catholic kings issued a new law punishing first-time blasphemers with one month of imprisonment. Subsequent offenses carried monetary fines, piercing of the tongue, and banishment.[46] As the empire came to face greater economic and political challenges, the Spanish Crown, and its representatives in colonial Mexico, would ratify and even expand these laws.

Denouncing Blasphemy: A Derivative Competence

Because punishing blasphemy was necessary for the well-being of the Christian community, theologians and moralists encouraged the faithful to denounce transgressors. In the Fourth Lateran Council (1214), Pope Julius III mandated that Christians denounce blasphemers. He even decreed punishments for those who refused to make a denunciation to the ecclesiastical authorities. In colonial Mexico, the Holy Office instructed people to report blasphemy during the promulgation of the Edict of Faith, which was supposed to occur every three years, on a Sunday in Lent or a feast day. The edict contained a detailed description of various crimes. Under penalty of excommunication, the audience was given six days to denounce anyone who possessed heretical books; was a follower of Mohammedanism, Protestantism, and Mystic Illuminism; or had committed crimes of blasphemy, witchcraft, bigamy, perjury, solicitation of women in confession, divination, or astrology. In the smaller towns, the *comisarios* (local representative of the Inquisition) were to read this proclamation aloud to the faithful.[47] In practice, however, the publication of the Edict of Faith was highly irregular because of sheer negligence and repeated conflicts between religious and secular authorities over matters of etiquette and social precedence. Nevertheless, preachers actively encouraged their parishioners to accuse people they had overheard blaspheming, and priests sometimes refused to grant absolution unless their penitents denounced the culprit or agreed to present themselves before the Holy Office if they themselves were the transgressors.[48]

Denunciations were crucial in blasphemy cases because, in a strict sense, it was not in the mouth of the utterer that blasphemy "originated," but on the lips of the denouncer. Indeed, in colonial Mexico, denouncers triggered a "blasphemy affair" by utilizing their own "religious competence" (generally a concern with "the honor of God") to interpret the blasphemy and then report it to the Inquisition.[49] Of course, the Inquisitors reserved for themselves the power to decide what was and was not blasphemous speech and to ponder the circumstances under which the crime was committed. As a consequence, not all denunciations resulted in prosecutions. Denouncers seem to have understood that their competence was subordinate to that of the Inquisition, since in describing the verbal transgressions when making the report, they frequently used terms such as *disparates* (atrocious remarks), *disonancias* (literally, dissonances; discordant or cacophonous speech), and *palabras escandalosas* (scandalous words) instead of the perhaps more doctrinal term *blasfemias and juramentos*. Similarly, the use of euphemisms that substituted *"tal"* for *"Dios,"* such as *pese a tal* (may so-and-so regret it) or *por vida de tal* (by the life of so-and-so), allowed the witnesses to denounce well-known expressions without repeating them exactly.[50] Moreover, it was not unusual to consult with priests and confessors, the "specialists" on religious matters, before deciding to go to the Holy Office.[51]

Although it was uncommon, some blasphemers denounced themselves to preempt a harsher punishment from the colonial authorities. Unfortunately, this stratagem did not always work. For instance, during the early years of the colony, several blasphemers confessed their crimes to priests and friars and were told to do penance, only to find out later that these clerics had no authority to forgive them.

Once a denunciation was received, the Inquisition investigated the charges in detail. The calificadores (appointed by the Mexican Holy Office) determined whether the evidence collected warranted prosecution. If so, an order was issued to arrest the culprit and confiscate part of his or her property. The identity of the denouncer and the charges were not disclosed to the defendant, so that when asked if they knew the reason for their trial, prisoners sometimes confessed to a crime different from the one the Inquisitors were prosecuting. After gathering additional evidence, the *fiscal* (prosecutor) articulated the charges, to which the defendant replied. Then, the Holy Office appointed a lawyer for the defense. Although uncommon, the Inquisition occasionally resorted to torture to obtain confessions from those suspected of major heresy.

After spending months (sometimes years) confined in the Inquisition prison, the accused was sentenced. In passing their verdict, the Inquisitors normally considered not only the seriousness of the crime but also the prisoner's social standing and willingness to repent. Offenders could be condemned to abjure their crimes *de levi* (for minor offenses) or *de vehementi* (for grievous ones). Although major heretics faced the possibility of being *relajados* (literally, "relaxed," that is, released to the state authorities) to be burned at the stake, blasphemers were normally sentenced to spiritual penance; scourging; public disgrace; forced labor in textile workshop, presidios, or on galley ships; or even exile. Sentences were often announced in an auto-da-fé, an elaborate private or public ceremony in which the culprits were displayed wearing penitential garb that included sanbenitos, *corozas* (cone-shaped hats), and gags. Designed to represent Judgment Day through an imposing drama of punishment and redemption, public autos were regularly attended by both secular and religious authorities to celebrate the Inquisition's achievements and promote religious conformity.[52]

Following traditional procedure, the delinquent was first required to publicly abjure the crime. Like other sorts of public apologies, public autos-da-fé were meant to ease the reincorporation of the individual into the body of the faithful and to symbolically restore the dominant power relationships by showing that the culprit publicly accepted "the judgment of . . . [the Holy Office] that this is an offense and thus, implicitly, the censure of punishment that follows from it."[53] Next, the now "infamous individuals," regardless of their gender, were placed on a beast of burden naked to the waist, gagged, and carrying a rope. In that state, they were paraded through the "customary streets," while a crier announced their transgression. They were then lashed, with offenders from the lower social echelons generally receiving a greater number of lashes than would their higher-ranking counterparts. It truly was a moment in which, "social values [were] not so much inculcated into the subject as etched upon the subject's body."[54] Not surprisingly, from the time the first auto-da-fé occurred in 1574, blasphemers were frequently punished in these edifying ceremonies.

Organization of the Book

This book is organized in five chapters, each dedicated to a different aspect of the use, prosecution, and representation of blasphemous speech in sixteenth- and seventeenth-century Mexico. Rather than building a chronological narrative, each chapter addresses a distinct facet of blasphemy with the purpose of offering the reader a sense of the many *simultaneous* ways in which different groups in colonial Mexican society used blasphemous speech. I analyze diachronically the changes in representation, prosecution, and punishment of blasphemous speech, but the specificity of the discourses, practices, and social scripts is discussed synchronically, in terms of the racial, gender, and class divisions in colonial Mexico.

In the first chapter, I discuss blasphemy and the Spanish imperialistic rhetoric that fashioned the conquest of Mexico as a holy enterprise to restore God's honor and God's right to be honored in New Spain. The Spaniards justified their armed intervention by constructing the idolatrous Indians as blasphemers, on the grounds that they showed Satan the honor that belonged only to God. The representation of the Indians as blasphemers did not survive after the first few years of conquest, however. Soon Franciscan and Dominican friars leveled that same charge against Spanish men, who blasphemed the God they were supposed to honor and whose excesses and brutality forced the Indians to "blaspheme" (that is, to reject) the Christian deity.

Chapter 2 discusses the fierce campaigns against Spaniards who had the audacity to endanger not only themselves but also the entire colony by blaspheming "with little fear of God." In discussing blasphemy as a performative anchor of male identity, this chapter explores in detail the relationship between this kind of deprecatory speech and male bonding in professions characterized by toughness and high mobility, such as muleteers, sailors, and soldiers.

Chapter 3 discusses the recurrent use of blasphemy by gamblers, through an exploration of the prevalent belief that gambling depended on God's will, not on the whim of chance. At a time when God's omnipotence was strongly emphasized, gamblers' angry reactions offer an interesting window through which to explore the widespread providentialism that prevailed in New Spain and the pervasive conviction that God's hand intervened in earthly affairs, ranging from the most insignificant turn of cards to the most devastating earthquakes, plagues, and floods.

Chapters 4 and 5 analyze blasphemous speech among subordinated groups, particularly Spanish and Creole women and Afro-Mexican slaves. In chapter 4, I explore the use of blasphemy by women in light of the gender conventions that related chastity and obedience with female control of speech. I explain that inquisitorial trials show that women resorted to blasphemy in order to make forceful statements aimed at fighting those who defiled their honor, defamed them, or unjustly confined them. Although women succeeded in commanding the attention of their audiences and even drawing the intervention of the Holy Office, they seriously compromised their status as Christians through their subversion of the gendered moral expectations that demanded verbal restraint in a pious woman.

Finally, in chapter 5, I analyze the use of blasphemy by slave men and women as a strategy to resist unbearable physical punishment at the hands of their masters. Claiming before the Inquisition to have blasphemed on account of cruel and unjust chastisement, Afro-Mexicans tried to find some leverage against their masters by displacing the responsibility onto them. In this sense, slaves used their "integration" into the Christian community to fight the abuses deriving from their marginality in a slaveholders' society.

In analyzing the different social uses and unintended consequences of blasphemous speech in colonial Mexico, this book departs from traditional anthropological analyses of "taboo words," which generally see the production of blasphemy as the result of a primitive and "naive confidence that one is in possession of a verbal formula which is bound to produce the desired effect."[55] The key to the social efficacy of blasphemous speech cannot be found in discourse itself, for there is little to learn from a catalogue of expressions removed from their historical context and the particular circumstances that imbued them with meaning and value. As Pierre Bourdieu wrote some time ago, to look within words for the power of words implies treating language as an autonomous object entirely detached from the social conditions in which it is employed.[56] Far from exhibiting a blind confidence in the "magical power" of blasphemous words, slaves, soldiers, seamen, gamblers, and women made use of blasphemy based on their knowledge of the colonial institutions, practices of punishment and denunciation, and discourses of Christian salvation that gave social force to their expletives.

In citing sixteenth- and seventeenth-century documents, I have kept the original spelling of names. Quotations of excerpts from Inquisition proceedings and other primary sources also respect the orthography and syntax of the original. Unless noted otherwise, all translations are mine.

1

From Defenders of God's Honor to Blasphemers

Blasphemy and the Rhetoric of Empire

> Those who honor me I will honor, but those who despise me will be
> disdained.
> —1 Samuel 2:30

> For, as it is written, the name of God is blasphemed among the
> Gentiles because of you.
> —Romans 2:24

*D*uring the final days of 1520, Cortés and his decimated army
arrived at Tlaxcala for a brief rest before undertaking the final campaign
against Tenochtitlán. They had barely overcome the sense of loss and un-
certainty following their defeat on the Noche Triste. No longer the master
of a new empire recently won for his king, Cortés was finding it harder
than ever to obtain royal approbation for his unconventional proceedings
in Mexico. Yet, in his *Second Letter*, penned in October in Tepeaca, Cortés
was bold enough to assure Charles V that the defeat had been only a temporary setback. Moctezuma, donating his realm to the king across the ocean,
had purportedly submitted voluntarily to Charles, and Cortés declared that
he would soon recover what legally belonged to Spain. The conquistador
quoted a now famous welcome speech, made in Tenochtitlán on November
18, 1519. In it, the master of Anáhuac identified Cortés as the descendant of
a great lord who had led the Mexica to the Valley of Mexico but who later
abandoned them. "We have always held that those who descended from him
would come and conquer this land and take us as their vassals," declared
Moctezuma, who then surrendered his domains to Cortés. As a result of this
astounding *translatio imperii* (transfer of rule), Cortés was able not only

to legitimate Charles V's claims to sovereignty over this territory but also to refashion his continuing military campaign as a reconquest. Needless to say, the Mexica, when they resisted the Spaniards on the Noche Triste, were regarded as being guilty of rebellion.[1]

Besides indulging the Iberian monarch's narcissism, the translatio imperii staged by Cortés brought several advantages for furthering Spain's imperial interests in America. It provided the king with a legal basis for his rule over Mexico by asserting that the Mexica Indians "voluntarily submitted" to the Iberian sovereign.[2] The translatio imperii also offered an alternative to the papal donation made in the 1493 bull Inter Caetera, which had been the Spanish Crown's principal claim to dominion in America. Pope Alexander VI's bulls assumed that the supreme pontiff was empowered to act as a temporal lord over both Christians and the heathen, something jurists and theologians found contrary to natural law.[3] In contrast, Cortés had been able to present his royal master with a way to assert jurisdiction over New Spain on secular grounds alone.[4] Whereas the bull Inter Caetera had sanctioned Spanish possession of the West Indies as part of the extension of the Christian world, Moctezuma's donation of his empire supported Charles's attempts to combine church authority and state power within the all-encompassing ideology of universal divine kingship, embodied in his own person.[5] Moreover, at a time in which Castile had become the capital of Christendom, the idea of "reconquering" lands previously "possessed" by Spain offered the additional incentive of establishing a chauvinistic continuity between Spain's national crusade against the infidels and its imperial ambitions overseas. It was only natural that Castilians like Cortés would see themselves as a chosen people, endowed with the superior mission of defending God's honor—and God's right to be honored—in the New World.[6]

Still lacking royal approval, however, Cortés decided to invoke the reconquest argument one more time before moving back into the Valley of Mexico. On December 22, he addressed his troops when issuing a series of ordinances to regulate his soldiers' conduct so that they could better serve God and king in New Spain. He told his men that the main purpose of Spanish warfare was to convert the infidels and redress the "disservice" that the Indians had done to God by worshipping the devil in his place. Following on this premise, Cortés's first ordinance prohibited his men from offending the god they were supposed to serve. Whoever uttered expressions like *"No creo en Dios!"* (I don't believe in God), *"Pese a Dios!"* (may God regret it), or *"Reniego de Dios!"* (I renounce God) would be condemned to pay a penalty of fifteen gold *castellanos* (a Spanish coin). Through its piety, the ordinance was intended to attract much needed sympathy in the highest Spanish circles for Cortés's cause. It was also intended to avert the possible dangers awaiting his men in the New World as a result of this crime. Blasphemy, Cortés clearly stated in his ordinances, "is the worst offense possible made to his most holy name, and this is why he allows people to be harshly punished [for it]."[7] Cortés himself had been admonished in a similar way in the instructions he received from Diego de Velázquez before his departure for Mexico in February 1519: "You must bear in mind from the beginning that the first aim of your expedition is to serve God and spread the Christian Faith. You must not, therefore, permit any blasphemy or lewdness of any kind, and all who violate this injunction should be publicly admonished and punished."[8] The prohibition against blaspheming was a precept a Castilian hidalgo and Christian knight was expected to follow, as is clear from the injunctions included in the *Siete Partidas* (1256–1263), a medieval code of military and legal conduct and an encyclopedia of law and theology, with which Cortés was familiar. Accordingly, decrees against blasphemy would frequently be issued before launching future *entradas* (military campaigns) in New Spain.[9]

Fighting for God's Honor: Idolatry as Blasphemy

If Cortés deemed it necessary to remind his soldiers of the requirement of honoring God's name, he also encouraged them to take up arms to avenge "offenses" committed by the Indians against God. On several occasions, Cortés told his companions that, as Christians, they had the duty of waging war against the "enemies of our Faith." Yet, in one of those instances, López de Gómara's account has Cortés adding to his habitual harangue that the Spaniards were obliged to uproot idolatry, "that great *blasphemy* against our God."[10]

The accusation of blasphemy against the natives is strange because it not only charged them with the same sin Spaniards committed but also, as López de Gómara probably knew, Christian theology considered idolatry and blasphemy to be two distinct sins. According to Aquinas, idolatry consisted in according divine honor to entities that are not God, thus constituting a sin against the first commandment. Blasphemy, on the other hand, denoted the (generally verbal) derogation of the honor due to God through malediction, reproach, or contumely pronounced against him, thus constituting a sin related to the second commandment. Although clearly differentiated, both sins related to the honor owed to God, which

is either "misplaced" (idolatry) or derogated (blasphemy). Aquinas himself left open the possibility of linking or even conflating these two sins
by distinguishing three ways of committing blasphemy: (a) attributing to
God something that does not pertain to him or is not consistent with his
nature (for example, saying "God is cruel"); (b) denying God something
that pertains to him ("God is not just"); or (c) attributing to an entity a
characteristic that pertains only to God.[11]

As we can see, this last form of blasphemy seems to be the point of
contact between the two religious crimes. It is likely, however, that Gómara—and probably Cortés himself—thought of idolatry as an act rejecting
God, which, in itself constituted a blasphemy (as in Ezekiel 20:27, where
the Israelites were told that by worshipping idols of "wood and stone,"
"your fathers have blasphemed me"). However, was it possible to claim
that the Indians had rejected God before they knew anything about him?
This became a major issue in the ensuing debate about the legitimacy
of the wars of conquest. Yet, during these first decades, warfare in New
Spain was justified both in defensive terms—as a response to the Indians'
"offenses" against the Christian god—and as a way to secure conversions
to Christianity. These aims were intertwined in Cortés's military campaign against the idolaters, as was clearly shown by an episode during the
summer of 1519 in Tepeaca.

Around mid-August in Cempoala, Cortés asked his troops after a pe-
remptory speech: "How are we to accomplish anything good if we don't
fight for God's honor (volvemos por la honra de dios)?" (my italics).[12] He
had just ordered the Cempoalans "to give up their idols" and allow the
Spaniards to dash the native gods to the ground. The moment was tense,
because the Indians did not simply refuse to comply but were ready to fight.
Yet, on Cortés's orders, fifty Spaniards ran up the steep steps of the temple
and hastily cast down the effigies. Later, in what would become a common
practice in the conquest, the Indians were ordered to whitewash the walls of
the temple. Then, the Spaniards deposited an image of the Virgin and Child
on the altar and brought in a big cross on a stand, after which, a priest said
mass. Surprisingly, the Spaniards put eight native priests and an old Spanish
soldier in charge of the Christian icons.[13]

The phrase that triggered this fierce scene of iconoclasm, *volver por la
honra de Dios*, had a double meaning in sixteenth-century Spain. It meant
to struggle for the honor *owed* to God as an acknowledgment of his power,
sanctity, and precedence, as well as carrying the meaning of avenging God
when he was not duly revered. The reference to precedence, characteristically

emphasized by anthropologists of Mediterranean societies, arises because God, like any other great lord, can be offended if he is not rendered due respect.[14] The Indians, it was widely believed, offended the Christian god by venerating the devil, attributing to him divine properties that *belonged only to God*.[15] Of course, the greater the magnificence of the temples dedicated to Satan, the bigger was the "disservice" the natives rendered to the Christian God. In this context, Cortés's act of replacing idols with crosses and icons seems to be endowed with the symbolic force of redirecting to God the reverence rightly owed to him. Moreover, since la honra de Dios meant both the honor owed to God and the honor God bestows on men, Cortés apparently believed that his actions would earn him the honor and prestige once reserved for the Christian knights in Spain, by virtue of the much-quoted promise of divine reciprocity: "Those who honor me I will honor, but those who despise me will be disdained" (1 Samuel 2:30).[16]

Although Spaniards seemed to believe that the Christian images were capable of inducing reverence by themselves, Cortés and his men were careful to place them in spaces that the indigenous people regarded as sacred and to leave them under the care of native priests.[17] This surprising gesture implied that the Spaniards were not only interested in colonizing the sacred geography of New Spain but also were attempting to "capture" the devotional patterns of the Indians for the service of the Christian god. In the eyes of the Spaniards, although the Indians appeared to revere Satan, they also lived "in a more civilized and reasonable manner than any other people" yet seen in the New World.[18] Ironically, the natives' idolatry itself was proof that these societies exhibited high levels of complexity and civilized conduct that could be redirected to Christianity. In his *First Letter* (1519), Cortés urged his king to convert the Indians to the Catholic faith so that "the devotion, trust, and hope that they have in these their idols [would be] transferred (*conmutada*) to the divine power of God; for it is certain that if they were to worship the true God with such fervor, faith, and diligence, they would perform many miracles."[19]

In this sense, to fight for God's honor implied not only fierce iconoclasm to avenge blasphemy but also a transfer of devotion from the demonic idol to the Christian god. Without reverence, there is no power,[20] and if God were to regain his "jurisdiction" in the New World, the Spaniards would have to reverse the blasphemous rejection of him that was implied in honoring the Evil One as if he had divine properties. Interestingly, Cortés's ambition of restoring God's dominion over the New World through an act of "transference" was later mirrored when the conquistador delivered to Charles V the land that he "legitimately" owned as a result of the questionable translatio imperii.

Blasphemy, Violence, and Just War

Despite Cortés's best efforts, not everybody in the Spanish elite was convinced that the Indians' idolatry was an act of blasphemy, that violence and destruction were needed to convert the natives to Christianity, and that Spanish soldiers were defending God's honor in the New World. Some Christian writers, notably certain Dominicans, even charged that their countrymen, by their violent actions, were inciting the Indians to reject the Europeans' religion and to "blaspheme" the Christian god. The unprecedented conquests between 1519 and 1532 revealed for the first time the highly developed cultures of Mexico and Peru, but this coincided with a growing tendency among theologians and legal experts to severely scrutinize the Spanish right to conquer and colonize the New World.[21]

Dominican Francisco de Vitoria was among those appalled by the enormous increase in excesses that accompanied Spanish expansion. In a famous letter to fellow Dominican Miguel de Arcos, Vitoria expressed his anger after receiving news of the recent massacre at Cajamarca and the execution of Inca Emperor Atahualpa (July 1533): "No business shocks me or embarrasses me more than the corrupt profits and affairs of the Indies. Their very mention freezes the blood in my veins." He condemned the cupidity of his countrymen, arguing that since those lands belonged to the Indians according to natural law, the only way in which Spaniards could legitimately claim these lands was by acquiring them as the spoils of a just war. And yet, as far as Vitoria understood, these people had never done "the slightest injury to the Christians, nor given them the least ground for making war on them."[22]

Vitoria also found the traditional accusation of religious infidelity to be an insufficient excuse for attacking and depriving the peoples of the New World of their natural rights. In *Relectio de Indiis* (1539), the Dominican claimed that since the rights of property and dominion depended not on God's grace but on his laws—hence the illegitimacy of the papal donation—the Indians' idolatry was not a legitimate pretext for dispossessing the natives of their lands. Besides, the Indians had known nothing of Christ before the arrival of the Spaniards, so they should be considered as "invincibly ignorant." In contrast to Muslims and Jews—who were "vincibly ignorant" for having received but then, in free will, having rejected the Christian message—the peoples of the New World were not *inimicos Christi* (enemies of Christ).[23] In Vitoria's eyes, the Spaniards could wage a "just war" against the Indians if one of three rights was obstructed: to travel and "trade" in the Indies (*ius peregrinandi*); to preach Christianity (*ius predicandi*); or to defend the innocent against tyranny. Depriving anyone of those rights constituted an injury, the vindication of which would justify war.[24] Vitoria discussed other grievances that also might justify waging war against the peoples of the New World, including blasphemy. Yet, he defined this crime in terms clearly unsuitable to the American context:

> If the barbarians were *publicly* to blaspheme against Christ, they could be compelled to desist from such blasphemies. This is conceded by the doctors and is true; we could declare war upon them if they put the Crucifix in ridicule, or in any way abused or ashamed Christian things, for instance by mockery of the sacraments of the Church or things of this kind. This is obvious, because if they were to do wrong to a Christian king, we would be empowered to avenge the wrong, even after the king were dead; so much more so, then, if they insult Christ, who is the king and Lord of Christians (my italics).[25]

In contrast to other offenses, such as cannibalism, sodomy, and human sacrifice, which Vitoria believed only God should punish as crimes against nature, not against men, the theologian considered it the Spaniards' Christian duty to defend "God's honor" by redressing the insults made against him. The wrongs done to God empowered the Iberians to initiate hostilities against the Indians as a defensive response and a means of revenge. There is no mention, however, of idolatry as blasphemy. As is obvious from Vitoria's reference to the classical accusations against the Jews (the desecration of the cross and mockery of the sacraments), the Dominican merely characterized blasphemy in terms of the Europeans' anti-Semitic anxieties.[26] The significance of Vitoria's emphasis on the *public* character of this crime is better illustrated in his *Lecture on the Evangelization of Unbelievers* (1534–35). There he commented on Aquinas's assertion that unbelievers could be lawfully warred against "so that they do not hinder the faith by their blasphemies." According to Vitoria, however, this applied only if unbelievers did not "keep their blasphemies to themselves" but offended the Christians by, for example, sending them "a letter full of blasphemies."[27] "We are all aware that both Jews and heathens blaspheme the name of Christ among themselves," he concluded, "but we cannot for this reason alone go to war with them." Like those deprived of grace and scorching in hell, Vitoria's unbelievers constantly blasphemed the name of God (Apocalypse 16:9). Yet, only if their blasphemies were publicly addressed to the Spaniards would it qualify as an "injury" against them. Obviously, since Indians did not engage in any of those condemned behaviors—not to mention the impossibility of their sending the invaders "a letter full of blasphemies"—the Spaniards had no justification to wage war against them.[28]

If Vitoria had proven that the Indians did not commit blasphemy and thus could not be justifiably attacked, his fellow Dominican Bartolomé de Las Casas went even further and blamed the Spaniards for driving the Indians to blaspheme the Christian god. Obviously concerned by Vitoria's conclusions, the Crown prohibited all further discussion on Spain's rights to occupy the Indies. Yet, when, on his return from America, Las Casas presented Charles V with a copy of his *Brevísima relación* (1542), the debate reignited. In this renowned tract, full of horrifying details of Spanish cruelty, the Dominican urged the king to abolish the *encomienda* system and charged the members of the Council of the Indies with corruption.[29] Las Casas not only underscored the unjustness of the Spanish war in America, as Vitoria had done, but also emphasized the noxious effects of violence on the task of evangelization. The Spaniards, he argued, had "brought the one true God into opprobrium," instead of procuring that the Indians honor him. In a fierce attack, Las Casas transformed God's "defenders" into an infernal pack of defilers, who by means of their countless atrocities, forced the Indians to blaspheme God's name.[30] Given the Dominican's preference for St. Paul as the image of the true apostle, as apparent in his previous tract, *Del único modo* (1538–40),[31] Las Casas was most likely echoing the saint's own angry reproach in his second letter to the Christians of Rome: "You who say that one must not commit adultery, do you commit adultery? You who abhor idols, do you rob temples? You who boast in the law, do you dishonor God by breaking the law? For, as it is written, 'The name of God is blasphemed among the Gentiles because of you'" (Romans 2:22–24).[32]

Las Casas's denunciations led Charles V to issue the New Laws (1542), but this attempt to suppress the encomienda system proved difficult to enforce in the New World. After receiving numerous memorials and petitions from both sides, in 1550, the king convoked a group of theologians and counselors to determine how to justly conduct new conquests. The ensuing debate between Las Casas and Juan Ginés de Sepúlveda in Valladolid, well known to scholars, contains specific implications for the Dominican challenge to Cortés's identification of indigenous idolatry as blasphemy and to the legitimacy of Spain's war to avenge God's honor. Ignoring Vitoria's contribution to the debate, Ginés de Sepúlveda asserted that, as established in Deuteronomy 9 and 12, the Indians should be attacked on grounds of their idolatry. He supported this by citing Augustine's letter to Count Boniface, in which the saint commended the use of force against the Donatists. Las Casas rebutted Ginés de Sepúlveda by noting that in Deuteronomy, the Canaanites, the Jebusites, and other nations had been attacked not because they were idolaters but because they occupied the Promised Land. Moreover, God only punished those who had received the divine Law but, by blaspheming his name, chose to ignore it. Thus, although Las Casas tacitly implied that the Indians might be idolaters, he argued this was not blasphemy because they had not known about Christianity. In his *Apologética Historia Sumaria* (ca. 1551), he would assert that far from constituting a rejection of God, idolatry was a natural—although misguided—expression of the human desire for God in the absence of grace.[33] Regarding Augustine's endorsement of the use of force, Las Casas replied that the saint referred only to heretics; pagans, in contrast, should be peaceably converted. To preach the faith to the heathen by means of arms (a proceeding he found Islamic in inspiration)[34] would only plant in the hearts of the pagans a great hatred for the Christian religion, leading to blasphemies of Christ's name. Since the original apostles never resorted to coercion, Las Casas concluded, Spaniards should preach solely by means of persuasion and good example.[35]

Las Casas's ideas on blasphemy, idolatry, and the right of conquest later matured in his *Historia de las Indias* (not published until 1552–61), where he expanded his criticism of the Spanish warfare in the Americas. In his eyes, the Spanish presence in the New World was justified only in missionary terms. In contrast to Vitoria, Las Casas reasserted the bulls of donation as the Crown's principal claim to dominion in America, but only to the extent that they represented a charter for evangelization. "If we are to talk and act as Christians, we cannot call this conquest, but rather commission and precept of the Church and Christ's vicar," he wrote.[36] Like his enemies López de Gómara, Oviedo, and Sepúlveda, Las Casas believed that Spain's providential destiny was to expand Christianity. However, the Spaniards had fallen short of God's design.[37] The task seemed easy given the Indians' "meekness" and "docility," yet the Spaniards not only failed to behave like Christians; their actions gave a terrible reputation to the Christian religion and the name of God. Atrocities obstructed the task of evangelization by "defaming and making [God's name] stink," to the extent that for the natives, the word "Christian" became code for "dangerous and suspicious people." He later remarked that even *idiotas plebeyos* (ignorant rustics) from Spain would have made excellent apostles in the New World had they behaved in a Christian manner.[38]

Saint Paul established a relationship between vile behavior and blasphemy among the heathen that Las Casas also stressed in an exemplum given in Cuba on Corpus Christi on an unspecified date. According to Las Casas, a Franciscan friar was preaching to the Indians on the virtues of God as *el Salvador* (the Savior) of the world. The friar had barely started to praise him, when the Indians reacted by spitting and shouting blasphemously that el Salvador was nothing but a cruel and evil man who tormented and killed them. As the Franciscan later learned, the Indians had confused Christ with a Spaniard named Salvador, whose diabolical actions had sullied God's own reputation among the natives. That very day, God's wrath manifested itself by inflicting a sudden death on the homonymous wrongdoer. The story offers an ingenious warning to the colonizers and a reminder that, in accordance with the papal donation, the legitimacy of the Spanish presence in America was contingent on the conversion of the Indians. In this sense, the actions of the Spaniards not only undermined the colonial enterprise in America as a matter of practical fact but also called into question the right of the Spanish Crown to conquer and occupy the lands across the Atlantic.[39]

Las Casas died in 1566, and on July 13, 1573, the Crown issued a new set of ordinances regulating all future discoveries and acquisitions.[40] Apparently influenced by the combative Dominican, the Spanish authorities forbade the use of the word *conquest*. However, the new approved term was not *commission*, as Las Casas had wanted, but *pacification*, a term that did not suggest the Christian mission that had been entrusted to the Spaniards but merely removed the association with the word *struggle*. The regulations clearly established that new discoveries should be made with "peace and charity,"[41] but they failed to justify the Spanish presence in America as a "precept of the Church and Christ's vicar." Nonetheless, the Crown accepted the Dominican's concern about the pernicious effects of violence on conversion, for the ordinance recommended dealing gently with the Indians from the outset, "so as not to scandalize them or prejudice them against Christianity."[42] As this document attests, the Spanish authorities found it increasingly difficult to justify warfare against the Indians on grounds of their alleged offenses committed against the Christian god.

Spanish Pollution

In colonial Mexico, Las Casas's Pauline attack found an unlikely but re-
ceptive audience in Franciscan missionaries, among them Jerónimo de
Mendieta. Like other Franciscans, Mendieta deemed the wars of con-
quest to be a cruel but necessary means to open the way for the Catholic
Church. However, the missionary coincided with Las Casas in denouncing
Spanish violence and its harmful effects on the task of evangelization.[43]
Whereas Vitoria and Las Casas had feared that the Indians would reject
the Christian god because of Spanish excesses, Mendieta went a step further by suggesting that the Indians were learning to blaspheme from the
Spaniards themselves. Indeed, far from acquiring "our civilized way of life
and good customs," as stated in a 1550s royal decree, the Indians were only
becoming contaminated by European vices through Spanish contact. "Who
could imagine," wrote Mendieta in his *Historia eclesiástica indiana* (1596),
"that not only the Indian men but also the Indian women would learn to
play cards and play the guitar?" The natives' communication with the "old
Christians" had only taught them to steal, drink, and give themselves to
the devil. Mendieta forcefully, albeit unsuccessfully, advocated the establishment of an independent church in New Spain, under the control of the
mendicants and linked with the Spaniards only by being subject to the same
viceroy. Many other missionaries shared Mendieta's opinion and tried to
keep the Spaniards and Indians apart even to the extreme of spreading the
use of Nahuatl, rather than Spanish, as a lingua franca among the diverse
Indian linguistic groups.[44]

The pervasive Indian moral corruption portrayed in Mendieta's turn-
of-the-century account had long been feared. In the 1535 *Información
de derecho*—an angry protest against Indian slavery—Vasco de Quiroga
was already urging the Crown to take all possible measures to reduce the
contact between Indians and Spaniards. Implicitly referring to Colossians
3:5, Quiroga accused the colonizers of teaching the Indians a new kind of
idolatry, by elevating to a "godly" status those human desires involved in
the sins of sexual immorality, lust, and greed.[45] The neophytes could gain
nothing, in moral or material terms, from their *conversación* (interaction)
with the Spaniards. Although Quiroga strongly disagreed with Las Casas
regarding the legitimacy of the wars of conquest, he nonetheless launched a
Pauline attack on his countrymen, decrying the deleterious consequences of
violence and abuse for the missionary enterprise in Mexico. In apocalyptical
imagery, the Franciscan harshly criticized the greedy colonizers for sending

the Indians to the hell of the mines, where the natives cursed the day they were born and blasphemed the name of Christ. With this Dantesque spectacle in mind, it comes as no surprise that, like Mendieta years later, Quiroga portrayed the Spaniards as fierce persecutors of the Indian religions.[46]

In the case of Mendieta, however, the criticism against the colonizers was also triggered by a bitter disillusionment and pessimism that characterized the second generation of missionaries in colonial Mexico. The Franciscan missionary project had, for some time now, been under siege: countless epidemics, onerous exploitation of Indians through the *repartimiento* (labor system), and a sustained decrease in the mendicants' privileges under Philip II (1556–98).[47] Gone was the euphoria of the early years' massive baptisms. Gone too was the political authority that allowed the Franciscans to undertake fierce campaigns to extirpate idolatry, which had targeted the offenders as heretics but not as blasphemers, as Gómara might have expected.

In the earlier period, prosecutors had typically accused backsliding Indians of "heresy," but they applied the category erratically. They charged the idolaters with returning to the "heretical life" they had led *before* becoming Christian (*"volver a la vida perversa y herética que antes que fuesen cristianos solían tener"*). Yet, heresy, in the sense of falling away from the Christian faith, could only be possible *after* Christianity had been promulgated.[48] Reports of the excessive severity of the friars who were acting as inquisitors in Oaxaca and Yucatán motivated Charles V's 1538 exemption of the Indians from the Inquisition. This did little, however, to diminish the coercive turn in Christian conversion resulting from the growing conviction that the Indians were easily deceived by Satan. Indeed, only one year later, Bishop Juan de Zumárraga sentenced don Carlos Ometochzin, the cacique of Texcoco, to be burned at the stake on charges of heresy. In 1562, Zumárraga's fellow Franciscan Bishop Diego de Landa conducted a violent three-month campaign against idolatry in Mani, Yucatán, in which more than four thousand Mayans were savagely tortured. Hundreds lost their lives as a result of the interrogations while many others took their own lives in despair.[49] The missionaries' disenchantment soon led to their paternalism toward the Indians. In the wake of two previous Church Provincial Councils (1555 and 1565), the Indians emerged from the third (1585) characterized as intellectually weak, vice-prone, and inconstant human beings.[50] In this pessimistic climate, Mendieta in his *Historia* leveled harsh criticism against the Spaniards, whom he depicted in the same dark colors employed by Las Casas.

Grounding himself in St. Paul's second letter to the Christians of Rome,

Mendieta criticized the Spaniards for despising the heathens and boasting of the law they had received from God, while, in reality, they lived in a more sinful state than the Gentiles themselves (Romans 2:22–26). The Franciscan was outraged by a prevailing tendency among Spaniards to distinguish themselves from the Indians by the term Christian, as if Indians were not entitled to call themselves "Christians" because of their recent conversion.[51] Moreover, those who labeled themselves Christian were in reality not worthy of it, for their works had brought God's name into disrepute. Since they engaged in killing, robbing, burning, and destroying, they transformed the name "Christian" into a cry of alarm among Indians, a synonym for "thieves, pirates, and enemies." Writing against his compatriots' interests, Mendieta defended himself by stating that he was not an enemy of his own country. He would not have dared to move the contents of these "stinky latrines," he wrote, had he understood himself to be damaging the reputation of pious and generous Spaniards. But this was hardly the case. In a clear allusion to the writings of Las Casas, he added that the faults of Spaniards were now infamous from East to West. He praised, in contrast, the "true Spaniards" who, by working for the salvation of the Indians' souls, added to the "good fame and honor of their nation." The rest should be considered enemies of their religion, king, and nation and be called "barbarians," "Caribbeans," and "degenerates," since it was because of their actions that God's name was blasphemed by the still unbaptized. Mendieta thought it indispensable to separate God's name from the Spaniards and their works, by liberating the term "Christian" from its natural association with "Spaniard." Only in this way could the holy name recuperate the necessary universalism to encompass not only Indians but mestizos and mulattoes as well.[52]

Like most missionaries, however, Mendieta was convinced that the only way of dissociating God's name from the Spaniards' actions and their moral pollution was to segregate the Indians completely from the colonizers. Early in the colonial period, the Crown manifested a keen interest in protecting the Indians from Spanish abuses by decreeing a policy of physical and racial separation that kept Indians and Spaniards in different settlements. Closely related to the medieval system of orders, the institution of two repúblicas (separate administrative and fiscal orders) recreated a hierarchically structured, corporate society. The Indians were allowed to retain their laws, provided these did not conflict with those of the Crown or natural law. However, the Indians were subordinate to the república of the Spaniards, the *gente de razón* (civilized and educated people). Advocates of the legislation creating the two orders based their claims on distinct views of the nature of Indians. Mendieta and most of missionaries believed that the Indians were childlike, and segregation could thus save them from corruption and physical extinction at the hands of Spaniards. Vasco de Quiroga and others were convinced that Indians were capable of governing themselves as civilized people and needed guidance only in religious matters. Although royal policy regarding this issue was occasionally erratic, in the course of the sixteenth century, the Crown issued a number of decrees that forbade Spaniards, blacks, mestizos, and creoles from inhabiting Indian towns.[53] In practice, however, demands for tribute and labor required constant contact between the two repúblicas, undermining the policy of segregation. Furthermore, vagrancy, miscegenation, and even illegal settlement of Spaniards in Indian towns augmented the already significant intermingling.[54] For all their interest in enforcing a policy of segregation, the metropolitan authorities never questioned that Indians should work for the Spaniards. The Crown's decision to reform the repartimiento system, further pressuring the Indian communities precisely when the native population was still decreasing, only confirmed that the Franciscan ideal of complete segregation was clearly impossible.[55]

The Crown's policy favoring religious instruction in Spanish for the Indians further undermined segregation by lifting the linguistic barrier between colonizers and colonized, which risked exposing neophytes to the invaders' recurrent blasphemies. Arguing that the Indians would be more easily indoctrinated, the Crown first issued a royal decree on this in 1550. Although the policy was reversed in 1565, the mendicants struggled against linguistic imperialism until the early seventeenth century, when the Crown came unequivocally to support the original decree.[56] The injunction from Madrid stemmed from some Christian writers' conviction that the necessary resources to explain the mysteries of Catholicism were lacking in the native languages. The wealth in number of those languages was matched only by their putative lexical poverty. That fact, it was believed, could lead only to a lack of understanding about utterly fundamental religious notions. Thus, the apparent absence of a term for "god" in Nahuatl led Jesuit José de Acosta to conclude in *Historia natural y moral de las indias* (1590) that the Indians hardly understood anything about the Supreme Divinity, "for they don't even know how to name him except by means of the Spanish term (*vocablo*)."[57] For the missionaries, however, the use of the Spanish term *Dios* in sermons and confession manuals was vested with different connotations. They knew of the word *teotl*, a Nahuatl term referring to a multiplicity of manifestations—images, ritual objects, and deity impersonators—which the Spaniards found difficult to apply to their own deity.[58] The missionaries thus left untranslated the Castilian word, and in doing so, they assumed "a perfect fit between the Spanish word and its Christian referent."[59] Given this wonderful correspondence between the Spanish language and the name of God, it was a scandalous irony that the Spaniards used their language to blaspheme. And yet the possibility that Indians might acquire a derogatory repertoire from the Spaniards was real: Hence the frequent warnings found in colonial texts against the moral disadvantages resulting from the Spanish contact with Indians.[60] In religious terms, the lifting of the linguistic barrier was a motive for constant anxiety and also a threat to the authority of the mendicants as intermediaries between the Indians and the rest of society. To indoctrinate the Indians in Spanish would only heighten the increasing competition that the regular orders were already facing from the secular clergy, who, in general, avoided learning Indian languages.[61]

The fear that the Spaniards would corrupt the natives was augmented by the widespread assumption that if left alone, the Indians were naturally incapable of committing any of the sins associated with anger, among them, blasphemy. This conclusion stemmed from an environmentalist understanding of the formation of temperament, which rested heavily on Hippocrates's theory of humors as elaborated and refined by Galen.[62] According to this conceptualization, human beings were composed of four basic fluids: blood, phlegm, black bile, and yellow bile. Depending on the relative predominance of each element in the individual, the combination was supposed to produce temperaments classified as sanguine (cordial and affable), phlegmatic (slow-moving and apathetic), melancholic (depressed and sad), or choleric (impulsive and hot-tempered). Since the formation of humors relied on the combination of the four qualities of hot, cold, dry, and moist, it was assumed that climate and terrain were decisive in the constitution of the temperament. Thus, the humidity and heat characteristic of the Americas led Bartolomé de Las Casas to conclude that Indians had a "sanguine" constitution. Unlike the "choleric" Spaniards, born in dry and hot conditions, the Indians were not prone to sudden emotions like anger. The Dominican interpreted this as a proof of their fitness to receive the Christian faith.

Yet, for chroniclers who regarded the Indians as naturally inferior, such as López de Gómara and Francisco Cervantes de Salazar, the natives' lack of choler had only negative consequences. These writers believed that Indians were in reality "phlegmatic," which clearly explained why they were cowardly, lazy, gullible, ungrateful, and without the honor, shame, charity, and virtue that characterized the Spaniards. Mendieta also assumed that Indians had an overabundance of "phlegm." Although the Indians lacked the Iberians' sinful predisposition to anger, lust, and greed, he conceded that the native inhabitants were perhaps too sluggish for the choleric colonizers. He also believed that after several generations, the Indians were unfortunately starting to develop the same "superfluous humors" that led the Spaniards to commit sin. He observed that after the Indians' traditional diet changed to a meat-based one, they tended to "misbehave" in the same way Europeans did. The fact that the Indians' bodies had begun to produce the same corrupting fluids as the Spaniards' bodies did only emphasized the invasive character of Spanish moral pollution.[63]

Coda: Colonialism, Scandal, and Danger

Clearly, the Spaniards had fallen short of their providentialist mission as the defenders of God's honor. However, the pessimism of Mendieta and other fellow missionaries cannot be fully understood without analyzing the notion of "scandal" and its relation to Spanish actions in a colonial setting. Commonly defined as a moral reaction to the knowledge of something shameful, scandal was of concern to moral theology in that it results from an action that incites someone to sin, in this case through blaspheming God. Since scandal was particularly grave when inflicted on the weak and ignorant by people who are expected to guide them, missionaries found the actions of Spaniards against the natives particularly reprehensible.[64] The colonizers, divinely chosen to expand Christianity in the New World, were expected to mirror the behavior of Christ as God incarnate in order to be a model to imitate. As Paul stated in his famous letter to the Corinthians, "be imitators of me as I am of Christ" (1 Corinthians 11:1). The link between imitation and salvation was perverted, however, when the Spaniards became models of impious behavior by abusing the neophytes in the name of Christ, thus triggering the spiritual ruin of the colonized by either inciting them to sin or, as Las Casas complained, driving them to reject the Christian god.[65]

Because the colonizers' actions were destroying the reputation of the God they were supposed to defend in the New World, both Franciscans and Dominicans urgently sought to break the association of the signifier "Christian" with that of "Spaniard." Undoubtedly, the missionaries still considered the wars of conquest as the opening of one more front in the expansion of the holy faith at the expense of the infidels. Nevertheless, the invaders were no longer cast in the same providentialist light that had characterized the early years of Spanish warfare in America. Gone were the days when

López de Gómara could write enthusiastically in his *Historia general* (1552), "conquest among the Indians began when conquests among the Moors had finished, so that there might always be Spaniards at war with infidels."[66] Clearly, the pious belligerence could not be easily translated into a civilizing mission along Christian lines. The Crown's policies of protective segregation, although not incompatible with economic exploitation, implicitly recognized the need to save the Indians from the worst aspects of European ways.

Policing the Spaniards' behavior and their allegiance to Christianity soon became a priority for the Spanish Crown. That a great part of this anxiety revolved around blasphemy by Spaniards indicates a general mistrust of the colonizers, in their role not only as "civilizers" but also as defenders of God's honor. Moreover, at a time in which blasphemy was deemed capable of calling down God's wrath upon the land, the king believed it to be in his best interest to punish the Spanish blasphemers, not only to avoid the moral pollution of the colonized but also to allow Spain to regain the favor of God in an era of increasing economic and political decline. Indeed, throughout the sixteenth and seventeenth century, in an effort to propitiate a god who seemed to have abandoned Spain, as evidenced by increasing economic and political setbacks at home and abroad, the Crown would repeatedly instruct colonial authorities to punish the blasphemers.

For those inhabiting the colonies, monitoring the production of pious speech became a way of preventing disaster and forging a moral community. In an era in which spiritual salvation was deemed a communal endeavor, made possible by corporate forms of worship, belief, and religious conformity, blasphemy was an intolerable source of "sacred contagion." The transgressors were deemed capable of endangering the well-being of the faithful. Paradoxically, as we will see in the next chapter, precisely because of its dangerous character, blaspheming became a way for Spaniards to prove their manhood to their audiences.

2

"He Who Doesn't Blaspheme Is Not a Man"

Blasphemy and Masculinity

> By God's body, he who doesn't blaspheme is not a man!
> —Rodrigo Rengel, 1527

On May 1, 1527, Rodrigo Rengel, a former captain in Cortés's army, was arrested on the orders of Inquisitor Domingo de Betanzos. Rengel, now a syphilitic old man of eighty, was accused by Fiscal Sebastián de Arriaga of having uttered so many "abominable blasphemies" as to raise serious doubts about his faith in God. Rengel had spoken the "five heinous utterances": *descreo de Dios* (I don't believe in God), *reniego de Dios* (I renounce God), *por vida de Dios* (By God's life), *pese a Dios* (May God regret it), and *malhaya Dios* (God be damned). He had even denied the virginity of Mary by calling her a whore.[1] When the pain from his syphilis was unbearable, Rengel would shout that God has no power to cure illness, as he spat with anger from his bed upon holy images and crucifixes. When he felt better, he would gamble, especially on horse races, and generally give himself to the devil. While serving as *alcalde* of Pánuco, Rengel had desecrated a church looking for his enemies, and he had prevented the Franciscans from destroying Indian shrines when they came to preach to his district. As alcalde, he annulled the marriage of a young woman to a silversmith so that he could have sexual access to her. He had often composed blasphemous songs, and he had even encouraged others to blaspheme, by saying with conviction, "By God's body, he who doesn't blaspheme is not a man!"[2]

Yet, Rengel was submissive and repentant when he faced the Holy Office. At first, he claimed not to know "what had been said," but he later admitted that he had blasphemed many times. He blamed this be-havior on exhaustion from participating in the conquest and pacification of New Spain. Moreover, as his long defense later proved, Rengel had been in great pain for several years, hence he was frequently "out of his mind." Being under suspicion of practicing Judaism for spitting at images and crucifixes, Rengel assured Inquisitor Betanzos he was the son of Old Christians and that heresy had never entered his mind.

Although this case constituted by far the most blatant infringement of his blasphemy ordinances, Cortés himself decided to intervene on behalf of his old campmaster and testify to Rengel's noble lineage and Christian-ity. Cortés's pressure probably caused Betanzos, a Dominican, to cede his jurisdiction of the case to a Franciscan, Luis de Fuensalida, who, in turn, delegated responsibility to Fray Toribio de Motolinía. Fuensalida asked Motolinía to consider Rengel's service in the conquest of New Spain, his noble origins, and his terrible health. These mitigating circumstances notwithstanding, on September 3, Motolinía ordered Rengel to pay the huge sum of five hundred gold pesos, to stand during mass with a candle in his hand, and to be incarcerated for five months in a monastery. He was also condemned to finish building the hermitage of the Eleven Thousand Martyrs in Tacuba using the labor of the Indians assigned to him as a reward for his service in the conquest.[3]

Like many other blasphemy trials in New Spain, Rengel's case illus-trates the strong contrast between the use of the active voice when insult-ing the divinities of the Christian pantheon and the use of the passive voice when disclaiming responsibility before the Holy Office ("I did not know *what was said*"). In contrast to the disclaimers made in the courtroom, Rengel and many other men asserted their responsibility for the words they had uttered before other audiences as a strategy of self-affirmation and performance of masculinity.[4] The transgressors usually blasphemed on occasions reserved for male sociability, typically exemplified by a card game at a gambling house or tavern. Spanish soldiers, sailors, and mu-leteers were among the usual offenders, suggesting that blasphemy was also related to a masculine culture of work. Finally, Rengel's case shows that blasphemy was also related to risk taking, sexual assertiveness, and menacing speech—behaviors associated in medieval Spain and, in gen-eral, in Mediterranean societies, with the ideal of "real" manhood.[5]

Nevertheless, using blasphemy necessarily placed the male individual at odds with the interests of the larger Christian community. Following a well-established Christian belief, the colonial authorities assumed that blasphemy could have devastating consequences for the community as a whole by subjecting it to the wrath of God. Since it was not only the sinful who were chastised, the pressure for religious conformity was substantial, and monitoring the colonists' speech was thus not only a moral concern but also an issue of security. As the ecclesiastical judge (provisor) for Oaxaca, Juan Núñez, stated in 1570, it was necessary to punish blasphemers because Spaniards were living "in dangerous times."[6]

In fact, on November 10, 1527, only two years before Rodrigo Rengel's conviction, an assembly of government representatives from New Spain had urged the king to end the widespread blaspheming, something the colonial judges had been negligent in addressing.[7] Thus, when the Dominican Fray Domingo de Betanzos was appointed head in 1527 of what is now known as the Monastic Inquisition (1524–1535), he devoted his efforts to punishing blasphemy among the conquistadores. During his short period as a minister (May 1527 to September 1528), Betanzos tried some twenty Spanish men, many of whom had been Cortés's comrades. This same keen zeal to punish blasphemy was exhibited during the Apostolic Inquisition (1535–1571) by Inquisitor Juan de Zumárraga. In 1536, he initiated a ferocious campaign that yielded about fifty-six cases, most of them against Spaniards, a trend that would continue well into the seventeenth century.[8]

This chapter will explore the use of blasphemy in New Spain as a cultural tool of gender self-fashioning and masculine assertiveness. For the period from 1527 to 1708, I analyze 141 cases against Spanish men and 3 cases against sailors from Portugal, Italy, and France. The charges were for uttering blasphemies in Mexico City (80), Oaxaca (27), Puebla (7), Veracruz (7), Guadalajara (5), Guachinango (1), Guajacatlán (1), Jocotlán (2) Michoacán (3), Colima (3), Mérida (2), Tabasco (1), Acapulco (1), and Zacatecas (1).

Building on recent feminist analysis of masculinity as the dramaturgical effect of cultural practices performed in the presence of others, I discuss blasphemy as a performative anchor of male identity in colonial Mexico.[9] Blasphemy was not only a verbal resource for the expression of emotions—such as despair, anger, and frustration—but also a language of combat, negative reciprocity, sexual assertiveness, and confrontation embraced by Spanish men in colonial Mexico to project an image of strength, bravery, and maleness in social settings that included both the domestic and the public sphere. In particular, I will discuss the relationship between blasphemous speech and a masculine culture of work in groups character- ized by high mobility, such as sailors, soldiers, and muleteers.

Blasphemy and Masculinity

As a specific style of speech, blasphemy has long been related to strate- gies of distinction and to the construction of social identities in terms of class and gender. In the late Middle Ages, blasphemy was invested with the necessary daring and arrogance to make it a preferred pastime of the nobility: "'What?' says the nobleman to the peasant, 'You give your soul to the devil and deny God, yet you are not a nobleman?'"[10] In the Span- ish court, the infamous Beltrán de la Cueva, Henry IV's favorite, was an enthusiastic organizer of blasphemy contests for the nobility. This may have prompted the Augustine Fray Martín de Córdoba to urge the future Queen Isabelle to combat blasphemy as soon as she came to the throne.[11] The plays of early modern authors, such as Shakespeare and Molière, reveal that a plebeian blasphemy could be distinguished from an aristo- cratic "good mouth-filling oath."[12] Even though class distinctions in New Spain shaped blasphemy—as will be shown in the discussion on slaves in chapter 5—strikingly, it remained a verbal practice mostly reserved to Spanish men. As Solange Alberro has suggested, perhaps because women were out of earshot in the sheltered domestic environment, their blasphe- mies were rarely heard by potential denouncers.[13] It is also true, however, that moralists, preachers, and confessors strongly pressured women to avoid deprecatory language and excessive loquacity, behaviors that fell short of the feminine ideal of the time.

Although blasphemy was widely seen as a risk-taking form of speech, religious authorities were aware that men used it as a verbal device to assert their masculinity in front of others. Sixteenth- and seventeenth- century religious literature either denounced blasphemy as a sinful "adornment" of male speech or decried it as a hellish strategy to show bravery by abusing the Christian god.[14] To counteract the idea that blas- phemy asserted "manliness," moralists described blasphemers as ani- malistic, satanic, and effeminate. Indeed, their tongues were depicted as scorpions,[15] and their insults were portrayed as the natural reactions of rabid dogs, language proper to those scorching in hell.[16] Christian writ- ers also emphasized that men who blasphemed behaved like *mujercillas apocadas* (gutless little women) for they resorted to their tongues—the weapons of women—when they saw they were not able to take revenge against God.[17]

Far from serving as an excuse, the anger many blasphemers expressed when attacking God was particularly disturbing. Indeed, defined by Aquinas as a "disorderly desire for vengeance," anger was understood as a passion triggered by the conviction that a person or an object had done one harm.[18] In the scheme of Gregory the Great, popular since the seventh century, anger was a cardinal sin and at the root of six other vices, "anger's daughters": indignation, quarreling, vanity, contumely, clamor, and blasphemy. However, moralists also pointed out that moral indignation or considered reason could provoke virtuous anger, as when defending the Christian religion.[19]

Most often, however, anger was an "appetite" of the soul, piqued by trivial and sinful things, such as losing a game or bickering. Moreover, by identifying God as the source of the perceived harm, the transgressors manifested a foolish and infernal desire to defy the Divinity out of hatred. Thus, although several authors of Inquisition manuals believed that anger could affect the rational faculties of men to the point making them swear, nobody considered the *calor iracundiae* (heat of anger) to be an excuse for blaspheming.[20] Moralists and preachers stressed the absolute powerlessness of these bragging, "fierce" men by repeating frightening tales in which male blasphemers were paralyzed, struck in the mouth by a bolt of lightning, or infected with a horrible disease, all believed to be manifestations of God's own anger.[21]

Seeking to break the tie between blasphemy and masculinity, moralists promoted a different kind of masculine excellence predicated on men's capacity to control their own speech and passions. "If any man sin not in word, he is a perfect man and able to bridle the whole body," says a commonly quoted passage from James (3:2). In describing moral perfection as the capacity to control one's tongue, moralists drew on a long Christian tradition that depicted this member as a dangerous inner enemy always ready to sin and cause harm if not subject to proper surveillance. Christian writers frequently commented that Nature had quite intentionally placed the tongue inside a chamber guarded by sharp teeth with the lips as a double door.[22] Although the "tongue literature" was normally addressed to women (see chapter 4), Christian writers also described the tongue as a deleterious two-edged sword that required a firm, virile hand to be properly handled.

"Irae Malum" (the evil of anger). An engraving representing the destructive force of uncontrollable anger, which is a cardinal sin and a source of blasphemous speech. From Borja, *Empresas morales,* 23. (Courtesy of the Biblioteca Nacional de México, Fondo Reservado)

"Thou hast conquered, oh Galilean." A representation of Julian the Apostate, the epitome of the angry blasphemer, showing his contumelious expletives as a flying sword. From Drexelius, *Orbis Phaëton*. (Courtesy of the Mandeville Special Collections Library, University of California, San Diego)

For instance, in his *Emblemas morales* (1610), Sebastián de Covarrubias included an engraving portraying the sword and tongue as two weapons, with a motto alluding to Proverbs 18:21: "Two weapons are the tongue and the sword, which if properly controlled, protect our person and bring about a thousand benefits. But when any of those weapons are used in excess and without reason, they cause the death of the foolish, and change the luck of the intelligent."[23] Although the motto urges the reader to control his "wandering" tongue, promising "a thousand benefits," the quasi-phallic engraving of the erect tongue suggests a more tangible reward of enhanced virility and sexual performance. For the prudent man, the tongue was not a slippery and capricious "flabby little organ," as it was for many slanderous and blasphemous men, but a "solid" signifier of masculinity.[24]

Effectively fitting into the Catholic Church's wider Counterreformation program of spiritual revitalization, confraternities were formed explicitly to praise the holy name of God and uproot the *dañada costumbre de jurar* (harmful habit of blaspheming). Dominican Fray Diego de Victoria, a member of the convent of San Pablo de Burgos in Spain, founded the first confraternity of this kind in 1550. In Mexico, however, the initiative belonged to the Augustinians, who received permission from the archbishop of Mexico, Dominican Fray Alonso de Montúfar, in 1561 or 1562. Pope Pius IV officially approved the first confraternity's constitutions in 1564. Headed by the future conqueror of the Philippines, Don Miguel López de Legaspi, the confraternity soon grew in prestige, counting among its members the viceroy and the archbishop themselves. Although the records of this confraternity apparently no longer exist, it is likely that its activities and constitutions closely mirrored those of its counterparts across the Atlantic. If so, it would have been involved in organizing processions on the eve of the holy day of Jesus's name, helping brothers during illnesses and securing them a Christian burial at death, and most important, requiring brothers to refrain from blaspheming.[25] Despite this devotional initiative, the constant warnings and exhortations, and the rewards promised by moralists and preachers, blasphemy remained a recurrent male offense throughout the colonial period.

First Trials: "With Little Fear of God"

During the late 1520s, blasphemy was the most prosecuted religious crime and the main reason for contact with the Inquisition. Many individuals who faced the Holy Office on blasphemy charges had partici-

CENTVRIA III.   266

SERVARE POTES TV PERDE

TV

RE

EMBLEMA 66.

Dos armas fon la lengua, y el efpada,
Que fi las gouernamos qual conuiene,
Anda nueftra perfona bïe guardada,
Y mil pronechos fu buen ufo tienes:
Pero qualquiera dellas defmadada,
Como de la cordura fe enagenes,
En el loco y fandio caufa muerte,
Y el cuerdo y fagaz trueca la fuerte.

Mm 2   Siē.

"Two weapons are the tongue and the sword." As a deleterious two-edged sword, the tongue requires a firm, virile hand to be properly handled. From Covarrubias y Orozco, *Emblemas morales,* 266. (Courtesy of the Biblioteca Nacional de México, Fondo Reservado) pated in the conquest of New Spain. Given that this military enterprise had been predicated on defending God's honor, it is understandable that early inquisitors, such as the Dominican Betanzos, were deeply disturbed by the conquistadores' frequent verbal and even physical attacks on the sacred. Beyond the religious zeal of Betanzos, however, these early campaigns may have been motivated by the multiple conflicts and local power struggles among Spaniards that characterized the early postconquest era. As Richard Greenleaf has pointed out, most of those tried by Betanzos and his fellow Dominican Vicente de Santa María had fought alongside Cortés in the conquest, and some had remained his staunch supporters between 1524 and 1526, when Cortés led a catastrophic expedition to Honduras. To be sure, most of the conquistadores tried by Betanzos were not personal friends of Cortés,[26] but as former combatants and early settlers, they were all significant players in colonial politics. Controlling them was undoubtedly a priority for the Spanish state. In this context, it is not farfetched to consider the first campaigns against blasphemers as being part of the Crown's early attempts to control the violent settlers and enforce cohesiveness in the midst of factionalism.

Although there is no record of it, Betanzos probably proclaimed the Edict of Faith upon his appointment as inquisitor, and, as was the custom, it is likely he pronounced a decree of anathema against heretics, *judaizantes*, and blasphemers during the third week of Easter. This recitation of heretical practices and offenses against Catholicism taught the assembled population about the boundaries of permissible behavior. It asked the audience to participate in the chastisement by denouncing transgressors.[27] In 1527, Betanzos tried eighteen conquistadores in characteristically brief and swift trials that rarely indicate the circumstances in which the accused had blasphemed or the identify of the denouncer. In his formal charges, Fiscal Sebastián de Arriaga regularly declared that the transgressors had blasphemed "with little fear of God," a formula that expressed both the lack of due reverence toward the Godhead and the audacity of endangering the colonizers' standing, and that of the whole community, before God.

A unique characteristic of this early, fierce campaign against blasphemy was the frequent sentencing of the culprits to make penitential pilgrimages to the shrines of Nuestra Señora de los Remedios, Nuestra Señora de la Victoria, Santa Fe, and San Marcos. In contrast to later years, when backsliding or particularly scandalous blasphemers were banished from Spanish settlements, Inquisitor Betanzos reconciled the transgressors to the Christian community by ordering them to look for grace in the sanctuaries of the capital city. Several of the conquistadores punished in this way had even been previously condemned for blasphemy by secular judges in other regions. Diego García, for instance, had been punished in 1526 by a judge in Villa Rica, Veracruz, for renouncing God and uttering "pese a Dios" and other blasphemies.[28] On July 10, 1527, Betanzos sentenced him to take part twice in the procession to the shrine of Nuestra Señora de los Remedios, fast for seven Fridays, deliver two pounds of wax for the church, and pay for the costs of his trial. In another case, the encomendero of Ixmiquilpan, Juan Bello, had already been punished by the secular authorities for saying "descreo de Dios" and "pese a Dios." Betanzos fined him twelve gold pesos, plus the costs of his trial, and sentenced him to make a pilgrimage to the shrine of Nuestra Señora de la Victoria.[29] By traveling the processional routes leading to the sacred shrines of Mexico City, the penitents not only expiated their sins but also propitiated God so that the colony would be protected and the dangers posed by their blaspheming would be averted. In this violent and unstable society, ritual punishments of this kind manifested a yearning for social order and cohesion on the part of the early colonial authorities, who felt a pressing need to suppress the conquistadores' sinful behavior for the well-being of the colony and the honor of the Christian god.

Besides the remarkable case of Rodrigo Rengel, the trials of Diego Núñez and Diego de Morales are particularly noteworthy because their crimes combined sinful locutions with acts of desecration. Inquisitors distinguished between blasphemy, which consisted of words, thoughts, or writings deemed derogatory to the Divinity, and sacrilege, which only involved "acts."[30] Mixing the two was particularly disturbing because it constituted a possible sign of Judaism, and the Jews were traditionally viewed as Christ killers and crucifix desecrators.

On August 2, 1527, Fiscal Arriaga accused Diego Núñez of offending God and the Virgin by throwing rocks at and breaking a crucifix. One month later, Núñez was arrested and his property confiscated. Since destroying a crucifix indicated he might be a judaizante, Inquisitor Betanzos ordered a careful investigation of Núñez's ancestry. Witnesses summoned by Arriaga testified that Nuñez was a converso from Gibraltar, who neither prayed, went to church, nor observed Easter. Moreover, while living in Chilapa, he had frequently exclaimed *"pese a Dios, descreo de Dios."* In addition, one Juan Guisado accused him of concubinage. His attorney, Juan Torres de Villafranca, called four witnesses who knew Núñez well, and they testified that Diego was a good Catholic and the son of Old Christians. When interrogated on September 3, 1527, Núñez himself claimed to be a baptized Christian. He admitted blaspheming but denied practicing any Jewish rites. He also admitting hitting a crucifix with a rock, but he explained that he had been throwing the rock at a fire in a small brazier nearby. Núñez claimed that Guisado was his enemy because Diego had testified against him in a trial involving the murder of an Indian. As the charge of being a judaizante went unproven, Betanzos sentenced Núñez as a blasphemer to thirty days in prison and payment of the costs of his trial.[31]

On July 14, 1528, various witnesses accused Diego de Morales—the brother of Gonzalo de Morales who would later die at the stake as a judaizante—of renouncing Christ and all his power and slapping a crucifix. Three years earlier, Leonel de Cervantes, the alcalde of Mexico City, had accused Diego of blaspheming and stepping on a cross. Despite being tortured during that trial, Morales denied having desecrated the crucifix and confessed only to blasphemy. He was sentenced to thirty days in prison and fined four thousand maravedís. Diego faced the Holy Office on the new charges on July 24, 1528. Before the Dominican Inquisitor Santa María, he denied being of Jewish ancestry, and he stated he was not close to his brother. He admitted having blasphemed, but he denied having slapped a cross. Morales's sentence was oddly lenient for a recidivist blasphemer: He was sentenced to attend a penitential mass, while gagged, shoeless, and carrying a candle. He was also fined fifty gold pesos plus the costs of his trial.[32]

In 1528, when the Dominicans lost control of the Inquisition, it ended the ruthless campaign against Cortés's supporters that had been motivated by factional politics and the Crown's need to control the colony in the conquistador's absence. The departure of the Dominicans, however, did not imply the end of the campaigns against male blasphemers. The Franciscan bishop had important political differences with his predecessors, but he was equally appalled by the frequency with which the colonizers resorted to blasphemy in fights, gambling, and during outbursts of anger. Between 1536 and 1543, under Juan de Zumárraga, the Mexican Inquisition tried approximately fifty-six individuals for blasphemy. Zumárraga's trials were brief and generally expeditious. In contrast to Betanzos, the Franciscan also had a "pedagogical" mission, which manifested in his warnings to transgressors about the magnitude of the crime of blasphemy. "Did you know that blasphemy is a mortal sin and an assault on the Divine Majesty, and that those who blaspheme risk being punished by the Holy Office?" asked Zumárraga to the gambler Juan de Villagómez on October 6, 1536.[33] Only days earlier, on August 25, 1536, he gave a similar warning to the blacksmith Lorenzo Hernández: "Did you know that it is a sin to use the name of God in vain, a great sin to commit perjury, and an even more horrible sin to blaspheme God's name?"[34]

Zumárraga also made sure that defendants understood that heretical blasphemy was a crime that only the Inquisition could punish and forgive. Indeed, several blasphemers received penance from priests or friars only later to learn that the clerics, while having the authority to forgive blasphemy, were not empowered to forgive heresies, including blasphemies involving a rejection of God or the Catholic faith, such as, "descreo de Dios" or "reniego de Dios." For example, Ecclesiastical Judge Rafael Cervantes had ordered Alonso Sánchez to buy a pound of candle wax for the church as a punishment for having said, "Descreo de Dios!" On November 8, 1538, Zumárraga declared that Cervantes did not have the authority to forgive Sánchez, for "this is a right restricted to the Holy Office." Zumárraga then fined Sánchez fourteen gold pesos.[35] Similarly, Francisco Maldonado of Castile had denounced himself at the cathedral for having said, "descreo [de Dios]!" and he had been ordered to buy candle wax for the church. On November 12, 1536, Zumárraga told Maldonado that "he who gave him penance had no authority to forgive him." Zumárraga then fined him twenty gold pesos and ordered him to pay for five masses in honor of Christ and three in honor of the Holy Trinity, and to pray the rosary three times.[36]

It is clear from these campaigns that the early inquisitors considered it crucially important to end the tendency of Spanish men to blaspheme. They did so not only through fines, imprisonment, and penitential pilgrimages, but also by showing the transgressors the magnitude of their crime, the risks of being tried by the Holy Office, and the necessity of averting God's wrath. At a time in which factional struggles among Spaniards threatened the colony, punishing blasphemers was an important way for the Spanish imperial state to exert much needed control over the men who were expanding and settling its colonial frontier. As R. W. Connell has pointed out, imperial states are gendered enterprises, and the creation of colonial frontiers is frequently characterized by a clash between forces pulling towards an ethic of violent conquest and expansion and a demand for the control of male violence.[37] But if disciplining Spanish men's behavior represented a daunting task in the early years of colonization, it would later become a nearly impossible endeavor.

Menacing Speech

Indeed, as a performative anchor of masculine identity, blasphemy soon became a recurrent and widespread ingredient of everyday confrontations between men. Seeking to make a strong impression on their audiences, angry men often blasphemed to show that they were capable of taking revenge and inflicting harm on their antagonists. It is common to find in inquisitorial records men like Hernando Ortíz, who renounced God in 1562 and assured those surrounding him that even if he had to go to hell, he would force Pedro Ruiz to pay him his money back.[38] Antonio de Sosa is alleged to have said to Francisco Ruíz in 1567 in the mines of Xocotlán, "I'll force you to pay me back or I'll renounce my [baptismal] Chrism!"[39] More creatively, Domingo Alonso threatened his debtor, Johanes de Mar, in 1560, in Antequera, that he would pay a higher price than Adam did for biting the apple.[40] Money was of course not always the issue when it came to matters of "payment." On February 6, 1566, the prosecutor of Oaxaca accused Vicente Martínez of threatening Cristóbal de Colmenares by saying, "By God's life, you'll pay for this!" without specifying the reason for this promise of retaliation.[41] In most of these cases, the defendant was sentenced to pay a fine that ranged between ten and twenty gold pesos, attend a penitential mass, and cover the costs of the trial.

Even more impressive as an intimidation tactic in daily confrontations was the use of a vast array of expressions of corporal combat against the Catholic pantheon. Male profaners frequently portrayed themselves as violent and dangerous, capable of "facing God *a campo raso* (in the open)," "breaking Christ's head with a stick,"[42] "stabbing their way into heaven," and "killing Saint John and the Guardian Angel." Discarding the idea of a transcendent and unreachable God, those who uttered these expressions were resorting to an imagery of physical struggle that stressed the speaker's bodily strength and ferociousness in challenging the Divinity. Consider the case of Gerónimo de Cuéllar, a thirty-four-year-old bricklayer, whom several witnesses described as being a *valentón jurador* (bullying blasphemer) who "led an evil life." In 1597, Cuéllar was desperate to kill Luis Martín, who had written a love letter to Elvira García, a woman Cuéllar also apparently had designs on. He looked for Martín in several places and told all those he encountered that the saints, Saint John the Baptist, and even God would not be powerful enough to deter him from killing his rival. Then, in an angry outburst, Cuéllar uttered an old favorite: Even if Martín managed to hide himself in the Virgin Mary's womb, he would still go after him to take his life.[43] The Inquisitors Lobo Guerrero and Alonso de Peralta clearly took offense at Cuéllar's pretension to penetrate the Virgin's holy body, and on April 20, 1603, they sentenced him to one hundred lashes, exile in perpetuity from New Spain, and four years of service as a galley slave.[44]

This same imagery of violent access and penetration could acquire arrogant overtones when the speaker was not a ruffian but an individual endowed with colonial authority. On October 19, 1658, Father Juan de Velasco denounced Pedro Mateos, the *alguacil mayor* (governor's constable) in the royal district of Cuautla. According to Velasco, Mateos had told people he encountered during his constable's rounds that he would "kill Christ himself if he gave him a reason to do it," "jail even the Eternal Father," "enter even the house of the Virgin Mary if he wanted," and "fight with the Guardian Angel," and that if a priest by the name of Cristóbal Pérez hid himself, even in Abraham's bosom, he would go after him to punish him. Many inhabitants of the town testified that Mateos abused his power as constable and frequently called them *cornudos cabrones* (cuckolded sons of bitches). Two years later, the Inquisition ordered an investigation into these charges, which was carried out in Cuautla between December 6 and December 16, 1660. Yet, as often happened with crimes in remote areas, the Inquisition's response was slow. Twenty-one years later, on January 25, 1681, Inquisitor Don Juan Gómez de Mier ordered the arrest of Mateos, who had already been dead for three years, having been shot with an arrow.[45]

Another example involving abuse of authority was Father Baltazar Márquez's denunciation on June 30, 1660, against Don Juan de Espejo, the *alcalde mayor* (district governor) of Nexapa, Oaxaca. Asking the Inquisition to end the scandal Espejo was causing in the town, the priest testified that the alcalde had physically and verbally abused the Indians of Nexapa. Like many other district magistrates at the time—alcaldes mayores and corregidores—Espejo had expected to make a good profit by advancing merchandise and cash to the Indians in exchange for their valuable export crop, cochineal. However, on June 21, the Indians— accompanied by priests from the Nexapa convent, with whom Espejo apparently had had some differences—returned the money Espejo had advanced them. Profoundly irritated, he shouted "By God's life!" and hit the Indian cacique in the face. This caused commotion among the Indians, who calmed down only when a squad of soldiers appeared. In the following days, the district governor, who had assumed his appointment on Saint John's Day, expressed his frustration at not obtaining the revenues he had expected from his administrative appointment. He declared he would fight with Saint John himself if he were to descend from heaven. He also called the saint a cuckold and son of a bitch and challenged him to show that he was braver than Espejo. Several soldiers testified that he had blasphemed "twelve thousand Christs and twelve thousand Holy Trinities." As if stressing the divine injustice that he, a brave man, had to suffer in Nexapa, Espejo also declared that if one could get into heaven by sword strokes, he would already have a living room, a bedroom and a kitchen up there.[46] Unfortunately, the records are incomplete and do not show if the Inquisition proceeded against him.

Only Great Fornicators Go to Heaven

Besides resorting to blasphemy to demonstrate their fierceness and bodily strength, Spanish men paraded their virility and manliness as qualities of their sexuality by using this kind of derogatory speech with regularity. By praising their sexual potency to the point of seeing themselves capable of penetrating celestial beings, and performing scandalous comparisons with the Christian divinities to emphasize their sexual precocity, male speakers attempted to portray themselves as endowed with unusual sexual vigor, even as "great fornicators" and *"garañones"* (stallions).

Take the case of Juan de Azpitia, a 30-year-old tailor, whom Juan de Campos denounced on February 22, 1614, in Mexico City. Two days before, Azpitia had been visiting the house of Isabel de Ordoñez, a married woman whose husband was in the Philippines. Isabel had a daughter, Catalina, who apparently was of Azpitia's liking. Sensing Azpitia staring at the girl, Isabel had asked him what he was looking at. "I'm looking at you," replied Azpitia. *"voto a Dios* that you're more beautiful than God the Father." Catalina told him that he was a pig, and he responded that his buttocks were so clean that the saints could kiss them. That afternoon, Isabel went out to visit a friend, and Azpitia hugged Catalina from behind, saying, "voto a Dios that you have such a beautiful ass that God himself could kiss it." Azpitia was fond of making such comparisons for he also said to a young woman, María de las Rosas, that she was more beautiful than God's mother, and while embracing her, he declared, "What a hug is missing here, God the Father!" The Inquisition was slow in responding to the denunciation, and only imprisoned Azpitia nearly a year later, on January 17, 1615. On March 8, they gave the tailor a stern sentence: He would hear mass with a gag in his mouth, a rope around his neck, and a candle in his hand, be paraded on a donkey, receive one hundred lashes, and be exiled from Mexico City for five years.[47]

Other Spaniards preferred to make their point in a straightforward and blunt manner. For instance, in September 1610, Diego de León was talking with other men about the women in the house of Gerónimo de Cuevas's father in Mexico City. León declared with great enthusiasm that he "wanted to screw (*darles un cimbrón*) all the women in the world," and he even asserted in a delirious image of sexual potency that he wanted "to screw the Virgin in the air (*darle un cimbrón en los aires*)."[48]

Similarly, around 1691, Don Bernardo de Benavente Quiñones, an overseer in the mines of San Pedro de los Pozos, was reported to have said that he "would screw even the Virgin." On February 16, 1691, Benavente's denouncer, Captain Juan Vélez de Guevara, declared to Lorenzo de Salazar y Zapata, a priest commissioned by the Inquisition to gather information in the case, that when drunk, Benavente had said that the Virgin was a whore like all women. Benavente's fondness for slandering the Virgin was an ongoing concern for the miners of San Pedro, who feared divine retaliation in the form of a disaster.[49] In December 1690, the miners rebelled against Benavente, who was forced to ask the mines' owner, Pedro de Arana, to help end the riot.[50] Although Arana had threatened to kill anyone who dared to denounce his compadre, on December 18, Captain Vélez wrote asking the Holy Office to end Benavente's "horrors and blasphemies" that had scandalized and endangered the mining town. Having gathered all the information, Father Salazar sent the testimonies to the Inquisition's headquarters in Mexico City. Yet, probably because of Arana's threats, the Holy Office received no further denunciations, and Benavente's case simply gathered dust in the tribunal.

Marital Abuse and the Domestic Sphere

A darker side of blasphemy as a kind of menacing speech was revealed when Spanish men used it to abuse their wives. In most cases, men blasphemed during marital disputes when their authority inside the household was challenged. Indeed, a cause of marital abuse involving blasphemy

was "entitlement thwarted," something sociologists today also cite as being behind other forms of domestic abuse.[51] For instance, Juan de Moya
had an inn in Mexico City in 1569. According to Father Francisco de Vea
and other unidentified witnesses, Moya fought frequently with his wife
because she refused to prepare the food for their guests and instead spent
her time in church or praying the rosary. "Voto a Dios that you won't go
to mass for the rest of your life," he told her once. On another occasion,
he threatened to burn her rosary if he saw her praying again. Reportedly,
Moya even spat at the sky and stamped his foot, saying, "May he who
created her be damned!" Denounced to the Inquisition, Moya was imprisoned and interrogated on May 21. He admitted making blasphemous
remarks, but he blamed his wife for provoking him: "You have forced me
to say what I did not want to," he allegedly told her.[52] Moya's attorney argued on June 3 that the innkeeper's utterances should be excused because
he was angry about his wife's disobedience. The attorney pointed out
that Moya lived a miserable life because his wife was *brava e indómita*
(truculent and indomitable). Despite the established Christian principle
that wives should obey their husbands, the inquisitor found Moya's behavior excessive, and on July 26, he sentenced him to receive fifty lashes
in prison, hear a penitential mass at the Hospital del Amor de Dios, and
pay thirty gold pesos.[53]

In a 1598 case, a tavern keeper in Cholula, Francisco de Garfias Abrego,
complained to one of his friends about his wife, Catalina de Loza. "*Vivo
mártir*" (I live like a martyr), he declared, claiming that Catalina refused to
obey his prohibition on visiting some of her female relatives who had bad
reputations. Like Moya, Garfias frequently fought with his wife. Cursing,
he would beat her and threaten her with a butcher knife. Probably tired
of her husband's debauchery, one night in September 1598, while he was
in Acapulco, Catalina denounced him to Diego de Coca Rendón, *familiar*
(a member of the Inquisition police) of the Holy Office in Cholula. Summoned on October 14, Catalina testified that Garfias had said many "heresies," and he had renounced God while playing cards at home. Warning
him that "the walls have ears," she had urged him to denounce himself to
the Inquisition. He refused, exclaiming "God is a faggot (*puto*)" and "his
mother is a whore."

Garfias was imprisoned on January 13, 1599. Four days later, he declared with tears in his eyes that he was drunk when he had renounced
God during the card game. After Fiscal Martos de Bohórquez made a formal accusation on January 23, Garfias claimed that his wife had falsely

denounced him in order to get rid of him and live as she pleased. Like Juan de Moya, Garfias presented himself before the Inquisition as a man whose authority had been unjustly challenged by his unruly wife. In the opinion of several witnesses, however, it was Garfias who had infringed the matrimonial pact by mistreating Loza. Francisco de Mosquera, Garfias's father-in-law, testified that he once had to intervene in one of the couple's frequent fights to prevent Garfias from killing his daughter. In the end, Inquisitor Alonso de Peralta sentenced Garfias in an auto-da-fé on March 25, 1601. Wearing the penitential symbols, he heard his sentence: to perform public abjuration de levi; to be led, gagged and shirtless, through the streets on a burro; to receive one hundred lashes; and to be banished from Puebla and Cholula for three years.[54]

In contrast to the tendency of Spanish men to blame unruly wives for "forcing" them to blaspheme, women often tried to present their husband's expletives as part of an abusive pattern of mistreatment and brutality (*mala vida*).[55] Canon and civil law granted husbands the right to beat their wives and children, but with the help of friends, relatives, or the local priest, women were occasionally able to negotiate limits to that.

On April 22, 1562, for instance, María Casarrubias denounced her husband, the innkeeper, Diego López, to the provisor of Antequera, Juan Ruiz Núñez. According to Casarrubias, her husband owed a great deal of money to his creditors. Seeking somewhere he could stay without being recognized, López had told her to ask another innkeeper if he would rent him a room. Although Casarrubias did as her husband had ordered, he refused to believe her when he arrived home. In a fit of pique, he smashed several objects and exclaimed that "even if God himself came down and told him that she went [to see about the room], he would not believe it." She also declared that López used to give himself to the devil and was fond of saying that not even half of the four thousand devils he believed lived in hell would come to take him off. Witnesses to these and other violent exchanges at the inn declared that López was constantly beating up his wife, dragging her by the hair, cutting off her hair with scissors, throwing objects at her, and threatening to kill her. Facing the provisor, López readily confessed to all these crimes with the hope of getting a merciful sentence. Yet, besides pondering the magnitude of López's blasphemies, the provisor found it particularly disturbing that the innkeeper treated his wife "as a slave." López's physical and verbal abuse showed an absolute lack of respect for the holy sacrament of matrimony. Thus, on April 28, 1562, Juan Ruiz was severe, sentencing López to take part in the procession to the church of San Marcos, hear a penitential mass, be paraded on a beast, receive two hundred lashes as he walked around the cathedral; pay for the costs of his trial; and undergo a one-year exile from Antequera.[56]

Although abused women did not always succeed in negotiating "the fine line between wise chastisement and endangerment of life due to violence," it is clear that familial intervention could make a big difference in their domestic lives.[57] Consider a 1568 case in Colima: Pedro de Trejo was denounced by his mother-in-law, sister-in-law, and several other of his wife's relatives, because he had uttered many blasphemies and verbally abused her. Witnesses appealed to the bishop of Michoacán, Antonio de Morales y Molino. They told him that on one occasion Trejo was beating his wife when his brothers-in-law intervened, and outraged by this intrusion in his marital affairs, Trejo then roared that "even if Christ himself came down from heaven and asked him on his knees to give a good life to his wife, he would still kill her in four months." Responding to these accusations from prison on July 29, 1568, Trejo correctly identified several of his denouncers, whom he described as his capital enemies. Since Trejo had identified his denouncers, he theoretically had the right to have his trial annulled. However, the prosecutor dismissed this legal argument by claiming that the prisoner was aware that these individuals had witnessed him committing the crimes, and so he was able to identify them. On March 21, 1569, Bishop Morales y Molino condemned Trejo to attend a penitential mass and pay four hundred gold pesos. He appealed his sentence on March 22, but there is no record of whether or not it was overturned.[58]

The most impressive case involving blasphemy as threatening speech, chronic mistreatment, and marital abuse was that of Manuel Fernández de Figueroa. This 28-year-old baker was denounced on October 10, 1667, to the Inquisition's comisario (local official) in Guadalajara, Felipe de Zavala. According to the testimony of his denouncer, the priest Gaspar de Medina y Padilla, and other witnesses, Fernández, in fits of jealousy, frequently insulted and beat up his wife, Mariana de la Cruz. One night, after Fernández had beaten Cruz, she decided to go to the house of her aunt, Petronila de la Cruz. On the advice of her aunt and uncle, Cruz asked the Provisor Baltazar de la Peña to grant her a divorce. After initiating the suit, the provisor ordered Cruz to be *depositada* (placed, or "deposited") at the house of her aunt. The next day, Fernández went to get his wife, and when he was prevented from doing so, he angrily exclaimed that he shit on the priests and their miters and on Saint Peter and his keys. Another witness, a mulatta, María de Lima, stated that when the provisor asked Fernández why he did not treat his wife well, the baker had answered that it was because she was a whore and that he was even jealous of the baby Jesus, for she would surely give him her *coño* (cunt) if he asked her for it. The wife's uncle, Nicolás Cordero, testified that Fernández had once scolded Cruz because she was standing at the door of the house, asking her, "Haven't I said to you that even if Saint Augustin comes to the door asking for something, you should not give it to him?" Knowing that he had been denounced to the Holy Office, Fernández de Figueroa presented himself voluntarily before Inquisitor Juan de Ortega y Montañez on December 12, 1667, in Mexico City. Although he referred to fights he had had with several of his wife's relatives, he did not confess to any of the blasphemies for which he had been denounced. Fernández managed to have Cruz returned to him, whereupon he decided to leave Guadalajara and start a new life with his wife in Mexico City. Unfortunately, this was not the end of Cruz's problems. Shortly before Easter 1668, Fernández again beat her up. Crying inconsolably, she reproached her husband, "What did you bring me here for? Just to beat me up?" While lying comfortably on his bed, Fernández answered that she was his wife and that he was going to do with her as he pleased. He added in a formidable scatological outburst, "I shit on the four Gospels, on your Guardian Angel, on your mother's tomb, and your father is burning in hell inside a horn, and the bishop is a cuckold. I shit on his miter and his consecration, and my shit is more truthful than your Guardian Angel."[59] As a result of that tirade, Mariana de la Cruz sought refuge in the Convent of Santa Catarina in Mexico City, where she stayed for a while. When Fernández went to see Cruz, Dominican Father Antonio Pedrique reproached him for mistreating her. Fernández replied that if his wife had abandoned him it was because she had fallen in love with either a saint or a demon.

On May 7, 1669, the Holy Office reopened Fernandez's case when Father Antonio denounced him to Inquisitor Ortega y Montañez. Two days later, Francisca de Garibay, Cruz's neighbor, offered an account of Fernández's latest beating, and Cruz herself declared on May 10 that her husband had called up the devil to take him off in body and soul, and among many other things, he had said that "not even God with all his power can stop me from doing as I please with my wife." Imprisoned on May 21, 1669, Fernández had his first hearing on May 24, 1669. Although he first denied having blasphemed, he gradually acknowledged his crimes in subsequent hearings. Listing all of Fernández's offenses in his formal accusation, the prosecutor stated that the defendant "seemed to have no other profession but that of a blasphemer." On December 7, 1670, the tribunal sentenced him to hear a penitential mass, while gagged, holding a candle, and with a rope about his neck; to be paraded on Mexico's streets while a crier broadcast his crimes; and to be exiled for four years to the Philippines.[60]

Although the inquisitors decided to punish Fernández's excesses, it is clear that the tribunal's main concern was not the brutal mistreatment to which he subjected his wife but the culprit's use of deprecatory speech against God. This notwithstanding, women like Mariana de la Cruz were able to set limits to their husbands' violence by framing their verbal excesses within a pattern of physical abuse. This was certainly not easy, for even *abogados* (defense attorneys) appointed by the Holy Office had no problem arguing that a defendant had been forced to blaspheme on account of his wife's behavior. It is probable that most men did not abuse or attack the women with whom they lived, but the available evidence indicates that those who did believed that their behavior was perfectly justifiable. As today's researchers on domestic violence have shown, "Husbands who batter wives typically feel that they are exercising a right, maintaining good order in the family, and punishing their wives' delinquency."[61] In colonial Mexico, men's sense of entitlement was so well established that husbands even used tropes of persecution (for example, claiming to live "like a martyr" in their own households) in order to depict themselves as victims of women who refused to know "their place." Because a woman's "unruliness" evidenced her husband's inability to control his wife, it is understandable that some abusive men felt emasculated to the point of challenging God (whom, significantly, they often called "faggot"). Blasphemy clearly represented a privileged tool that men used in the domestic sphere to enact and reproduce the structure of gender inequality in the larger society. However, the pervasiveness of blasphemy within the household is the best proof that the structure of domination did not go unchallenged.

On the Move: A Culture of Work

Outside of the domestic sphere, men engaged in blasphemy as part of what can be called a mobile culture of work. Subjected to frequent dis-

placements for occupational reasons, soldiers, sailors, and muleteers constituted figures uprooted from customary social relationships, and occasionally, the imperial state had difficulty controlling them. Their work
called for endurance, strength, and toughness, important ingredients
in the definition and display of their masculinity through labor. These
men "on the move" frequently resorted to blasphemy as an expression
of displacement, risk taking, and self-estrangement from the Christian
community. Like other men, they used this powerful speech as a tool for
challenging, disputing, and asserting dominance. For these mobile men,
gender identity and work culture were closely linked, so blasphemy also
became an element of the performance of the toughness associated with
their trades. Under these conditions, blasphemy represented a language
both of male bonding and solidarity and of estrangement and social detachment. The balance between these two countervailing forces was fragile, for these workingmen and their audiences also shared the conviction
that blasphemy was a source of danger on the road, at the fortress, and at
sea. Frequently, it was in the midst of that tension that denunciations to
the Holy Office were made.

Among the occupations most typically associated with high mobility
in colonial Mexico was that of *arriero* (muleteer). Muleteers established
inland communications, transported merchandise, and generally reduced
"the friction of distance," so these men played a fundamental role in the
creation and maintenance of the social fabric that connected different regions in New Spain. Muleteers not only traveled well-worn roads, such
as the one leading from Mexico to Veracruz, but also ventured to mining
towns and marginal areas, which, in the process, they helped to develop
and later consolidate as communities. And yet, moving constantly from
one place to another, and sleeping one night here and another there, muleteers were also regarded with suspicion as liminal or "floating" members
of society. As Richard Boyer has pointed out, arrieros were suspected of
delinquent behavior and religious transgressions, such as bigamy, which
involved the abandonment of kinship ties and a certain degree of up-
rootedness.[62] This was not entirely true, however. As recent research has
shown, muleteers were enmeshed in a dense network of kinship ties that
allowed them to get initiated in the business, acquire necessary resources
for their trade through loans or inheritance, and even get new clients
through recommendations of relatives.[63]

The image of the arriero as an uprooted and crime-prone individual
was a stereotype, but muleteers did tend to blaspheme on the road. Most

attributed this to the inherent harshness of this occupation. Indeed, life for the muleteer was extremely hard. The roads were in bad condition and were almost impossible to use during the rainy season. Bandits and robbers were very active, especially on the main roads. The *ventas* (inns) were relatively expensive and not particularly clean. The valuable pack animals could collapse on the road from being overloaded or lacking rest, or they might have to be shot after breaking a leg. As interregional trade grew in importance, many Indians from pueblos near the main routes became arrieros, thus increasing the overall level of competition and causing the transportation fees to drop.[64] It was in the midst of this difficult environment that some muleteers felt prompted to blaspheme the Christian god.

In 1537, Francisco Jiménez denounced himself before Zumárraga. Three months earlier, a herd of oxen had scared his pack train, making the horses dump their cargo. Seeing the resulting chaos, Jiménez hit himself in the head and then with deep anger and frustration, he uttered "pese a Dios!" Despite Jiménez denouncing himself and using the strenuous nature of his trade as an excuse, Zumárraga sentenced him to pay twenty gold pesos and attend a penitential mass.[65]

The harshness of his work was also the excuse the muleteer Juan Moreno offered when he presented himself before Inquisitor Zumárraga on August 4, 1537, after Juan de Cura and Alfonso de Gallego denounced him for blaspheming on the road. Moreno traveled the route between Mexico and Veracruz transporting various kinds of merchandise, including wine, grains, and nuts. Around June 20, Moreno loaded one of his horses in preparation for a trip, but the animal lay down, refusing to make the journey with such a heavy load. Moreno then lost his patience and yelled at the horse, "Don't do that, *canalla* (you bastard)! I renounce San Francisco!" Facing Zumárraga, Moreno declared in his second hearing on August 12, 1537, that his trade as muleteer was so harsh that he could not help saying something against God, as he frequently did during his numerous trips. Like Jiménez, he was forced to pay twenty gold pesos and attend a penitential mass.[66] Three years later, muleteer Juan Cabezas also blasphemed, saying "pese a Dios!" when a sack ripped, spilling its contents of hazelnuts on the road. He was sentenced to pay six gold pesos and the costs of the trial.[67] The harshness of this trade was also probably to blame for gaining the Galician Gonzalo de Santiago a reputation as a contumacious blasphemer in the town of Antequera in 1566. He was sentenced to pay twenty gold pesos and attend a penitential mass for saying,

"pese a Dios [up] there where he is!" He was warned not to blaspheme
again lest he receive one hundred lashes.[68]

Clearly, muleteer was a difficult occupation that required skill and endurance. A muleteer frequently found his resources taxed when trying
to cover losses resulting from accidents, bad weather, and even robbery.
Despite the tribulations and risks of this occupation, it was perceived as
being relatively lucrative. This was certainly true for the *señores de recuas* (masters of mule trains) who owned carts and wagons that could
carry large cargoes.[69] For Ambrosio Pareja, a forty-year-old arriero born
in Jaen, Spain, this perception was not only wrong but also utterly annoy-
ing. In September 1570, Pareja, en route to Mexico City, stopped by the
banks of the Cuitzeo to water his horses. There he struck up a conversation with some other men who commented in passing that he must make
good money in his trade. Profoundly irritated, Pareja swore to God that
if somebody were to give him one hundred pesos for his train of horses
and the black slave who worked with him, he would happily abandon his
trade and turn into a heretic. Six months later, one of audience denounced
Pareja to the provisor of Guadalajara, Melchor Gómez. On April 3, 1571,
Pareja confessed to his crime and was sentenced to buy a pitcher of oil for
the Eucharist, a very mild punishment.[70]

Muleteers usually needed to meet deadlines, which occasionally forced
them to work on Sundays or holy days. In colonial times, failure to observe religious holidays was a serious offense, indicating that the individual in question did not show the respect due to the Christian calendar
and was someone who refused to participate in the religious rituals that
would mark him as a member of the community. On July 5, 1573, muleteer Hernán Pérez denounced himself to the comisario of Oaxaca for
blaspheming and failing to observe a holy day. As in many other cases,
Pérez denounced himself as a preemptive strategy to avoid a sterner punishment, by confessing before someone else could accuse him. Several
days before, Pérez explained to the comisario, he was on the road transporting merchandise to the harbor of Huatulco. He wanted to arrive at
the port as soon as possible because his sacks were in poor shape, and he
was afraid he might lose his cargo. Night fell, and he was forced to sleep
at the town of Miacuatlán. He planned to leave early in the morning but
since the next day was a holy day, he asked the vicar of the town, Diego
Trujillo, for permission to work. The priest refused to authorize that and
told Pérez to go to church like everybody else or face excommunication.
Pérez hit the road and swore to God that he would hear mass with a

different priest. He then uttered other, unspecified "ugly words" against the Catholic Church. On July 11, 1573, Pérez was sentenced to attend a penitential mass and pay twenty gold pesos, and he was explicitly ordered not to work on Sundays or holy days.[71]

The trials discussed here involved only Spaniards, but it is likely that throughout the colonial period, arrieros of all ethnicities were generally seen as being prone to blasphemy. Indeed, as late as 1796, muleteers were depicted as habitual blasphemers in a popular ballad, "The Trip of the Muleteer." It describes the eventful journey of an arriero who, among other things, allows his mule to eat a cargo of papal bulls to later shit them as indulgences. The muleteer also slashes and insults the image of the thief Gestas in a shrine near to the road, after realizing he had confused him with Christ and mistakenly prayed to him.[72] The story line was mirthful, but its elements clearly reflect the harshness of the lives these tough arrieros led.

If muleteers were considered to be, metaphorically, "floating" members of their communities, sailors were literally part of a floating community. In contrast to arrieros, seafarers were expected to work on Easter, holy days, and Sundays. Even though the sixteenth-century Franciscan writer Antonio de Guevara claimed that sailors frequently ignored the religious calendar, that claim is not entirely true. Although Mass was rarely celebrated because only large war galleons carried a chaplain, crewmembers were accustomed to praying twice a day, at morning break and in the afternoon, and they even said a Hail Mary on Saturdays.[73] As an experienced traveler, Guevara also observed that when in danger, sailors often prayed and tearfully promised to undertake pilgrimages if they were saved, but that once the peril had passed, they relaxed, gambled, and even blasphemed the name of God.[74] This apparently was not seen as being contradictory as long as prayers and blasphemies were each uttered at appropriate times, a condition not always respected, to the dismay of other members of the crew. In 1557, for example, a Spanish ship was caught in a powerful storm on its way to the harbor of Huatulco, close to Puerto Angel in Oaxaca. Fearing the worst, some members of the crew were praying for God's mercy when the pilot of the ship unexpectedly roared, "Come demons! Take me off, and take this ship with me, because God has no power to help us!" As might be expected, the alarmed crewmen denounced the pilot, Francisco Roldán, to the Inquisition as soon as they came ashore. When he was interrogated in Antequera on September 14, Roldán confessed to having summoned the demons, but he denied expressing any doubt about God's power. Two days later, he stated that it would be unthinkable for him to say such words, because he had been sailing for years and so knew the risks of engaging in such behavior at sea. Questioning the veracity of his denouncers, he added that those who testified against him were mere sailors, vile men *de baja suerte* (of the lower echelons), who should not be believed. He, on the contrary, was a hidalgo and a God-fearing Christian. The inquisitor clearly found such arguments unconvincing, and Roldán was sentenced to pay eighty gold pesos and attend a mass with the symbols of the blasphemer: a gag in his mouth, a rope about his neck, and a candle in his hands.[75]

Although the House of Trade in Seville prohibited recruiting foreigners as crewmembers, continuing difficulties in obtaining seamen led *maestres* (shipmasters) to disregard this law and include in their crews people of many nations. As Pablo E. Pérez-Mallaína has pointed out, in the final years of the sixteenth century and the first of the seventeenth, the Spanish Crown required between seven thousand and nine thousand seamen to guarantee regular communication with its colonies. Understandably, foreigners constituted a large portion of the average crew, starting with Columbus's first trip to Hispaniola, and their presence reached more than twenty percent in the last quarter of the sixteenth century. Many were hired for their precise technical knowledge, as was the case of gunners, also known as *lombarderos*, but most were employed simply because they were a source of cheap manual labor. For their part, enrolling in the Spanish fleet appealed to foreigners as a way to bypass the House of Trade's control on immigration to the New World.[76]

In terms of nationality, about one in every two of the foreigners was Portuguese, and one in four was Italian. The presence of French and English sailors was rare, since they were suspected of not being Catholic and their homelands were traditional enemies of Spain.[77] The Inquisition was particularly severe when it came to punishing foreigners who blasphemed the Christian god in their mother tongues.

Gerónimo Pullo was a young French sailor who worked on a galley ship that departed from the Canary Islands bound for Veracruz. On a night in 1571, while he was sleeping, some sailors tied one of his feet to a rope and using a tackle, abruptly jerked him up in the air. The startled Pullo became extremely angry and shouted to the sailors to let him down. When they refused, Pullo yelled in exasperation, *"Je renieu Dieu!"* (I renounce God). Unfortunately for Pullo, some of the sailors knew French and denounced him when the ship arrived at San Juan de Ulúa, an island fortress in the port of Veracruz. He was accused of setting a bad example and being a source of scandal on the ship. Pullo confessed to this crime in his first hearing with Inquisitor Pedro Moya de Contreras and was sentenced on February 8, 1574, to attend a penitential mass with the symbols of the blasphemer and to receive one hundred lashes.[78]

Like Pullo, many other foreign sailors were denounced during the customary *visitas de navíos* (ship inspections) carried out by the Inquisition. Indeed, following royal injunctions, representatives of the Holy Office inspected ships on arrival at San Juan de Ulúa to investigate if crimes had been committed by either crewmembers or passengers. Accompanied by a notary and a constable, the deputy of the Inquisition would summon the shipmaster, the pilot, and one or two passengers, and he would ask them "if the passengers, or any crewmember had blasphemed repeatedly and contumaciously." If so, the individual in question was imprisoned and his possessions seized by the Holy Tribunal.[79] This was how crewmembers of the galley *San Lorenzo* denounced Marcelo Miravello to the Holy Office on July 10, 1597. According to the constable of the galley, Miravello, a Neapolitan gunner, had lost a sizable amount of money in a card game sometime in May. When this officer asked Miravello what had happened, the Italian told the constable to leave him alone, and later he added, "*Reniego di dio!*" (I renounce God). Others heard him say "*putana di dio*" (whore of God) and insult his patron saint, San Marcelo. Miravello was denounced to the ship's captain, Salvador de Heredia, who ordered him to remain with his mouth in contact with the floor for one hour and to pay for two pounds of wax for the church. The Italian's punishment was relatively lenient, the fleet's military authorities often condemned for occasional blasphemers to spend a month with their feet in the stocks, a punishment that left many of them half crippled.[80] But Miravello's troubles did not end there. Later, Heredia instructed Sergeant Gil Martín de Pareja to gather the necessary information to denounce Miravello to the comisario of the Holy Office as soon as they arrived at San Juan de Ulúa. Initially jailed in Veracruz, Marcelo was later transferred to Mexico City because he had no money to pay for his expenses in prison. He stated in his first hearing, on August 18, 1597, that he was the son of Old Christians, but when the authorities asked him to make the sign of the cross, he did not know how. He was thirty-eight years old and had been working as a sailor on Spanish and Italian ships since the age of ten, when he had left his parent's home. Although he was married, he had not seen his wife in a long time. After the third hearing, the prosecutor stated in his formal accusation that by saying "putana di dio," Miravello had depicted God as imperfect insofar as it suggested that he had the same weaknesses as human beings. Besides, the prosecutor charged, Miravello was supposed to show special reverence to his patron saint. Since Miravello was too poor to pay for his stay in prison, the inquisitor sent him to work in the *obraje* (textile mill) of Juan Álvarez in Mexico City on October 13, 1597, pending his trial. It seems that he toiled there for an incredibly long time, nearly four years. He was finally sentenced on March 25, 1601, in an auto-da-fé. His sentence was exile from New Spain for an undetermined period, and he was returned to his wife on the first ship leaving San Juan de Ulúa for Europe.[81]

A similarly lengthy trial, showing the excessive severity with which foreigners were treated, was that of thirty-year-old Pedro Hernández, a sailor and fisherman temporarily living in the town of Alvarado in Veracruz. Like many other sailors at the time, Hernández was highly mobile. Born in Prado, Portugal, in 1567, Hernández had lived with his parents until the age of twelve, when he moved to Braga, where he learned to read and write. He later returned to Prado, but after his father died, he moved again, now to Evora, to work as a shepherd. He worked for five years in several towns in Portugal. In 1587, wanting a change, he crossed the Atlantic as a sailor on the ship of Francisco Pérez Granillo, which was headed to New Spain. He returned to Spain on a different vessel. Later, he again embarked en route to San Juan de Ulúa. In the intervals between his trans-Atlantic trips, Hernández found temporary work on both continents, as a fisherman in Almería and Alvarado. In July 1596, Hernández was in Alvarado, where he apparently got into a fight. Somebody wounded him in the right hand with a knife, and in an angry outburst, Hernández called up the demons, saying that they were cowards because they did not take him off in clothes and shoes. He went on to say that he did not believe in God or any of his saints, and that God had no power at all to heal. Several fishermen who heard his utterances advised him to denounce himself to the Holy Office, or they would do it. When he failed to report himself, he was denounced. From July 11 to July 14, a notary of the Holy Office gathered the pertinent information, which he forwarded to the Inquisition. An arrest order was issued on June 7, 1597. Comisario Francisco Carranco arrested Hernández, and on October 11, he was incarcerated in the Inquisition's prison in Mexico City. The sailor confessed to his crime during his first hearing, on October 20, and in his second hearing, three days later, he said that he had nothing more to add. Yet, on

October 24, at the end of the third hearing, when the prosecutor had formally charged him, Hernández tearfully asked for mercy and assured the Holy Tribunal that he had blasphemed in anger but that he never desired to drift away from the Catholic faith. He was interrogated once more on October 25, but he did not add anything new to his confession. Between January 19 and June 6, 1598, Hernández had three more hearings in which he was admonished to confess his crimes fully. Finally, on June 12, 1598, Hernández could not endure any more pressure and asked for a new hearing in which he assumed full responsibility for his blasphemies and while crying on his knees, he begged again for forgiveness. Strangely, on July 2, 1598, Inquisitor Peralta prolonged things by sending Hernández to work in Gaspar Gutiérrez's obraje in Mexico City. Hernández was probably still working there when Peralta finally sentenced him in an auto-da-fé on March 25, 1601. The punishment consisted of the usual spiritual penance, two hundred lashes, and three years of exile from the town of Alvarado.

As the case of Pedro Hernández indicates, many sailors engaged in blasphemy not only on the high seas but also at the port of San Juan de Ulúa, where they generally wintered over until February or March. At port, the sailors busied themselves working on the deck, cleaning the ship, and loading their vessel for the trip back to Spain. The port was perpetually busy, because ships also normally departed at the end of August or the beginning of September.[82] During the months in harbor, the population of Veracruz almost tripled, with between two thousand and four thousand sailors, plus muleteers, merchants, and workers who repaired the damage that had been done to the ships in their passage through the coral reefs surrounding the port.[83]

One inn, La Casa de las Mentiras (The House of Lies), was quite popular with the sailors as a place to eat and drink, have casual conversations, and occasionally engage in male bonding and socializing. It was there in February 1572 that a ship's officer, Iñigo de Lozoya, born in Vizcaya, was reported to have blasphemed the name of God. On March 24, Juan Ramírez, a thirty-year-old sailor from Triana, Seville, denounced Lozoya to Comisario Francisco Pérez Rebolledo, for another incident. In this one, Lozoya had uttered, "Pese a Dios!" when his subordinates refused to carry out his orders to punish a member of the crew. Witnesses working on other ships, the *San Francisco* and *Nuestra Señora de la Candelaria*, also declared that Lozoya, who suffered from a painful inflammation in one of his legs, had once told to the harbor chaplain "that he loved his leg more than God." Yet, when the comisario ordered him to be imprisoned, the captain of the fleet, Don Cristóbal de Grasso, twice refused to turn him over. Although Lozoya was finally fined one hundred gold pesos and severely reprimanded, his sentence was much lighter than that endured by French, Italian, and Portuguese sailors who dared to blaspheme.[84]

Indeed, as we have seen, corporal punishment seemed to have been reserved mostly for foreigners. Yet, even a Spaniard could be physically punished if he dared to defy the Holy Office by attempting to escape. On November 17, 1605, Marcos de Betanzos, a sailor on the ship *San Pedro*, denounced Juanes de Olachea. At dinnertime on the ship, after another sailor had read a prayer to the Holy Ghost, the Holy Trinity, the Virgin, and the Saints, Olachea had claimed that he did not believe in any of those entities. Reprimanded by other crewmen, Olachea told those who disagreed with him that they were a bunch of *cabrones* (assholes). On November 21, after more than ten witnesses had testified against him, Olachea presented himself before Comisario Francisco Carranco. He did not deny what he had said, but he claimed he had been angry with the other sailors. Moreover, he explained, they envied his appointment as *despensero* (steward), so they falsely reported him to the *contramaestre* (shipmaster's assistant) for stealing food.

The animosity against Olachea was probably not unfounded. As the least prestigious of the officers on board, stewards were in charge of distributing food rations. Protests over the poor quality and quantity of the rations were common, and stewards played an important role in suffocating such rumblings before they turned into mutinies. These officers also had exclusive access to the food-storage areas, and as presumably was the case with Olachea, often yielded to the temptation of trafficking in the ship's supplies.[85]

Ignoring Olachea's excuses, the inquisitors ordered him to be imprisoned. Between December 15 and December 19, he was interrogated three times. While waiting in prison for his final sentence, Olachea shared a cell with Pedro Núñez, who convinced Olchea that his case must be a serious one since he had been imprisoned even though he had admitted to his crimes. Núñez suggested that they should escape to Spain and then go to Rome to ask the Pope for forgiveness. Convinced of the feasibility of making such an incredible journey, Olachea helped Núñez to dig a hole in the wall with a nail. The inmates left the prison at around one in the morning on February 6, 1606. In the town of San Diego, an Indian helped them to remove their chains. From there, they went to San Juan, a town in Tacuba, where they decided to stay for a while. Probably riding on stolen horses, Núñez and Olachea also crossed Tlalnepantla in direction to Toluca. It was then that Olachea learned from Núñez that he made a living as a highwayman and had already escaped from prison once. The sailor decided to part ways with his companion, and go on, on his own, to Veracruz. There he was captured on April 13. On May 9, 1606, he was sentenced in punishment for escaping to be paraded in public and lashed two hundred times. Finally, on May 13, Inquisitors Gutierre Bernardo de Quiroz and Alonso de Peralta sentenced him to attend a penitential mass and receive instruction in the Catholic Faith for six months.[86]

We do not know if Olachea ever returned to being a sailor, but if he did, it is unlikely he found living conditions at sea much different from those he had endured in prison. That was the opinion, according to Pérez-Mallaína, of a good number of sailors at the time. Indeed, in the early modern period, comparing Spanish ships to "wooden prisons" became one of the most common topoi among seamen. The similarities were striking. Crammed into a small area for months on end, sailors lived and worked in an environment characterized by a dreadful lack of hygiene, comfort, and privacy. This situation was compounded by the harsh climate, meager food, lack of water, and disease. In such oppressive circumstances, sailors often engaged in fiercely competitive and abusive relationships that involved playing practical jokes on each other, engaging in brawls, and even subjecting each other to sexual abuse. Clearly, surviving in this environment was not simple, and as is also the case in modern prisons, many men felt compelled to adopt a swaggering style that involved exhibiting physical prowess and engaging in risk taking, such as blaspheming, if they were to stand a chance of surviving.

Closely related to the sailors as a group were the soldiers, who also experienced a mobile and active life working both in the harbors of colonial Mexico and on board ships, either as crewmen or passengers bound for Spanish fortresses on Caribbean islands and in the Philippines. Like the sailors, soldiers frequently resorted to blasphemy to project an image of daring, strength, and bravery before their fellow soldiers. For instance, on February 13, 1595, Gabriel de Ortega and Cristóbal de Yllescas denounced Pascual de Castro, a *cabo* (petty officer) from the squad of one Captain Pacheco. According to their testimony before the Holy Office in Mexico City, Castro, about to set sail to the Philippines with his squad, was not happy with the idea of leaving New Spain. His comrades had gibed him, saying that he was going to a terrible place. The officer feigned indifference by stating that there were as many storms in New Spain as in the Philippines: "Let there be tempests, thunder, and lightning," he added in anger, "and if the sky itself comes down, I will raise my sword so that God himself could get stuck on it." Knowing the gravity of his utterances, Castro denounced himself two days later. Given his profound repentance and his orders to embark for the Philippines, the inquisitor took pity on him and simply reprimanded him.[87]

Cowardice and fear were deemed emotions particularly despicable in a soldier and, like Castro, other military men boasted of their bravery through blasphemous remarks. Captain-Lieutenant López Patiño, another case in point, was denounced in Campeche on April 18, 1566, for saying that he wanted to set sail despite bad weather, and that he did not need God's help at all. He defied the Divinity to sink the ship when it left the harbor. This was only one example of López's inventiveness for, according to his denouncer, soldier Francisco Gómez, the captain was "always looking for new ways of blaspheming (renegar)." Facing the Holy Office on June 2, 1566, López confessed to having said everything, "sometimes out of anger and sometimes because of a despicable habit (ruin costumbre)." The inquisitors may have deemed the "bad habit" more relevant when considering the magnitude of López's crime, for they sentenced him to spend twenty days in the monastery of San Augustín in Mexico City, to fast on several Fridays, and to pay one hundred gold pesos plus the costs of his trial.[88]

Like López Patiño and Pascual de Castro, most soldiers tried for blasphemy in sixteenth- and seventeenth-century New Spain worked at the harbor of Veracruz, particularly on the island fortress of San Juan de Ulúa where many of them were stationed. At this time, almost all Atlantic commerce in New Spain was concentrated in San Juan de Ulúa. Between 1550 and 1600, for instance, an annual average of 52 ships arrived at San Juan de Ulúa, transporting approximately 11,082 tons of merchandise, including food, wine, books, animals, and plants. Since Ulúa had no storage facilities, the commodities had to be taken to Veracruz for sale and distribution.[89] The frequency with which soldiers resorted to blasphemy in the lively fortress was a constant source of scandal. Voicing what was probably the opinion of many at the port, in 1606, the comisario of Veracruz, Juan Arias, despairingly wrote to the Holy Office that San Juan de Ulúa was full of gente perdida y rematada (evil and degenerate people), who frequently blasphemed without fearing God or the secular justice.[90] Indeed, in this incredibly active port, Spanish soldiers found multiple reasons to blaspheme as an angry response to the challenges they endured at the hands of their peers and superiors in this masculine culture of work.

One case was that of Blas Pérez de Rivera, a 18-year-old soldier stationed at San Juan de Ulúa. In 1589, when someone stole his sword, he raised his hands skyward and renounced God. He was so angry that he yelled loudly that he would not go to mass until he recovered his weapon, and that even if Saint Paul himself had taken the sword he would force him to give it back. Two years later, he was sentenced to receive one hundred lashes, and to be exiled for two years from Mexico City in addition to the customary penitential penalties.[91] Similarly, Bernardino Alfonso, the young petty officer of the *nao capitana* (flagship)[92] commanded by Pedro Meléndez de Márquez, blasphemed God in 1595 because somebody stole a hen he had taken to the Casa de las Mentiras to have it cooked for his dinner. When Alfonso asked a constable about his hen, he said that a poor, hungry man who was roaming around the establishment might have taken the bird. Alfonso then angrily uttered, "I swear to God that I will beat up that beggar if he took my hen, and even God himself if he did it." Denounced to the comisario of Veracruz, Friar Francisco Carranco, Alfonso was imprisoned by the Holy Office on January 12, 1596. Judging that Alfonso was too young to punish sternly (the documents simply state that he was *muchacho*, that is, a boy), from an Old Christian hidalgo family, and that he had repented while admitting his guilt before the comisario, Inquisitors Lobo Guerrero and Alonso de Peralta simply reprimanded Alfonso and ordered him to confess and take communion on February 2, the feast of Our Lady of Candles.[93]

Several other cases occurred inside the fortress of San Juan de Ulúa, where the *castellano* (commander) enforced a harsh disciplinary regime on his soldiers. In the face of abuse, a sense of impotence frequently drove victims to blaspheme God in a futile attempt to regain their self-esteem before the other members of the armed forces. On April 21, 1659, Diego Rodríguez, a thirty-four-year-old artilleryman, denounced Alonso de Arango to Veracruz Comisario Bernardo Aguilera. Arango was a soldier drafted for the Armada de Barlovento or Windward Fleet, which Philip IV created in 1629 to patrol and defend the Gulf of Mexico and the Caribbean Sea. When it was finally assembled nine years later, the fleet had twelve galleons and two smaller vessels. It was in constant need of soldiers, and the viceroy issued frequent decrees of recruitment. Arango was probably drafted as a result of one of these.[94]

According to Rodríguez, two days earlier, Arango was fighting with

somebody in the armory. When Rodríguez went to see what was happen-
ing, he found an angry Arango hitting his head repeatedly against the cis-
tern. Believing that he was sick, Rodríguez and another soldier helped him
to stand up, but when they asked Arango what was wrong, he renounced
God. Alarmed by his response, Rodríguez and the other man tried to beat
him into silence, but Arango managed to add that he renounced Christ
and even three thousand Christs. Informed of Arango's sinful utterances,
fortress commander Francisco Castejón ordered Arango to be tied to the
capstan of the castle with a stick in his mouth as a gag. Then, for sixteen
days, he was forced to carry lime and sand for the construction in prog-
ress at the fortress, while spending the nights in the stocks.[95] The Holy
Office, for its part, ordered Arango to be imprisoned in Mexico City.

Almost a month later, on June 24, Arango was brought to the Inquisition's headquarters. In two long hearings, on June 30 and July 1, he
described the incredibly mobile life he had experienced as a nineteen-
year-old soldier, staying for short periods in Madrid, Seville, Cádiz, Cartagena de Indias, Portobello (Panama), Havana, Caracas, Jamaica, Puebla,
Campeche, Alvarado, and finally San Juan de Ulúa. Arango explained to
Inquisitor Bernardo de la Higuera y Amarilla what had happened on April
19 in the armory. Being a conscript, he had tried to escape along with a
mestizo soldier, Juan Martín. Although both of them were later caught,
the commander punished only Arango. Thus, when Martín imprudently
came to Arango to ask for the return of a sleeping mat, which Martín
claimed was his property, they started to fight. Seeing, however, that he
could not take revenge on Martín, Arango lost his temper and swore that
he renounced God, Christ, his mother, the Holy Virgin, and the saints. At
trial, Arango fell to his knees crying and begged for clemency, stating that
he truly regretted having committed these crimes, and that he had been
"drunk with anger" when he blasphemed. Nevertheless, Bernardo de la
Higuera sentenced him on October 14, 1659, to attend a penitential mass
and to be paraded on the streets on a donkey. In addition, he was exiled to
the Philippines for six years where he was to work under the orders of the
governor of those islands. Arango begged the tribunal to spare him the
shame of being paraded publicly and to reduce his time in the Philippines,
arguing that he had already been punished in the fortress and that he had
blasphemed "blind with rage" for having been mistreated (vejado). He
further stated that since he was born in Asturias, that most Christian of
towns, his Christian convictions should be understood as being beyond
suspicion. The prosecutor retorted, however, that the sentence should be

confirmed because, besides constituting heretical blasphemies, Arango's utterances were scandalous in the extreme. Moreover, because Arango had been born in Asturias, it was expected that he would avoid offending the Catholic faith. The sentence was upheld, and Arango publicly abjured de levi of his crimes on November 22. Some time later, he was sent to the Philippines.[96]

If Rodríguez blasphemed out of despair and frustration, other soldiers attacked the Divinity publicly in a pragmatic attempt to draw the attention of the Holy Office in order to be able to get away from the fortress. However, as Joseph de Mendoza, a soldier born in Puebla, soon found out, being denounced did not always guarantee the prompt intervention of the Holy Office. Like many other soldiers at the time, displacement characterized Mendoza's life. He became a soldier when he was fifteen years old by joining a company that was part of the Armada de Barlovento in 1687. After staying one year in Veracruz as member of another company, he went back to the Barlovento fleet as an artilleryman. He returned to Mexico City for two years and obtained an appointment at the fortress of San Juan de Ulúa. He also served as a soldier in the viceregal palace, and he went to Darien, Panama, to repress a rebellion. After the military campaign, Mendoza stayed in Havana for a while, and then he returned to the viceregal palace and, finally, he served for four years as a castle guard at San Juan de Ulúa.

It was while he was there that his problems with the Holy Office began. Everything started when Mendoza left the fortress without permission to visit his sister in Mexico City. He was captured, and, after being imprisoned in the capital for fifty days, Mendoza was sent to San Juan de Ulúa to do hard labor. Three months later, he was placed in the fortress brig. In an attempt to force his jailors to release him, Mendoza renounced God and the saints, and he said that he had no other Lord than the devil. He also tried to hit a painting of Ecce Homo.[97] As a consequence of these and other acts, Lieutenant José Galván denounced him to the Holy Office on November 14, 1703. The prison priest sent a letter to the Holy Office on November 29, 1703, in which he informed the inquisitor that Mendoza had publicly stated that he could get mercy only from the devil and that he wished he had insulted God even before having been born. A few days before, during the earthquake of November 25, 1703, Mendoza had further horrified the prisoners and guards at the fortress when he called up the demons in a loud voice while everybody else was invoking God and the Virgin and soliciting the intercession of the saints. Mendoza was sent to the prison of the Holy Office in Veracruz, but because he was a source of constant scandal to the other prisoners, Comisario Camacho asked the tribunal to order his relocation to the public jail in Veracruz.

Sent to this prison on January 16, 1705, Mendoza attempted to escape one more time with two other men. He was captured and put in the stocks, but he was able to cut the lock, so he was moved to stocks with fetters. Seeing that the prison of Veracruz was not secure enough, on January 21, 1705, the tribunal prosecutor asked that Mendoza be put in the Holy Office prison in Mexico City. On July 13, 1705, the prosecutor presented the tribunal with a long list of Mendoza's crimes, including blaspheming God and the Catholic pantheon and also spitting at holy stamps, making a pact with the devil, stating in writing that Christ was not in the Holy Eucharist, and other heretical remarks.

On July 20, 1705, four months after entering the Holy Office prison, Mendoza had his first hearing. After describing his varied experiences as a soldier, he admitted putting in writing blasphemous remarks against the Holy Eucharist, as well as saying many disparates while in the castle prison, but he claimed that he was only trying to get himself removed from there. Three days later, in his second hearing, Mendoza confessed to making a pact with the devil to kill the commandant. He sealed that pact by taking a knife and carving on his left arm, "I belong to the devil." Repenting that he had done this thing, he later used a piece of broken glass to shape those words into an awkward crucifix. After his fourth hearing, on December 4, 1705, the prosecutor formally accused Mendoza. For some unknown reason, he had to wait almost three years for sentencing. On July 3, 1708, he was ordered to hear a penitential mass with the symbols of a blasphemer (a candle in his hand, a rope about his neck, and a hood). He was also forced to carry his sinful writings hanging from his neck. The tribunal also sentenced him to abjure de vehementi, be paraded on the streets, and receive two hundred lashes. Moreover, Mendoza was exiled for ten years from New Spain, during which time he would work as a galley slave. Finally, he was ordered to pray part of the rosary of the Holy Virgin every single day of those ten years and confess during Easter.[98]

Throughout history, few occupations have been so closely associated with aggressiveness and the monopoly of violence than has that of the soldier. Writing in 1578, the Irish theologian and former soldier Barnaby Rich clearly articulated the prejudices of his time, "If you would call a tyrant, a blasphemer, a murderer, a robber, a spoiler, a deflowerer, and oppressor in one short name, you may call him by the name of soldier."

Barnaby was certainly exaggerating, but many agreed with him that soldiers were nothing but vile, armed brutes in need of constant supervision.[99] Although it is unlikely that brutality was the norm, it is well known that unchecked troops frequently caused havoc among the civil population. In the colony, as late as the second half of the eighteenth century, troops assaulted citizens in parks and theaters, caused trouble and property damage, destroyed crops, invaded Indian towns and abused the residents, and generally wreaked havoc.[100] Not all soldiers were "armed criminals," of course, but it is clear that in the purely masculine environment of the colonial Mexican army, a combination of physical robustness, pride, courage, and a good dose of insolence came to symbolize ideals of masculinity expressed in male bonding and homosociality. In a dangerous occupation characterized by the amalgamation of violence and masculinity, soldiers learned to test and prove their manhood through multiple displays of one-upmanship and verbal aggression epitomized by insults, slander, and blasphemous speech. But no army could exist without rigid discipline, and from the first decades of colonial rule, the authorities took harsh measures to keep soldiers from harassing civilian society, preying upon each other, and endangering the colony with their blaspheming. Undoubtedly, the Inquisition played an important role in attaining those goals by punishing blaspheming soldiers, but discipline would prove to be a daunting task throughout the colonial period.

Conclusion

Between 1520 and 1700, blasphemy constituted a widespread and frequent religious crime committed by men in New Spain. As inhabitants of a colony, both the authorities and common people were interested in repressing this crime, which was believed to be an affront to God's honor that could endanger the colonial enterprise. However, men in colonial Mexico blasphemed precisely because such speech was seen as confrontational, combative, and daring, in both the domestic and the public spheres. As derogatory speech addressed to the Divinity, blasphemy exhibited characteristics that anthropologists would call *agonistic*, that is, related to struggling, fighting, or resisting "the Other." Furthermore, by staging these acts of verbal jousting before an audience, Spanish men attempted to affirm, establish, or manifest their manliness to others.

As a strategy to display bravery and strength, blasphemy played an important part in the assertive masculine style that characterized male working culture in colonial Mexico. Like the English factory workers analyzed by Paul Willis, Spanish soldiers, muleteers, and sailors in New Spain shared in a culture of work that associated the performance of an assertive masculine style with the ability to meet the challenges and dangers of manual labor.[101] The display of bravery and strength was undoubtedly related to the need to survive in hostile conditions while doing difficult work. But, as Lyman L. Johnson has recently shown, the lives of plebeian workers in colonial Latin America were also enmeshed in a masculine behavioral pattern characterized by ritualized insults, practical jokes, and other forms of intimidation. In this context, Johnson notes, "A man who failed to defend himself against the challenges of his peers found life intolerable. He was, in essence, feminized."[102]

Like the "fighting words" among men of central and southern Mexico analyzed by William B. Taylor, blasphemous speech was often used as a prelude to physical violence, but there was an important difference. In the criminal cases studied by Taylor, men confronted each other directly by uttering expressions such as, "Now we'll see who is a man" or even "You're a bunch of *pendejos* (assholes)—I'm the only man." In contrast, blasphemers addressed their audiences indirectly by aiming their attacks at the Divinity to intimidate the others.[103] True, some, like Rodrigo Rengel, directly challenged their audiences by stating that being a man entailed blaspheming. However, workingmen often engaged in this kind of verbal jousting to demonstrate their courage and establish their autonomy after being challenged or humiliated by their peers or superiors.

Blasphemy seems to have been part of a cultural script of male risk taking, but as is particularly clear in the case of workingmen, it could be used both as a language of male bonding and as a resource to manifest social detachment. As part of a rough masculine culture, blasphemy constituted a common ingredient of homosocial reproduction, particularly among those living and working in dangerous conditions. As sociologists have shown, workingmen in male-only peer groups often view linguistic conformity as a form of submission. In this sense, exhibiting a swaggering masculinity is frequently accompanied by the use of transgressive speech. As Pierre Bourdieu has written, "Linguistic license is part of the labor of representation and of theatrical production which 'tough guys' . . . must pursue in order to impose on others and assume for themselves the image of the 'lad' who can take anything and is ready for anything, and who refuses to give in to feelings or to sacrifice anything to feminine sensitivity."[104]

As a powerful speech style, blasphemy provided men with a strong means of expressing threats, opinions, and aggressive attitudes that were understood as expressly masculine.[105] By claiming the use of blasphemy almost exclusively for themselves, Spanish men reinforced their position of gendered strength in the colonial world, for they commanded more attention and were more likely to be taken seriously than were female speakers who normally did not state their views in this forceful way. Nevertheless, precisely because male blasphemers were capable of commanding the attention of an audience, occasionally they found themselves before the Inquisition, charged with being a source of danger and scandal for the Christian community.

Notably, by the end of the sixteenth century and throughout the seventeenth century, transgressors were increasingly denounced not only as blasphemers but also as *hombres deslenguados* (men with uncontrollable tongues), *valentones* (bullies), and troublemakers. This seems to suggest that blasphemy charges were now intertwined with references to a wider spectrum of delinquent behavior and verbal violence, which included perjury, defamation, and insults. Indeed, as Alain Cabantous commented on a similar trend in early modern Europe, the blasphemer was increasingly perceived as a threat to social order rather than as a source of cosmic danger for the Christian community.[106] Finally, it is possible that the gradual emphasis on the repression of emotions (which gave rise to the civilization of manners as studied by Norbert Elias) helped to break the tie between blasphemy and masculinity among men in the higher social echelons.[107] Self-restraint and control were now part of a dignified ideal that wealthy men embraced in New Spain as an expression of moral discipline and excellence and as a new strategy of social distinction. In this way, blasphemy was transformed from a risk-taking form of speech that had currency among people of high socioeconomic standing to just one more example of verbal incivility. But if men commonly resorted to blasphemy to defy, challenge, or scandalize their audiences, there were occasions in which recovering their self-esteem constituted their most pressing need. By exploring the male culture of leisure in colonial Mexico, and the gamblers' tendency to blaspheme to protest God's designs in the games, chapter 3 offers another facet of the complex relationship between blasphemy, masculinity, and providentialism in New Spain.

3

On Divine Persecution

Blasphemy and Gambling

> The lot is cast into the lap, but its every decision is from the LORD.
> —Proverbs 16:33
>
> They think God is on the rogues' side.
> —Pedro de Covarrubias, *Remedio de jugadores* (1543), xxxvi

On August 27, 1596, Diego Flores, an inhabitant of Jalapa, Veracruz, lost a good deal of money playing cards. Facing the second day of a losing streak, Flores was visibly frustrated. "God's not tired of punishing me (*hacerme mal*)!" he uttered in despair. To the dismay of Colonel Luis Pérez, who would denounce Flores, his frustration soon transformed into defiance. Flores angrily exclaimed, "*Voto a Dios!*" And looking heavenward, he went on to say, "By now, he should be tired of punishing me (*era razón de que estuviese cansado*)!" and "I swear you'll get tired (*pues de cansaros tenéis*)!" That same day, the defiant gambler was imprisoned on orders of Comisario Francisco Carranco. However, it took the Holy Office eight months to initiate an investigation. When prosecutor Martos de Bohórquez finally reported on this case on March 13, 1597, he complained that Flores had blasphemously depicted God as a whimsical creature who acted without reason and was subject to human passions. Bohórquez grounded his demand for a thorough investigation on Flores's misattribution of human characteristics to the Lord, but the prosecutor never contested the gambler's conviction that God's hand actively intervened in the games. On the contrary, Bohórquez's main motive for outrage was Flores's suggestion that, even at the seemingly trivial scale of gambling games, God could conduct himself without a purpose. Accordingly, the Holy Office issued an arrest order. In the meantime, Diego had managed to escape from prison in Jalapa and could not be found. Neighbors heard a rumor that while serving a sentence as a galley slave on a ship from Havana, he was executed by hanging. In any case, Diego Flores was seen no more.[1]

This story is only one among many in the Mexican Inquisition's archives. Other gamblers also erupted in insults and blasphemies against God, the Virgin, and the saints, evidencing their conviction that their repeated losses were not randomly effected but divinely ordained. Paradoxically, the same providential premises that led gamblers to blaspheme—the belief that God enjoyed supreme clairvoyance but also actively intervened in the affairs of this world—were also the basis on which moralists and theologians condemned gambling. Indeed, even at the gaming table, Divine Providence manifested, and players were expected to be content with their lot. Although this extreme version of providentialism was not universally shared, it was sufficiently common to override ancient notions of a capricious Fortune, Fate, or "Chance"—this last concept, as will be seen, being an uncomfortable and ambiguous one for Christian writers.

This chapter explores the relationship between blasphemy and gambling as a social practice in colonial Mexico. Normative and prescriptive sources relating to the control and condemnation of gambling games and the secular and religious risks assumed by the participants are reviewed. I also discuss the roles of the contrasting notions of chance and providentialism in gaming, the expectations and reactions of gamblers both in verbal and paralinguistic terms (gestures), strategies of self-control and denunciation, social differences and stratification in private and public gambling, and changes in the colonial authorities' perception of gaming at the end of the seventeenth century. My discussion is based on the analysis of 32 Inquisition proceedings against gamblers that occurred between 1526 and 1695. The defendants lived in Mexico City (23), Puebla (3), Veracruz (2), Toluca (1), Oaxaca (1), Acapulco (1), and Cusiguriachic, in today's Chihuahua (1). With the exception of the sad case of the Portuguese man, Francisco Tijera, all these proceedings were against Spanish men.

Blasphemy and Gambling

Christian thought has long associated blasphemy and gambling. Medieval writers often pointed to the quarrels and blasphemies concomitant with gambling as a reason to condemn games involving betting. Gaming presented moral dangers for the gambler, so canon law prohibited betting games from the earliest moments of Christianity. In 306 CE, the Council of Elvira threatened to excommunicate gamblers, although they could be restored to communion after a year of amendment. The Fourth Lateran Council (1215) also prevented clerics from playing or being present at games of chance. The Council of Trent (1545–1563) was no less severe in its denunciation of gambling, but it left it to the discretion of the bishops to rule on what games were to be considered illicit. Particular councils drew up lists of games, on which dice and some forms of cards were normally banned. Although moralists frequently exalted the virtues of "honest recreation" or *eutrapelia*, which provided rest and relaxation for the participants, gambling was always censured.[2] Christian writers argued that those indulging in reckless gambling not only could lose considerable amounts of money and precious time but were also easily led into fraud, theft, cheating, an idle life spent in bad company, and blasphemy.[3]

Sixteenth- and seventeenth-century moralists were convinced that "no other human dealings or interaction (*trato o conversación*) [existed in which] the admirable name of God and his saints [was] so regularly blasphemed as in the games."[4] As Bishop Juan de Palafox put it in his posthumous *Luz a los vivos* (1661), "To play and to blaspheme (*jurar and jugar*) are twin brothers and the legitimate offspring of vice."[5] Following John Chrysostom and Bernardino de Siena, spiritual writers commonly depicted gamesters as faithful celebrants of a satanic mass in which oaths and blasphemies played the part of litanies and exclamations of hallelujah and in which the creed expressed their conviction that they were not going to die and pay for their sins.[6] Whereas Chrysostom believed that "it is not God who gives us the chance to play, but the devil," Bernardino de Siena was convinced that Lucifer had invented gambling as a parody of transubstantiation. Indeed, since *substantiae* (the goods) of one player were transferred to the hands of another, gambling could be considered as a wicked imitation of the utmost sacred mystery of Christianity.[7] In Francisco Luque Fajardo's *Fiel desengaño contra la ociosidad y los juegos* (1603), a repentant cardsharp, Florino, even goes to the extreme of declaring that for gamesters, the biggest incentive to play was having the opportunity to blaspheme.[8] Similarly, in *Tratado del juego* (1559), Francisco de Alcocer estimated that gamblers transgressed all the commandments and committed every mortal sin. He described their games as infernal gatherings in which threats were common, lies and perjury regularly occurred, and promises were rarely kept.[9]

Given this diabolic imagery, it is hardly surprising that moralists and writers referred to the deck of cards as an anti-Bible of forty-eight sheets, *el descuadernado* (the unbound book) read by idle people of all classes who scandalously intermingled while playing cards. Indeed, as Luque Fajardo reminded his readers, the word *"baraja"* (deck of cards) originally meant a "fight" or "confusion." The baraja confused social order by leading nobles to mingle with plebeians, just as *oros* (coins) and *bastos* (batons), two suits in the deck, were intermixed when shuffling the cards.[10] According to moralists, the suits of these early playing cards revealed the nefarious character of gaming: The coins represented the sin of greed and the skin color of those who spent day and night at the gaming table; the cups, the drunkenness and gluttony that occurred in the card games; the batons, the bestiality and brutality among the players; and the swords, the often mortal hatred and disputes triggered by gaming. Clearly, cards were nothing but instruments the devil put in the hands of human beings to create social disarray and offend the Supreme Divinity.[11]

In New Spain, preachers and moralists also used rhetorical strategies, such as distortion, exaggeration, and antithesis, to warn the faithful about the moral dangers that awaited those who gambled.[12] Animating their sermons with an exemplum (the rhetorical device popularized in the twelfth and thirteenth centuries when preaching underwent a renaissance), preachers aimed to instruct their audience by means of a short, moving, and convincing salutary lesson. The exemplum was an appeal to the audience to imitate the protagonist's moral success and to avoid his or her moral failure.[13] Indeed, probably no more powerful argument against playing cards or dice existed for Catholics than the case histories of the disasters that supposedly befell gambling blasphemers.

At the end of the sixteenth and the beginning of the seventeenth centuries, the religious genre of exempla received new inspiration in the hands of Jesuits, who expanded the already vast Christian collection. Jesuit Fray Alexandro Faya de Saona offered one of those new exempla to his readers in the second part of his *Suma de exemplos de virtudes y vicios* (1633). Like other cautionary tales, the story left unspecified when the events took place, but the social scenario was clearly recognizable to the audience for this macabre story:

On a Holy Tuesday, a Jesuit friar of the Holy Company went to preach at a Mexico City prison. There he found a young man, about twenty-two years old, who was playing and blaspheming at the same time. The friar reprimanded him with love and tenderness, but the gamester ignored him and blasphemed with even more audacity, saying that he was going to blaspheme even more because he had been reprimanded. The friar then said, "Is there not perchance Justice so that the tongues of such blasphemers can be gagged? God will gag you, for I have seen even greater miracles than this!" A moment later, the friar left the prison. Around eleven that night, the young man saw three imps, two of them big and a third one smaller, coming out of a corner of his cell. After putting out the prison's lights, the two big imps started to play with him like a ball, while the little one pummeled the gambler in the face whenever he fell to the ground. The imps inflicted bruises over the man's entire body, and his face was covered with blood. Finally, they stuck the young man's tongue to his palate. The next day the same friar was called to the prison to see the extraordinary case. The young man threw himself at the friar's feet and kissed them in tears. He gestured asking for ink and paper, and he wrote down what had happened. Then, he confessed. The friar saw the tongue stuck to the gamester's palate and the red bruises on his body. He put his finger into the gambler's mouth to get the tongue unstuck, but to no avail, for, as the imps had told the young man, he had suffered this punishment for resisting the friar's advice and disobeying his own mother.[14]

This account was intended merely as an outline. It was the preacher's job to take this already impressive story and dramatize it, using his voice and gestures. The gifted Jesuit preacher Juan Martínez de la Parra delivered an undoubtedly skillful version of this tale at some point in his series of homiletic sermons delivered in the early 1690s at the church of La Profesa in Mexico City.[15] In his rendition, however, the gamester died without confessing, a logical consequence of having lost the use of his tongue. Having freely chosen vice over virtue, despite a "fraternal correction," the young blasphemer, becoming a mere plaything in the hands of the three demons, had to face the dramatic outcome of losing the agency to secure his own salvation. The Martínez de la Parra version also has the young man imprisoned as a transgressor of society's laws for having challenged parental and ecclesiastical authority by gambling and blaspheming during Holy Week. Thus, in a strong denunciation of gambling, the preacher aptly linked social disarray and moral decay. At the end of the story, it is now the imps who speak, to "thank" the gamester for his blasphemies, before beating him up and provoking his eventual death and condemnation. "Death and life are in the power of the tongue," Martínez de la Parra reminded his listeners, alluding to Proverbs 18:21. He concluded, "Let us thus free our tongue only to confess our sins and praise the Lord, so that it can be the helm that will lead our ship to the glory."[16]

This infernal imagery, which often suffused the moralists' attacks on gambling in treatises on blasphemy, was not unwarranted. Christian tradition had long held that blasphemy was the speech act of hell par excellence (Apocalypse 16:9). Thus, by engaging in it, gamesters established a bridge between earth and hell, bringing into this world the language of those who inhabited the kingdom of shadows.

Although some moralists, such as Nicolás de Avila, believed that the devil himself instigated gamesters to blaspheme, or even spoke through their mouths against God, most rejected this idea as being merely a way to deflect the transgressors' responsibility for their own utterances.[17] As the wandering specter of a gamester explained to the nun Francisca del Santísimo Sacramento in Juan de Palafox's *Luz a los vivos* (1661), the devil "can bark but he cannot bite" (*latrare potest, mordere non potest*) without human participation.[18] Indeed, like a rabid, barking dog at the end of a chain, which can only harm those who enter its restricted space, the devil was also thought to be divinely constrained and incapable of forcing anyone to sin without his or her consent. "He bites [only] fools (*stultis mordet*)," reads one of the popular *Empresas morales* of Sebastián Covarrubias y Orozco published around 1680 (see figure on page 84). In *Declaración magistral* (1615), Diego López wrote about a similar emblem by Andreas Alciati, "If somebody gets bitten, it is because he himself looks for it and also wants it (*a quien mordiere, será porque él lo busca, y él lo quiere*)."[19] Because sin was based on human intention, moralists urged Christians to avoid places and occasions where they could at will endanger their own salvation, such as those in which gambling or "forbidden games" took place and with them, blaspheming, that diabolical form of "prayer."[20]

Forbidden Games in New Spain

Despite repeated references to *juegos prohibidos* (forbidden games) in treatises on blasphemy, their definition remained imprecise and slippery throughout most of the colonial period. The moralist Pedro de Covarrubias described them as being games that paved the way to blasphemy, mockery, anger, fights, pain, despair, lies, curses, and perjury, but he made no attempt to offer a clearer definition.[21] Spanish law designated forbidden games as being those in which *envite* (betting), *azar* (chance), or *suerte* (luck) were involved. Under this broad classification, most table games were banned, but

"The passion for gambling." An infernal representation of a gambling den, depicting the gamblers as riotous satyrs. *La passion du jeu* by Claude Gillot (1673–1722). (Courtesy of the Biblioteca Nacional, Madrid)

Gillot Pinx.

Audran sc.

Craignez ces Furieux, et Concevez leurs maux.

Qu'on verroit le ravage

Qui cause leurs transports, verroit toute la rage

Et des Vents, et des flots.

LA PASSION
du Jeu

Exprimée par des Satyres
Joueurs

Le Ciel, pour se vanger de ces Cœurs impies,

Disperse t-il icy les Flambeaux des Furies?

Le souffle d'Alecton irrite t-il le Feu

Qui les a pénétrez de la fureur du jeu?

A Paris chez Audran Graveur du Roy en l'Hotel Royal des Gobelins

Avec Privilege du Roy.

4

"He bites [only] fools." Like the fearful Cerberus, who barks at the end of his chain, Satan can only harm those who enter his restricted space. He is thus incapable of forcing anyone to sin without his or her consent. From Borja, *Empresas morales*, 101. (Courtesy of the Biblioteca Nacional de México, Fondo Reservado)

royal decrees frequently used the expression "dice and cards" as a synonym for forbidden games. Whereas dice games were always proscribed, some card games were allowed on condition that the amount of money gambled did not exceed ten gold pesos in twenty-four hours. In truth, even the forbidden games were allowed if the bets placed did not exceed two reales, and the amount collected was used to buy food for those attending the games. These conditions were, of course, rarely if ever met.[22]

In 1511, Governor Diego Colón was instructed to forbid gambling on the island of Cuba, and in 1518, the Crown tried to eradicate gambling in the Antilles, or at least, to tone down the passions involved by limiting the bets to ten ducats. In 1525, the Mexico City *cabildo* (town council) banned card and dice games, including those played in the viceregal palace. For his part, in 1538, Viceroy Mendoza (1535–1550) ordered the closure of the *tablajerías* (gambling houses).[23] Despite these prohibitions, gambling continued everywhere because those in charge of enforcing the regulations were often themselves players.

A good case in point was Hernán Cortés. As the fleet was departing for Mexico, Diego de Velázquez had clearly instructed Cortés to prevent his men from playing cards or dice to avoid scandals and blasphemies against God and the saints as well as the detrimental effects gaming would have on military discipline.[24] However, shortly before the Noche Triste, when the Spanish invaders were forced to quit the Aztec capital, Pedro Valenciano, one of Cortés's soldiers, made a deck of "playing cards, as good and well painted as those of Castile, using the hides from the drums."[25] In his own decrees of October 30, 1520, the conquistador permitted card playing and other games that did not employ dice, a fact his detractors duly denounced to the first Audiencia. Indeed, after hearing evidence that Cortés not only allowed gambling while he was captain general and governor of New Spain but also organized card games at his own house, the courts fined him more than four thousand ducats. Witnesses also testified that conquistadors Julián de Alderete, Pedro de Alvarado, and Rodrigo Rengel frequently visited Cortes's house and often blasphemed in his presence without being punished for it. Cortés not only charged a house commission but also prohibited gaming anywhere else in Mexico City. His servant, Martín Vázquez, was in charge of providing gamblers with cards and dice and collecting the *coyma* (a commission paid by gamblers to the gambling-house owner). In his defense, Cortés argued through his attorney García de Llerena that by arranging the games, he was ensuring that enough Spaniards were together to offer a swift military response in case of an Indian attack.[26] The Crown apparently found his excuse credible, for a royal decree dated March 11, 1530, ordered the restitution to Cortés of twelve thousand gold pesos that had been confiscated on the grounds that they were his card-game winnings.[27] Yet, not everybody was convinced about his "strategic reasons" for gathering his men around a gaming table. Indeed, some believed that this practice clearly endangered the colonial enterprise. As Inquisitor Domingo de Betanzos saw it, it was not accidental that a bolt of lightening hit the very table at which Cortés and his blasphemous friends were playing cards. Apparently frightened by this divine warning, from that moment onward, the conquistador stopped organizing games at his house.[28]

Corregidores and governors also successfully exploited the passion for gambling. Hosting frequent *tertulias* (social gatherings), these high magistrates transformed their mansions into gambling houses for the well-to-do. They would charge the players the coyma and even obtain monetary gifts from the guests on their departure.[29] In contrast to people in the lower echelons of society—blacks, mulattoes, and mestizos—who were thought to gamble as one more expression of their "evil ways of life," elite Spaniards allegedly attended the magistrates' soirees for the sole purpose of entertainment.[30] Since these leading citizens ostensibly did not engage in the games for money but only to socialize and relax, Jerónimo Castillo de Bobadilla wrote in his *Política para corregidores* (1597) that the rigorous measures against gambling should not apply to the elite.[31] However, the Council of the Indies found offensive the torrid social life in the magistrates' homes, for the card games often went on for days, while the players left unattended their duties as *oidores* (Audiencia judges), corregidores, and governors. More strikingly, although licensed gambling houses had been again outlawed in 1609 and 1618, some corregidores were so bold as to establish their own tablajerías and to prohibit any other gambling establishments, thus assuring themselves of a source of revenue. Such blatant abuse of authority was not without its critics. Like other moralists, Fray Antonio de Ezcaray, a priest of Santiago de Querétaro who spent fifteen years in the New World, deemed that governors and corregidores who profited from gambling were committing mortal sin, and they could be forgiven only upon complete restitution of their gains to the players.[32] However, despite such severe criticism, the clerics themselves were sharply divided on the issue: While some decried playing for money as a sinful activity, many others were addicted gamblers. Thus, in the same way that royal legislation admonished the magistrates not to organize or take part in any gambling, in every Provincial Council

(1555, 1565, and 1585), the Church flatly warned clerics not to gamble under penalty of excommunication.[33]

Despite all the efforts to eradicate gambling, even the Spanish Crown and the Inquisition benefited from the practice. In frank contradiction of its high moral standards, the Crown reaped an economic advantage from its subjects' taste for cards by instituting an *estanco de naipes* (playing-card monopoly), which controlled the production and distribution of card decks in the Iberian world. Spain had been importing playing cards from France, but in 1528, the Crown decreed that all decks must be manufactured in Spain. Ten years later, Seville's House of Trade banned the export of cards and dice to the Indies except for those that were produced at the royal factories in Madrid and Málaga.[34] Each pack carried a royal seal, normally printed on the ace of coins. In 1576, the Crown decreed that all gambling cards used in New Spain had to be printed in the colony, but the price of a pack was still far higher than for a deck clandestinely produced in Mexico or imported from elsewhere.[35] Although royal decrees banning tablajerías and gambling games clearly affected the demand for cards in New Spain, the monopoly yielded good profits until its fusion with the tobacco monopoly in 1768.[36] The Inquisition also profited when chronic players took and then broke an *escritura de compromiso* (solemn oath) that they would never gamble again. Such an action had not only legal but also spiritual consequences, so the Inquisition could intervene to penalize the transgressors, a practice that secured a small but important source of income for the tribunal.[37]

It is clear that although royal and colonial authorities frequently voiced concerns about gambling in New Spain, they benefited from the widespread practice, which existed at all levels of society, and they even organized and participated in games. Only women were explicitly banned from playing card, dice, board, and other games. However, an ordinance issued by the Mexico City cabildo in 1583 indicated that female players were not unusual, although moralists and colonial authorities found that to be utterly scandalous and most damaging for the colony.[38] From the elegant soirees of corregidores and *gente principal* (members of the elite) to "infernal" gatherings at inns, taverns, obrajes, prisons, and tablajerías, gambling went on everywhere, thus becoming one of the first and most extensive modes for circulating money in New Spain. As will be seen, however, the thrill and attraction of gambling in colonial Mexico frequently arose from much more than the possible transfer of wealth between the participants.

Chance and Providentialism

Aside from the money involved, rolling dice and playing cards were also attractive activities because people believed the outcome depended not on the whim of chance but on God's immediate will. At a time in which God's omnipotence was so strongly emphasized, it was simply impossible to attribute a game's outcome to chance. To be sure, medieval Christians, such as Boethius, Dante, and even Aquinas, had emphasized that the belief in Divine Providence did not rule out the action of chance or luck, but many post-Reformation theologians contended that nothing could take place without God's will. Undoubtedly, this Christian conviction endowed the idea of "chance" with enough ambiguity to make the colonial authorities uneasy about the extent of gambling in the New World.[39] After all, as Aquinas himself and many others after him had argued, the idea of chance merely suggested that events could occur irrespective of the intentions of human beings but never independent of God's all-embracing purpose. Given the belief that nothing occurred without a design, "chance" was just shorthand to acknowledge our ignorance regarding God's plans.[40] In this context, participating in gambling clearly implied an appeal to Divine Providence, made for trivial and utterly inappropriate reasons.[41]

Although it is difficult to establish to what extent the Church's official eschatological thinking coincided with the perspective of ordinary Christians regarding this matter, it is clear that this kind of providentialism was widespread among people of all classes. In medieval and early modern Europe, a pervasive custom referred potentially contentious or urgent decisions to the drawing of lots as a way of discovering God's will. According to William Christian, the casting of lots was widely used in Castile to find helper saints in times of need.[42] Augustine and Aquinas accepted the practice if there was urgent necessity, provided due reverence was observed. The method had long been sanctioned by Judeo-Christian tradition, as is clear from the numerous examples offered in the Bible. In Leviticus 16:8, Aaron cast lots on goats, while God informed Moses in Numbers 26:52–56 that the Promised Land would be divided according to lots. Saul was also elected king by the casting of lots (1 Samuel 10:17), and this method was also used to pick candidates to join select groups (Nehemiah 11:1) and governors of sanctuaries (1 Chronicles 24:5). The New Testament shows several cases in which the casting of lots decided difficult issues. In Luke 1:9, Zechariah, John the Baptist's father, was chosen by lots to offer incense, and Matthias was similarly chosen as a new disciple to replace Judas in Acts 1:26. Moralists and theologians regularly classified all these instances of divine intervention in three broad categories: *sors divinatoria* (God's aid was invoked in order to know what was going to happen), *sors consultoria* (what ought to be done), and *sors divisoria* (what was to be given to whom). As procedures involving the distribution of wealth, games of chance fell into the last category. The blaspheming during games aside, this implied that gambling was often seen as a mockery of the sors divisoria and an illegitimate and sinful way of asking for divine intervention. As moralists saw it, resorting to divine judgment for trivial and unlawful reasons amounted to tempting god. Yet, people in Europe and America threw dice and drew cards as a way of engaging in a both ludic and mystical experience that rested on a providentialism, aptly summarized in the often quoted dictum of Proverbs 16:33: "The lot is cast into the lap, but its every decision is from the Lord."[43]

Given the widespread conviction that divine order operated in the midst of the apparent randomness of the games, it is understandable that losing gamblers engaged in blasphemy as a desperate reproach against the Divinity who "loaded the dice." Indeed, although moralists frequently defined blasphemy as nothing less than a naked act of vengeance against a guiltless God, gamesters in New Spain often broke out in insults against the Divinity because they attributed the outcome of a game to him. As seen in several blasphemy trials in the first decade of colonial society, Divine Providence was understood as God's active intervention in this world, not just his supreme clairvoyance and foreknowledge. Players witnessed more than God's unchangeable decisions at every turn of cards; they also experienced his power.

Take the 1536 case of Pedro de Sosa, who, losing hand after card hand, despairingly cried out, *"Reniego de quien lo hace!"* (I renounce he who does it). In a further gesture of defiance, he gave himself to the devil.[44] Similarly, Alonso de Carrión ascribed his repeated losses during 1526 to God, and looking heavenward, he also uttered, *"Pese a Dios que tanto mal me hace!"* (may it spite God who does so much harm to me).[45] Ten years later, Carrión again voiced a similar utterance, and he added rhetorically, as if trying to protect himself, "I do not believe in you, nor can you hurt me any more (*ni me puedes hacer más mal*)!"[46] That same year, in 1536, Archbishop and Inquisitor Juan de Zumárraga also tried and sentenced Juan de Porras for crying in despair that God could not punish him more than he already had (*no puede hacerme más mal*) after he lost badly at cards.[47] Some gamesters may have believed themselves to be the victims of God's whims, but those who repeatedly lost—like Porras, Carrión, and Sosa—were certainly convinced that they had been singled out for divine retribution. For them, blasphemy seems to have been a means for self-protection against a divinity that persistently "punished" gamblers with defeat.

Nevertheless, in recognizing the work of a supreme power, the players were not necessarily surrendering all agency and submitting to God who controlled the outcome of the games. They often attempted to influence the Supreme Divinity through an array of activities and artifacts, among which blasphemy may have been the most radical. Joseph de Messa, alias El Semita, gambled with a rosary about his neck during 1670,[48] and other players carried gold medals and crucifixes, which, in case of extreme necessity, could also be used to place a bet. That is what Juan Baeza did in Mexico City in 1545, and Diego Moreno in Guachinango in 1569.[49] Winning gamblers also gave *baratos* (monetary gifts) to bystanders. Sometimes they gave alms to beggars. They thus used their money as both an amulet and a way of attracting God's favor through token Christian charity.[50] Prayers and spells were also used at the time, although not always successfully. In 1695, while playing an *albur* (a game of chance),[51] Joseph de Saucedo prayed before turning the card face up, "May the Holy Virgin be there!" Yet, when he saw his opponent's card instead of the expected trump, he shouted, "What a shitty faith (*qué fe de mierda*)! What's the purpose of believing if it's of no use at all?"[52] For his part, Gonzalo Hernández de Figueroa went to the prison chapel before a game started and threatened a Christ figure on a crucifix, "There you are, you hunch-back (*encorvado*)! You better favor me now in the games or I'll do it!" without specifying what he intended to do in retaliation. The use of these strategies hardly enabled the players to force a favorable outcome in the games, but by symbolically standing up to the Divinity, gamblers were at least able to retrieve their self-esteem in the eyes of others.

A Persecuting God

What about those who repeatedly lost when gambling? How could they avoid feeling persecuted when Divine Providence seemed to rule against them in game after game, as they bankrupted themselves and beggared their families? Certainly, under such conditions, the player's power to influence circumstances was readily transformed into one more way of confirming his impotence before a God he perceived as rarely giving but almost always taking away. As might be expected in such cases, blasphemy constituted a particularly dramatic and confrontational act of verbal defiance that went far beyond its occasional production as an outburst of anger and frustration.

Take the case of Gonzalo Hernández de Figueroa, the proud son of conquistador Gonzalo Hernández de Mosqueda, who was condemned on an April morning in 1571 to an unusually severe sentence: public infamy and abjuration, four hundred lashes, and a life sentence as a galley slave. For Hernández de Figueroa, an inveterate gambler who had been reduced to absolute poverty, this was the final episode in a long affair with the Holy Office. He had already faced the tribunal on five occasions, on recurrent charges of blaspheming God when losing at cards. The Mexican Inquisition first tried him in 1559, when he was only seventeen years old. He had been accused of bragging after losing a game that he wanted to fight with God a campo raso. Because of his young age and his father's political influence, he was released after spending time in the stocks. Three years later, he was tried again for renouncing God and uttering other blasphemies after losing the huge amount of three hundred gold pesos in a card game. In his defense, he stated that as a Christian and the son of a conquistador, who had greatly assisted in the expansion of the Catholic faith, he could not have blasphemed. Although he also claimed to be an hidalgo and a close relative of Viceroy Antonio de Mendoza, Inquisitor Luis Fernández de Anguis condemned Hernández de Figueroa to pay five gold pesos plus the costs of the trial, and to hear mass in the cathedral while holding a candle, a sentence his attorney considered "unjust and ignominious."

This punishment notwithstanding, between 1565 and 1569, Hernández faced the Inquisition three more times. A frequent visitor to gambling houses, taverns, and private homes where forbidden games were played, the conquistador's son recurrently engaged in heated disputes over gambling debts, which occasionally ended in insults, fist fights, and cursing. As might be expected, several of his denouncers and prosecution witnesses had participated in those violent encounters. Attempting to mitigate the severe sentences that resulted from the often lengthy and costly trials, his father wielded his political influence fully. Undoubtedly, he was dismayed when the inquisitors got increasingly hard on Hernández. On August 27, 1565, Inquisitor Francisco Barbosa condemned the gamester to spend two years in exile and pay six gold pesos because Hernández had shouted, "I don't believe in the Catholic faith" and other sinful statements during a card game. One year later, Hernández was denounced for stating that God had no power to do him any good. For this, Inquisitor Barbosa sentenced him to pay eighteen gold pesos, to contribute two jugs of oil for the Holy Eucharist, and to be banished from Mexico City for three more years. Leaving his wife and children in his father's house, he went into exile in Acatzingo. However, in 1569, one year before concluding his sentence, he was seen in a Mexico City tavern. As the alguaciles arrived, Hernández escaped to his father's house. While his mother and sisters despairingly kept the constables at bay, he ran to a nearby church seeking sanctuary. Despite his efforts, he was finally apprehended and disarmed in the church. He looked then at the cross on the altar and uttered in anger, "*Pese a tí* (may it spite you) because I know who is doing this!" a phrase he also used at the gaming tables. On July 26, 1569, after a four-month trial, Inquisitor Esteban de Portillo condemned Hernández to pay fifty gold pesos and to receive one hundred lashes. Although he was to be whipped in a secret chamber, the sentence clearly debased Hernández's social standing since corporal punishment was normally reserved for individuals from the lowest social strata.

When Hernández faced the Holy Office yet again in September 1570, the prosecutor alleged that the gambler was now eligible to be burned at the stake as a heretic. However, the Inquisition sentenced him to pay thirty gold pesos and to serve five years as a galley slave. Since Hernández claimed to be completely destitute and incapable of supporting his wife and children, the inquisitor cancelled the fine. However, he ordered Hernández to be imprisoned until he could be transferred to San Juan de Ulúa, where he would be assigned to one of the king's ships on which he would serve out his sentence. Two months later, the inquisitor learned that Hernández gave himself to the devil while playing cards in jail, so he increased the sentence as a galley slave by one year. This only added to the gamester's already strong resentment and despair. In the months preceding his final sentencing, Hernández often said, among other things, that he would prefer to have money than to be canonized as a saint, and that, even if God gave him the glory of heaven, he would not accept it. Given his profound conviction that God's hand intervened in every turn of the playing cards, his anger and frustration at the gaming table were understandably acute. As the outraged inquisitor later learned, Hernández, looking up at heaven, had frequently uttered, "May it spite you, Jewish bastard (*pese a tí bellaco judío*), for you . . . persecute me so much, one day you'll regret this!" Almost a year later, having engaged in and lost countless battles against superior forces in the card games, a destitute Hernández received from the lips of Inquisitor Esteban Portillo his unusually severe sentence.[53]

Many other losing gamblers claimed to be persecuted by Christ just as

Hernández had claimed to be. Indeed, other divinities of the Catholic pantheon, such as the Virgin Mary, Saint Peter, and Saint Stephen, were praised, invoked, or vilified in the games, but Christ was a favorite target of chronic losers. In a reversal of the teachings of Catholic theology, the angered gamesters transformed Christ, the persecuted and sacrificed bearer of humanity's sins, into a relentless and cruel persecutor himself.

Consider the case of Domingo de Yrregui, who was denounced on November 13, 1612, for blaspheming. While playing cards in Acapulco during a celebration in honor of the viceroy, he exclaimed "that he knew God for his works better than his own hands, and that God did not help him but only persecuted him." Conflating the Son with the Father, Yrregui claimed that God did not get along with people of good birth, but only with Jews because he also was a Jew. "What good came from whipping him?" Yrregui asked, "He deserved even more lashes!" Besides, God had not reciprocated Yrregui's respect, because ever since he had confessed for the first time in ten years, he had been losing at games. On November 13, Isabel María de Gonzalo Rodríguez testified before Comisario Pedro García de Herencia that Yrregui had also called Christ a *bujarrón* (sodomite) and had said that he would not confess, hear mass, or fast ever again because God did not do anything for him. Nine years later, Yrregui once again scandalized his neighbors in Acapulco. According to a letter from Comisario Agustín de Mejía, dated August 18, 1621, Yrregui, looking heavenward, had uttered, "Oh Nazarene, neither you nor anyone of your race has ever done me any good!"[54]

In addressing Christ as a Jew, both Yrregui and Hernández distanced themselves from the martyr, while they also denied the passion as a source of a perpetual indebtedness to God. As Yrregui saw it, Christ did not reciprocate the faith of his believers. Indeed, partaking of the sacraments, a key ritual in which believers acknowledge their irredeemable debt to God for his son's death, was seen by Yrregui as a way of compromising God himself. Thus, the gamester probably reasoned that if he continuously lost in the games, it was because God was not paying up the debt contracted with those who were faithful to the Divinity.[55] The cases of Gonzalo Hernández and Domingo Yrregui were obviously outside the norm, but their expressions of outrage, impotence, and indignation were only extreme manifestations of feelings that were shared by many other gamblers, for what they deemed an undeserved punishment from the Supreme Divinity.

Gesticulating Gamesters

Moralists such as Pedro de Covarrubias pointed out that the impossibility of exerting any kind of control over the outcome of a game was usually mirrored by the lack of self-control players exhibited at the gaming table. In the dangerous theater of disguises that constituted the real world, gambling games were deemed an occasion in which the participants' "true self" was revealed and their secret vices were exposed, not only by blaspheming but also through derogatory gestures.[56] As apparent movements of the body, gestures had been considered since antiquity to be *expressions* of the inner movements of the soul. Consequently, gestures have been used to judge the moral inclinations of the person performing them. However, if duly disciplined, bodily gestures could contribute to the improvement of the human soul. Accordingly, a strong emphasis on self-restraint and control formed part of the moral discipline of the Counterreformation according to the dignified ideal of Spanish "gravity." Obviously, nothing could be farther from the disciplined decorum of the Iberian model than a gathering of *hombres rabiosos y desesperados* (desperate and furious men), as moralists such as Pedro de Covarrubias described gamblers.[57]

Insofar as they constituted a language of the soul, gestures began to arouse a great interest starting in the twelfth century, and they received renewed attention during the early modern period. Following a monastic tradition that went back to the Middle Ages, Christian writers paid special attention to those parts of the human body considered to be most "expressive," such as the hands, the face, and the eyes (in the form of gaze). This tradition is still alive in contemporary efforts of scholars from diverse disciplines to compile "dictionaries of gestures."[58] Yet, given that gestures have a meaning only through interaction, when they occur in a spatialized situation where communication happens, it seems a mistake to reduce gesture analysis to a description of body parts' movements as decontextualized, signifying units. As Jean-Claude Schmitt and Jacques Le Goff have convincingly argued, gestures acquire a social significance only when performed before an audience, in compliance or defiance of moral and social norms, and in relation to hierarchical spatial orientations, such as right and left, front and back, or, more significantly, high and low—undoubtedly, the most important of the spatial orientations for Judeo-Christianism.[59]

Indeed, since the source of cosmic power was in the heavens, whereas Satan inhabited the underworld, it was only natural that the high/low dichotomy would play a crucially important role in the performance and appraisement of irreverent gestures made during gambling games. For instance, turning the eyes heavenward, a bodily movement normally associated with prayer, was often a corporal means of identifying God as a referent of one's words or actions. Thus, even euphemistic expressions such as "pese a tal" (literally, "may so-and-so regret it") could be considered blasphemous if uttered while looking skyward.[60] Similarly, gestures that normally belonged to the recurrent repertoire of ridicule and offense, such as giving a "fig" (thumb protruded between clenched index and middle or middle and ring fingers),[61] or biting one's thumb (presumably, as a symbol of the adversary's penis) acquired blasphemous connotations if performed while gazing heavenward.[62]

Spitting, a gesture associated with profound contempt and disdain, was especially significant as a metaphor of contumelious speech. As noted in the second of *Las Siete Partidas* (1256–1263) of Alphonse X: "Those who revile (*denuestan*) [God and the saints] are similar to those who spit toward heaven and get their spit back in their faces."[63] Surely more than the force of gravity was at stake here: Since celestial beings could hardly be harmed by the invectives of aggressors, this bodily disgorgement—like all blasphemous speech—came back to haunt its producers. This metaphorical depiction notwithstanding, spitting seemed to have been a gesture that was aimed most often at the ground, that is, a "low" gesture, usually accompanying derogatory speech. For instance, in 1565, Hernando de Rivera was denounced in Mérida: After throwing his cards on the ground and spitting, he had looked heavenward and given his parents' souls and his own to the devil.[64]

The apparently trivial gesture of spitting could have grave consequences if its performance involved sacred objects. In what constitutes one of the rare cases in which a blasphemer was condemned to lose part of his tongue, Francisco Tijera was tried in 1564 for spitting against a painting of a crucifix and uttering "many blasphemies and offenses against God our Lord and his saints." According to his denouncer, Francisco de Ventanilla, he and Tijera had spent a whole night playing cards in Toluca. Having gone to the extreme of wagering and losing his own shirt, a doublet, and a cloak, Tijera spat with anger at the canvas that hung on one of the walls, while exclaiming, *"Pese a quien te pintó!"* (may he who painted you regret it). Writing from his prison in March of the same year, Tijera asked for mercy because he was the son of Christians. He claimed that he had not realized that a crucifix was in the room, and he had been acting only out of anger. The tribunal remained unconvinced. As a sailor in the fleet of the king of Portugal, Tijera had spent three years imprisoned in Algiers after being captured by the Turks. Knowing this, the provisor of Toluca suspected that the sailor had renounced the Christian faith during his imprisonment, and he even asked Tijera what he had said in the "Moorish language" when he spat at the painting of the crucifix. Some time later, on March 18, 1564, mounted on a donkey, Tijera was paraded in the streets of Toluca, naked to the waist, with a rope around his neck, while a crier announced his crime. Arriving at the public gallows, an executioner administered three hundred lashes and cut out part of his tongue.[65]

Casting objects to the ground was another recurrent gesture among angry gamblers. Although rosaries and medals with images of the Agnus Dei were occasionally sent to the floor, gaming cards were among the first objects to hit the ground.[66] Denouncers and witnesses usually reported this action to illustrate the frustration or despair of a blaspheming gamester. In 1555, while playing with a deck that had a cross printed on the back, Alguacil Antonio Márquez hurled his hand to the floor. The other players were so outraged that they denounced him to the provisor of Oaxaca. In his formal accusation, the prosecutor stated that after the game ended, Márquez also cast to the ground other cruciform objects, such as his *vara de justicia* (staff of office) and his own sword. He broke his staff in several pieces and gave it to the devil, and he also threw his sword to the floor and uttered, "Let the devil take this sword with its cross included!"[67] Like other players, Márquez performed these acts of angry jousting against the supernatural in such a way as to make it difficult for the others to miss them. In the same way that participants of rituals and social dramas created personae by performing before an audience, losing gamblers like Márquez used irreverent gesticulations and utterances against the Supreme Divinity to create an image of strong belligerence. In a sense, it was as if players thought it was necessary to assert their personal independence and autonomy precisely when a superior force had just shown that it was an impossible claim to make.

Not all gestures made in despair and frustration over gambling losses were directed against the Godhead. Besides pulling their beards, biting their hands, and crying, gamblers could undergo fits, convulsions, and tantrums that made it appear they were possessed by the devil. At least that is what Matheo Pardo de Soto, priest of the Cathedral of Mexico, thought one cold November night in 1694. Pardo and a colleague were summoned to a gambling house to see an *endemoniado* (possessed person). When they arrived at the place, they found Balthasar de los Reyes lying on the ground making strange faces and contorting violently, while exclaiming "many blasphemies and reniegos" and calling up demons. This destitute gambler had fallen into a trance after losing everything at cards. After the arrival of the priests, he continued in this lamentable state for three hours until he was so exhausted that he fell asleep right on the floor. Seeing him sleeping, Pardo and his colleague decided to go to have dinner. When they returned, they carried the book of exorcisms by Father Benito Remigio, a receptacle of holy water, a cross, and a stole.[68] They then asked Balthasar to kneel before an image of the Virgin of Dolores to start his act of contrition. He performed the ritual in a proper manner, although he also mixed in some *impertinencias* (unidentified exclamations) in his prayers. Reporting on these events five days later, Pardo told the inquisitor that Balthasar had a reputation for going into this kind of trance every time he lost. However, in his own deposition, Balthasar asserted that he had never experienced such a thing before, and that he had lost his senses only because he felt an enormous grief in his heart upon losing. Similarly, he also stated he had no recollection of what had happened, and he claimed no responsibility for the words and disorderly gesticulations he had exhibited in the gambling house. Like other individuals possessed by demons, the gambler had experienced corporal automatism—manifested by a multiplicity of tantrums and contortions—and had uttered blasphemies apparently authored by someone, or something, else.[69]

However, by the end of the seventeenth century, the Holy Office was beginning to view cases of demonic possession with great suspicion. Only two years before Balthasar's hearing, the Mexican Inquisition had dismissed a spectacular case of mass possession in a Querétaro convent, by stating that the purported demoniacs had feigned their possession "as a mere pretext to blaspheme and utter heretical remarks, thus causing great and unnecessary scandals."[70] Luckily for Balthasar, the inquisitor merely dismissed the case. Balthasar's youth (he was only twenty-four), his depression from the loss of a child, and his absolute poverty probably influenced that decision.[71] The entire matter was forgotten.

Private Homes and Gambling Houses

It is clear that gamesters failed to exhibit the cultivated stoicism of Renaissance courtiers, who lost huge amounts impassively as a way of demonstrating that they did not have an immoderate or base attachment to money. On the contrary, gambling among the popular classes was a social event in which passions and violence often erupted, and in which quarrels, fighting words, and blasphemies could lead to the intervention of both secular and ecclesiastical authorities. Knowing this, Renaissance writers as disparate as the gambling scholar Gerolamo Cardano and the philosopher and moralist Juan Luis Vives recommended some restrictions on social intercourse at the gambling table. Stressing the importance of carefully choosing place, time, and opponents, Vives warned his readers against gambling houses and against playing cards with troublemakers, irascible individuals, or scandalmongers. For his part, Cardano emphasized the relevance of playing with opponents "of a suitable station in life," for short periods and low stakes, in respectable places (such as the house of a friend), and on suitable occasions (as at a holiday banquet).[72]

Although some players in New Spain took the caveats of Vives and Cardano to heart, in general, these were "ideal" (but infrequently attainable) conditions. Surely, the best way to prevent quarrels and avoid drawing the attention of the colonial authorities was to play with people one knew and trusted and, if possible, at the house of one of the participants. Besides, since gambling for high stakes was illegal in New Spain, only the privacy of the home could guarantee that the gaming would remain secret. Playing at private homes also had other advantages, such as avoiding the fees paid to owners of gambling houses and the fines for high-stakes gambling—or the cost of bribing the authorities who occasionally raided gambling houses. Finally, by gambling at the house of friends, players could avoid using the expensive cards marked with the royal seal by playing with decks that had been clandestinely printed or imported from another country.

Since it was in their interest to avoid drawing the attention of the authorities, it is unlikely that players were particularly eager to denounce their opponents. There is evidence that gamblers tried different strategies to avoid blasphemous utterances by exerting some control over risky conversation, punishing players who cursed, or even fining blasphemers.[73] Even if all these strategies failed, an immediate denunciation did not necessarily ensue. For instance, in the 1536 blasphemy trial of Ángel de Villasaña, Juan de Alvarado stated that Villasaña had renounced God a year before, and that seven or eight years earlier, the defendant had said either pese a Dios or no creo en Dios.[74] Similarly, two of the witnesses against Juan de Porras declared in 1536 that the defendant was a "consummate blasphemer." They testified that they had heard him blaspheme every time he played and lost, a candid statement indicating that they had been at the gaming table with Porras on at least several occasions, and that they had chosen not to denounce him.[75]

Of course, the primary reason we know about these cases is that serious conflicts eventually arose among the players. Both Villasaña and Porras were tried by Bishop Juan de Zumárraga as part of a group of gamesters who had known each other for some time and who had frequently played at the same table. However, for some unknown reason, the group had a falling out, which triggered multiple denunciations before the tribunal. On a single day, July 7, 1536, Diego Palma denounced Ángel de Villasaña, Juan de Villagómez, and Alonso de Carrión, all of whom, he assured the inquisitor, were in the "habit" of blaspheming. Juan de Alvarado testified against both Ángel de Villasaña and Francisco de Maldonado. Hernán Pérez de Carrión presented himself voluntarily to declare against Ángel de Villasaña, Juan de Villagómez, and Alonso de Carrión. Finally, Alonso de Carrión was said to have witnessed Villasaña's blasphemies, and Juan de Villagómez was mentioned as a possible witness against Pedro de Sosa.[76]

Although we cannot know what triggered the denunciations on that July day, the accusations probably had their roots in bitter disputes over money and gambling debts. Given that high-stakes gambling was illegal, debts were not recognized by the state and were only as good as a gambler's word. Christian theologians and critics of gambling emphasized the importance of honoring debts, for although gambling was utterly condemned, welshing would only compound, not cancel, the sin.[77] However, a possibility always existed of finding a way to avoid paying up or, more strikingly, trying to get one's money back, through the intervention of the Holy Office.

For example, in 1557, Bernardo Ortíz went before the Holy Office to denounce Juan Mejía for uttering "many words of blasphemy," such as "By God's life," while gambling. After the arrest, Ortíz visited Mejía in prison as he awaited trial. According to witnesses, Ortíz asked Mejía to return clothes he was holding in pawn. Because Ortíz still owed him money, Mejía refused. Ortíz retaliated by saying that he would do as much harm as possible to Mejía, a clear allusion to the accusation he had made before the Inquisition.[78] Similarly, in a 1567 trial, Gonzalo Hernández claimed that Gonzalo de Arciniega was his enemy and had testified against him only because Hernández had refused to return items Arciniega had left in pawn since money was still owed on them. Hernández added, however, that other witnesses were also his enemies, but this, he explained, was because he himself had refused to pay what he owed them, a decision he rationalized by saying that they were cardsharps. Two years later, Hernández slapped Rodrigo Calderón in the face, calling him a "thief" for not playing fairly. Calderón then swore he would get Hernández arrested by the Holy Office, an endeavor in which he succeeded.[79]

Besides the quarrels and conflicts between players, complications arose when bystanders or witnesses were present, as was usually the case at the popular gambling houses. Money circulated not only in the form of bets but also as tips (*baratos*), gambling fees, and bribes. Failure to meet these various economic obligations, or even refusing to give alms to the occasional beggar, could provoke serious conflicts.

For example, on February 8, 1662, a group of women were begging at a gambling house in the street of El Portal de la Acequia in Mexico City. Ana Muñoz Vera, a poor thirty-eight-year-old, joined them, and she asked one of the gamblers, Jaime Viadel, for money. The gamester threw half a *real*, but another women grabbed the coin, claiming that she had been waiting longer than Ana. A third woman, María de la Rúa, then begged Viadel to give her a coin, "for the love of the Virgin," but he irritably answered, "Get away from me, whore, and go fuck yourself with the Virgin's prick!" Perhaps looking for revenge but also profoundly scandalized, both Ana and María denounced Viadel to the Inquisition. The owner of the gambling house, Pedro Fernández de Quiróz, denied that blasphemies were ever uttered in his establishment, although he later admitted that Viadel had had words with the beggars, including using the term "puta" (whore). For his part, the prosecutor charged that the gamester was a "vicious man contaminated with heresy," and a warrant was issued. After a trial that lasted for several months, Viadel was finally sentenced during a public auto-da-fé: He would hear mass while gagged with a rope about his neck and, most strikingly, he would hold a *green* candle (indicating that his remarks had been heretical). Suspected (although not convicted) of heresy, he would have to abjure de vehementi. Then, while a crier proclaimed Viadel's offenses, he would be paraded naked to the waist on a beast of burden, which would carry him to be lashed two hundred times. Lastly, he would serve as a galley slave for ten years, during which time, the prison priests would carefully instruct him in the basics of Christian doctrine.[80]

The case of Viadel was not isolated. Throughout the colonial period, frequent fights, quarrels, and blasphemies brought gambling houses to the attention of colonial authorities. In sermons, preachers often characterized these establishments as plebeian places of social disorder and moral corruption. As late as 1691, from his pulpit in La Profesa, the popular Jesuit Juan Martínez de la Parra decried those "infernal caverns," "caves of dragons," and "homes of demons," which contaminated the inhabitants of New Spain and were "the reason for all sorrows." He severely criticized the *coymes* (gambling-house owners) for making a living from their blaspheming clientele.[81]

This moral preoccupation with declining standards of behavior, represented by widespread gambling, acquired more dramatic overtones after a pivotal event in Mexico's colonial history. On June 8, 1692, a roaring mob of Indians, mestizos, and mulattoes rioted against the Spanish government to protest a shortage of wheat and corn. The mob set the viceregal palace aflame, burned the *ayuntamiento* (municipal council) buildings, and sacked merchants' shops, while shouting, "Down with the Spaniards and the gachupines . . . who are eating up our corn!" "Death to the viceroy and his wife!" "Death to the corregidor!"[82] The skittish colonial authorities executed nine individuals, ordered nearly thirty public floggings in the space of two-and-a-half weeks, and orchestrated a policy of racial and social segregation that excluded Indians from the center of the city and other areas. "From then on," writes Juan Pedro Viqueira, "the authorities and the elites perceived the dissipated customs of the people as a potential seed of social subversion that needed to be weeded out."[83] As might be expected, colonial authorities regarded places of plebeian subculture, such as taverns, markets, *cofradías* (confraternities), and gambling houses, as a breeding ground for rebellious behavior. Thus, after an Indian was robbed and killed in a gambling house, Viceroy Albuquerque ordered the suppression of all gambling establishments on June 21, 1707, and he canceled all licenses previously issued for organizing games. Of course, as the angered administrator of the playing-card monopoly, Juan Unzueta, pointed out to the king, the decree did not apply to the most important gambling houses, whose clientele were leading citizens and the wealthy. The viceroy had clearly targeted a locus of popular socializing in an effort to enforce order and control over what were deemed to be centers of vice, disorder, and crimes. His successor, the Marqués de Casafuerte, was no less severe, and his repressive policy reduced the number of gambling houses in Mexico City from thirty-six to fourteen.[84] Clearly, although an activity that the Christian religion continued to criticize, popular gambling came more and more to be considered a secular danger, a ludic practice that led to the financial ruin of the participants and their families and the corrosion of social order and hierarchy. However, the increasing revenues from the sale of cards and the participation of the authorities in gaming outweighed the desire to combat gambling, as expressed in decrees issued against it in 1745, 1768, and 1771. By the end of the eighteenth century, the playing-card monopoly was one of the more lucrative ones for the Spanish Crown, and gambling, clandestine or not, went on everywhere.

Conclusion

For all their harshness and obsessive preoccupation with order, the Bourbon authorities' social concerns are undoubtedly closer to the modern rhetoric of gaming as a self-destructive madness and source of social disorder, than they were to the religious convictions that informed both the condemnation of gambling games and blaspheming at gaming tables in the Habsburgs' New Spain. Once closely related, games of chance and religion had become in modern times rivals for the promotion of what the scholar of play Brian Sutton-Smith calls "altered states of consciousness," that is, states of mind that make it possible to transcend everyday cares and concerns and be "lost" in play.[85] Today, chronic gamblers are no longer seen as sinners but as pathological addicts to an activity that allows them little or no control over their winnings, losses, or psyches.[86] Indeed, trying to exert some influence on the outcome of games by means of amulets, prayers, or threats has come to be considered by modern scholars, such as Roger Caillois, as a "corruption" of the games, for the results are ruled by an "impersonal neutral power, without heart or memory, a purely mechanical effect. With superstition, the corruption of *alea* is born."[87]

In the eyes of sixteenth- and seventeenth-century moralists and inquisitors, the real corruption of games started when the legitimate need for entertainment before returning to one's labors was transformed into a way of tempting God in games of "chance"; of robbing him of precious time by playing on Sundays rather than going to Church; of leading to thefts, quarrels, and other crimes; and most importantly, of transmuting the human voice into a diabolical source of contempt, reproach, and blasphemy against God.

In his famous essay on Balinese cockfights, Clifford Geertz contrasted gambling for money, which he labeled "shallow play," with gambling related to social status, which he defined as "deep play." Although most gamblers bet on cockfights "just for the money," a select group wagered their esteem, honor, dignity, and respect.[88] In New Spain, however, the denial of the possibility of luck or accident frequently transformed playing for money into "deep play," since the believers in Providence could hardly account for a bad outcome in the games without jeopardizing their self-esteem. Since God was behind each turn of the cards, an unhappy outcome could mean either punishment for past offenses or undeserved reproach from God. Under these conditions, blasphemy constituted not only a cultural tool to express anger and frustration but also a way of "fighting back," if only symbolically, against the Supreme Divinity and his celestial court. Losing players could use blasphemy to regain self-esteem, even if only for a moment.

Aside from the free men analyzed in the previous two chapters, there were other groups, such as women and slaves, for whom resorting to blasphemy was a more risky endeavor. Chapter 4 explores the use of blasphemous speech by women, and chapter 5 analyzes the dramatic circumstances in which slaves of both genders blasphemed the Christian god. Blasphemy acquired its most dramatic overtones in colonial Mexico in these subaltern groups.

4

Through Eve's Open Mouth

Blasphemy and the Woman's Voice

> Women should maintain the house and silence.
> —Fray Luis de León (1583)

*I*n August 1541, news reached Santiago de los Caballeros de Guatemala that Pedro de Alvarado, the experienced captain of Cortés's army, had been crushed under a horse in Nochiztlán, Mexico, during a military campaign against the Indians of Nueva Galicia.[1] When his second wife, Beatríz de la Cueva, learned of his death, she cried in despair that God had punished her beyond measure in taking her husband's life, and to the horror of her neighbors, she exclaimed that *ya no tenía Dios más mal que hacerle* (God could not punish her any further). As a gesture of grief, Doña Beatriz ordered her palatial home to be stained inside and out with black clay, and she arranged for nine days of ostentatious mourning. After the last mass was celebrated on September 6, the members of the cabildo debated and then elected the young widow to succeed Alvarado as governor and captain general. Meanwhile, a three-day thunderstorm was raging over the city. On September 9, around two in the morning, an earthquake triggered an avalanche of mud, trees, and boulders, which descending from the Agua volcano, bore down upon Santiago at great speed.

Awakened by the roar of the approaching water, Doña Beatriz, with Alvarado's five-year old daughter, ran to her private chapel on the roof of her house. Seven other women also tried to reach it, but the mudslide swept them away. Only four would be found alive outside the city the following day. Inside the oratory, Doña Beatríz commended herself to God as the powerful current destroyed the building. She was found dead in the morning.

Some neighbors reported having heard strange voices and horrible screams during the storm. Others said they saw demons in the tumbling rocks; a cow, with a broken horn, that attacked those who tried to help Doña Beatríz; and two black men, who made strange faces and gesticulated, while yelling: "Forget it! Forget it (*dejadlo, dejadlo*) because everything is bound to perish and die!" When the waters abated, more than seven hundred Spaniards and six hundred Indians were dead among the ruins of the colonial city.

Several versions of this popular story found their way into the work of secular and religious authors in Spain and colonial Mexico. These writers decried the blasphemous speech of this powerful woman by emphasizing the momentous consequences of Doña Beatriz's transgression. "It might be possible," wrote Gonzalo Fernández de Oviedo, "that God was served by her corporal martyrdom . . . [and decided] to make her an example to the living so that nobody dare to utter contemptuous words, for blasphemy is a sin against one of God's commandments."[2] This conviction was also shared by Francisco López de Gómara who, as in many other things, was specifically contradicted by Bernal Díaz del Castillo in his *Historia verdadera de la conquista de la Nueva España*. Díaz did not deny that God's wrath could manifest in the form of natural disasters, but he insisted that only God knew if the storm and earthquake were divine punishment for Doña Beatriz's blasphemies. Most of Bernal Díaz's contemporaries agreed, however, with Franciscan Jerónimo de Mendieta: God had sent the torrent of mud racing "directly to the house of the governor" in order to kill Alvarado's sinful wife. Mendieta's disciple, Juan de Torquemada, even charged Beatríz de la Cueva with idolatry for having loved her husband as if he were a god himself, to the point of forgetting the reverence owed to God and his designs.[3] As proof of Beatriz's unfitness to rule over men and women and guide the Christian community, Torquemada noted that it was the arrogant defiance of God by colonial America's first woman ruler that had triggered the horrid disaster.

Despite the popularity of this story, which implied that the blasphemies of women were more serious than those of men, women were rarely accused of blasphemy in New Spain. Using the Mexican Inquisition's records to research the types of accusations made against women, historians have found sexual transgressions (prostitution, bigamy, and general sexual misconduct) and religious crimes (heresy, judaizing, witchcraft, and mysticism) to be the most prevalent.[4] Rather than adding to the literature on the activity of the Holy Office, this chapter interprets the use of blasphemy in light of the gender conventions at the time, women's various ways of using blasphemy, the representations of women blasphemers in Christian literature, and to a certain extent, the infrapolitics behind the denunciations of women to the Holy Office. This chapter is based on the study of 21 inquisitorial proceedings that took place from 1564 to 1689 against Spanish female blasphemers, 13 of whom lived in Mexico City, with the remainder living in the towns of Puebla (4), Oaxaca (1), Pachuca (1), Cholula (1), and Veracruz (1). During the sixteenth and seventeenth centuries, most denunciations and trials of women on charges of blasphemy involved either Spaniards or black slaves. Spanish women blasphemed in a variety of contexts and for purposes involving not only defiance and resistance but also, paradoxically, the assertion of their honor and reputation, as those concepts were interpreted by the gendered moral standards of the time. By contrast, women slaves committed blasphemy for essentially the same reason as male slaves: as a strategy to resist their masters' brutality. Their cases are thus discussed in the chapter dealing with slavery, and this chapter will focus on the analysis of the trials and denunciations of Spanish women.

Female Loquacity, Blasphemy, and Miraculous Water

In New Spain, the concern of the godly about the cosmic and social dangers posed by women's blasphemy was deeply rooted in the Judeo-Christian conviction that the female's tongue had an incredibly malign potential, as first demonstrated in the Garden of Eden. If the serpent had seduced Eve using its tongue, she had in turn seduced Adam by using her own tongue, thus bringing about the divine estrangement and disgrace of the human race. Grounded in this biblical tradition, moralists also decried evil-speaking and garrulity as the most irritating of female transgressions, which also included instability, disloyalty, pride, vanity, avarice, seditiousness, greed, vindictiveness, gluttony, drunkenness, and licentiousness.[5] Indeed, the pious production and control of female speech was a crucial element in the prescription and enactment of Christian womanhood. In his widely read *Instrucción a la mujer cristiana* (1524), the philosopher and moralist Juan Luis Vives commended verbal restraint as one of the cornerstones of female virtue which, however, proved difficult to attain given women's frequent lack of self-control:

> Now the bridle must be put on the tongue, which is easily done if the mind is bridled. The reason why many women have no control of their tongue is that their mind is uncontrolled. Anger takes hold of them, car-

ries them away and renders them powerless over themselves. As a result, there is no limit to their quarreling and no logic in their abusiveness since there is no room for reason or judgment. . . . Then unrestrained rage of emotion and tongue bursts forth, which I have often marveled at in good women.[6]

The idea of woman's alleged incapacity to control her speech and senses was based on Galen's and Aristotle's physiological theory of humors. According to them, men were composed of hot and humid humors, whereas women were constituted by cold and humid humors, which endowed them with a changeable and deceitful temperament. In addition to these psychological effects, deriving from their natural coldness, women were prone to irrationality and unrestrained passions because of the influence of the uterus. Garrulity or loquacity was also said to be an effect of hysteria, and a host of illnesses stemming from the womb was listed as evidence of women's weaker powers of mind when compared to men.[7] Thus, the alleged difficulties women experienced in restraining their tongues were closely related to their physiological and moral inferiority.

This conceptualization did not imply, however, that women's disorderly speech was to be tolerated. "Putting a bridle" on the tongue was recommended for both men and women, but women were most commonly reproached for uncouth speech. Even Erasmus, who discussed the perils of the use and abuse of the tongue in his extremely popular *De lingua* (1525) ("Of the Tongue," which referred, somewhat unusually, to male speakers), resorted to the deeply influential writings of Saint Paul to condemn women as "natural" chatterers, whom men should discipline rather than attempt to surpass.[8] Lacking the necessary strength and reason to govern their own passions and speech, women were in need of patriarchal vigilance in order to control both their tongues and their bodies. Thus, men should endeavor to impose on them the Christian female virtues of silence, chastity, and obedience. Indeed, as Fray Luis de León wrote in *La perfecta casada* (1583), a widely read and frequently reprinted manual for wives, women were expected to "maintain the house and silence."

Drawing from Solomon's Proverbs, Saint Paul's letters, and the writings of Juan Luis Vives, Fray Luis asserted that to prevent women from "rushing around," God had endowed them with "little strength and delicate limbs." Thus, only a "bad" woman would roam the streets, engaging in public matters she did not understand, or occupying herself with petty and trifling things that might compromise her reputation. In contrast, the ideal woman would gladly surrender her physical mobility to guarantee her chastity, and she would exert control over her speech. In women, modesty and silence should be "not only a pleasant condition but a required virtue": "For, just as nature, as we said and we shall say, made women so that shut away they should protect the home, so it obliged them to shut their mouths; and just as it freed them from business and dealings outside, so it freed them from what these dealings entail, which is many discussions and words."[9]

Women who "roamed about" and talked publicly infringed on the Christian ideals of silence and confinement and also violated their own nature and subverted the social and sexual order.[10] It is not by chance that talkative women were often suspected of also being sexually available to men, their open mouths being "the signifier for invited entrance elsewhere."[11] As Lynda E. Boose has recently pointed out, the common association of silence with chastity was predicated upon the construction of female bodies as endowed with margins and open orifices whose vulnerability could endanger the whole social body. After all, it had been through Eve's open mouth that sin and disorder had invaded this world after Adam's seduction.[12]

In stigmatizing female public speech by stressing the ideals of chastity, silence, and confinement, moralists also stressed the responsibilities of honest women in the production of pious language inside the domestic unit. Writing for the future Queen Isabella, Augustinian Fray Martín de Córdoba included a discussion of blasphemy in his *Jardín de nobles doncellas* (ca. 1460), a small moral treatise published in 1500 and reissued in 1542. Since blasphemy constituted an attack on God's honor, Córdoba asked Isabella, as queen and mother, to punish blasphemers, for "parents do wrong in not chastising their children when they blaspheme."[13] He then told an exceedingly popular story, which had been included the *Dialogues* of Gregory the Great (d. 604): A five-year-old child had the habit of blaspheming but was never reprimanded by his father. Infected during a plague, the child was dying in his father's arms when he saw several black demons approaching to take his soul. "Protect me, father! Protect me!" he cried in despair. "What do you see my son?" asked the father. "Several black men are coming to take me off," said the child; moments later, he blasphemed one more time and died.[14] Like Fray Martín de Córdoba, many other moralists used this exemplum to stress the responsibility of parents to secure their children's salvation by monitoring their speech and mores.[15] Contrary to this cautionary tale, however, some Christian writers believed that mothers were to blame for their children's blasphemies. In his *Tratado de juramentos*

(1569), Dominican Felipe de Menesses decried the tendency of children to blaspheme "from the moment they learn to speak." Given the bad habits of some women, he wrote, it was not a surprise that their offspring offended God, for they acquired this bad habit with their mother's milk. And since bad habits learned in childhood only get stronger as a person grows up, Menesses accused women of being responsible for the blasphemies of adult men.[16]

Other Christian writers held women responsible for male blasphemy not only as mothers but also as wives. By engaging in quarrelsome fights with their husbands and using their "bitter tongue," women exasperated their partners to the point that the men would lose control, and while hurling insults and uttering blasphemies, they would beat their wives.[17] Far from arguing with her husband, a Christian wife was expected to endure her partner's outbursts in silence and avoid fueling his anger. The vicious and scolding woman, wrote Juan Luis Vives, made "two madmen out of one," she and her husband.[18] In his *Coloquios matrimoniales* (1552), the moralist Juan Pedro de Luján compared women's mouths to the volcano Etna and recommended the use of violence to silence a *mujer brava* (truculent woman).[19] Preaching at La Profesa in 1691, Jesuit Juan Martínez de la Parra also stressed the importance of women's silence in marital relations by telling a tale about some "miraculous water." According to the story, a woman had an unbearable husband who habitually gambled, got drunk, and came home late. Not knowing how to put an end to this, the woman complained to a "very prudent man," who gave her a container with water as a remedy to her problems. He instructed her to put a small amount of the liquid in her mouth before opening the door to her husband. He also advised her how to use it, saying, "Don't swallow it because it will make you sick." "Don't spit it out," he added, "because it will do you no good." Several days later, the woman came back to thank the man for the miraculous water, for her husband was now incredibly tractable. Obviously, Martínez explained to his audience, it was the forced silence of the woman and not the "miraculous" liquid that had finally brought peace to her home.[20]

Responsible for the production of pious speech in the family, the Christian woman was thus expected to control her own "unruly member" to avoid not only committing blasphemy but also setting a bad example for her children or driving her husband to blaspheme. In the end, moralists pointed out, women's verbal restraint would guarantee the maintenance of domestic peace, the enactment of feminine Christian decorum, and the preservation of the gender hierarchy and social order.

A "beautiful woman" becomes a monster after blaspheming God. The story depicted here was first published in 1678 (see Ettingham, *Noticias del siglo xvii*). From the title page of an anonymous work, *Relación verdadera de la más admirable maravilla* (1754). (Courtesy of the Biblioteca Nacional de México, Fondo Reservado)

"Foulmouthed" Women and Standards of Femininity

Given these gendered Christian ideals, it is understandable that women who blasphemed would be perceived as both engaging in sinful behavior and failing to "do gender" in the right way.[21] As several Inquisition cases indicate, a woman who frequently resorted to blasphemy was often depicted as a *mala hembra* (bad woman), *deslenguada* (loose-tongued or foulmouthed), or *temeraria* (daring). This implied that blasphemous women were held socially accountable both for derogatory speech and for falling short of the moral standards of Christian femininity. Indeed, the witnesses who denounced female blasphemers often commented on the reputation of those they accused. That is, they gauged the extent to which the women's sexuality conformed to the ideals of chastity, abstinence, and fidelity expected of them as wives, widows, or daughters. In this sense, although nobody viewed female blasphemy as necessarily stemming from sexual misconduct, these two gender transgressions were closely associated.

For instance, in 1610, Francisco del Castillo denounced Bernardina de Esquivel, the wife of Gonzalo Carvajal, a fruit merchant who lived in Puebla. Del Castillo informed the comisario that Bernardina was a "scandalous and foulmouthed woman (deslenguada)" who frequently fought with her husband, and her sexual behavior filled him with sorrow and jealousy. In particular, during the couple's short stay at the del Castillo home two months before, Francisco had heard Bernardina exclaim, "By the life of God's blood!" "By the life of God's mother!" and similar blasphemies while she was scolding her slave. Scandalized, del Castillo asked Carvajal to reprimand his wife, but to no avail, for "her husband could not manage her (no puede con ella) because she had been a prostitute (mujer pública)." In del Castillo's opinion, she enjoyed excessive freedom and was shameless. The denouncer himself was apparently afraid of her, because he had dared to report this intractable woman only as he was about to leave Puebla to go to live in Veracruz.[22]

The failure to live up to the standards of honor and seclusion expected of married women caused Juana Rodríguez's mother-in-law, Leonor de Morales, and sister-in-law, Juana Segura, to denounce her. The comisario of Puebla summoned them to testify against Rodríguez in a blasphemy hearing on June 18, 1606. In the opinion of Leonor, Rodríguez was constantly exhibiting "bad behavior (mal proceder), and [she led an] evil life (morbo de vivir)." For concrete evidence, Leonor recounted that around 2 o'clock on the afternoon of January 11, Juana Rodríguez was standing at the door of the Morales's house, gazing out at the street. This was unacceptable behavior for a married woman, so Morales told Rodríguez to come inside, warning her that if Juana's husband happened to see her at the door, he would reprimand her. Rodríguez protested the social etiquette of seclusion by angrily renouncing God and the saints three times. "Why should God be blamed for what you're doing? How can you say such words?" exclaimed Segura. In response, Rodríguez called up the demons, saying, "Don't be cowards; come and take me off in clothes and shoes!" a daring utterance, commonly used by workingmen. According to Juana Segura, her defiant sister-in-law was a habitual blasphemer who used to call up the demons "for whatever sorrow she had."[23]

On January 22, 1604, Captain García Pérez de Salas, a Spaniard living next to the Plaza del Volador in Mexico City, made a striking denunciation that clearly associated blasphemy and sexual misconduct. García Pérez went to the Holy Office's headquarters to denounce his lover, Doña Catalina de Chávez. He told Inquisitor Bernardo de Quiroz that fifteen days earlier he had had sex with her *en mala parte* (in a sinful setting). At the point of ecstasy, his lover blasphemed the name of the Almighty, saying: "I don't do this with you, but with God Himself! You're my eternal God, and I renounce God!" Horrified, García Pérez told her to shut up. This was the second time Chávez had uttered such things while having sex, the pious captain informed the inquisitor. Bernardo de Quiroz then asked if Doña Catalina was of sound mind when she spoke, or what could possibly have "moved" her to say that. "Perhaps the Devil blinded her," answered García, "or she was just trying to overstate (*encarecer*)" how much she loved him. García declared that Catalina had nothing against the Catholic faith. However, in his opinion, she was a rash woman, *una mujer temeraria juradora* (a woman fond of uttering oaths), for Chávez had already been imprisoned once for having said, "*Por vida de Dios!*" (by God's life).[24] The documents do not reveal what prompted the hypocritical captain to bring his bedroom conversations to the Holy Office, but other cases show that García was not alone in regarding the mixture of blasphemy and sexual situations as especially alarming.

Consider, for instance, the case of forty-year-old Teresa Rodríguez. On March 6, 1575, Rodríguez received a sentence that was unusually severe for a Spanish woman: She would have to attend a penitential mass while barefoot, be carried on a donkey gagged and naked to the waist while a crier announced her crime, and receive one hundred lashes. She would also be exiled for four years from the archbishopric of Mexico. Rodríguez had been denounced on August 3, 1572, by Melchor de Aranda, a peddler. Two months earlier, when passing through the town of San Juan, near Zacatecas, Aranda had stopped at an inn Rodríguez owned to sell his merchandise. Aranda sold a piece of cloth and two small figures representing Christ and the Holy Virgin to Isabel de Spíndola, one of Rodríguez's customers. "Look what I bought!" said Spíndola to Rodríguez. Teresa Rodríguez regarded the figurines, and while looking at the one representing the Holy Virgin, casually remarked, "This one is good to hang from my pubic hair (*pendejo*)! And this other one," she added now looking at the image of Christ, "is good to put in my ass!" Probably scandalized by these unusual methods of obtaining holy protection, Aranda reported the episode to the Holy Office. He stated, however, that Rodríguez had a reputation as a *chocarrera* (teller of coarse jokes). Two years later, when Rodríguez was imprisoned in the Mexico City headquarters of the Holy Office, she tried to excuse her behavior by claiming that she had not recognized the faces of Jesus and Mary in the little figurines. Rodríguez also claimed that Aranda had denounced her because she had ruined the reputation of a woman with whom he had had an affair. Nevertheless, almost a year later, the inquisitors handed down Rodríguez's stern sentence.[25]

These cases indicate that denouncers of female blasphemy frequently referred to the ideology of gendered morality that informed men's attempt to regulate both the verbal conduct of women and their sexual and physical behavior. Female blasphemy was perceived as an act of irreverence, just as it was in the case of men who blasphemed, but it was also understood as an act of gender subversion. As Pedro de Arganda suggested in 1607, when denouncing Francisca del Castillo in Puebla, a woman with a *mala lengua* (sharp tongue) could also be considered a *mala hembra*.[26]

Female Emotions

Since blaspheming not only affected their reputation as pious Christians but also subverted the gendered expectations about women's speech, female defendants who faced the Inquisition needed to provide a convincing explanation for their behavior. Asking for mercy, some women resorted to gender stereotypes, by depicting themselves as "ignorant women" with feeble minds in need of male guidance and forgiveness—a traditional argument for reduced responsibility based on the classic characterization of women as belonging to the *sexus imbecillus* (weaker sex).[27] Women defendants also used a rich vocabulary of emotions rooted in the conceptions of feminine physiology and psychology of that time.

Like their male counterparts, women also asked for forgiveness by claiming that they had expressed the blasphemous words in an angry outburst (see chapter 2). Yet, as Natalie Zemon Davis has pointed out, female anger was particularly reprehensible and a deadly sin. Whereas men could legitimately use anger in fighting for just causes—doing so would only enhance their appearance of valor and courage—women's anger could hardly be put to good use, for they were thought to be both powerless and not in control of their emotions. Besides, being cold and damp (humid) according to humoral theory, women were believed to be excessively obstinate when angry because of the deleterious influence of phlegm and melancholy on choler.[28] In contrast to the French women studied by Davis, however, women of New Spain occasionally claimed before the Holy Office that they were "drunk with anger." Yet some women also placed this emotion within a constellation of more complex and widely recognized "female conditions," such as melancholy and *mal de corazón* (heartsickness), which allowed them to argue that they were *fuera de sí* ("out of" or "beyond" themselves) when they had made the sinful utterances.

On January 15, 1575, for instance, Dominican Fray Diego de Osorio denounced Doña María de Peralta in Mexico City. The friar told Inquisitor Hernández de Bonilla that eight days earlier, Osorio had ministered to Peralta's sister as she lay dying. To Peralta's deep consternation, her sister died that very night. "So many sacrifices, so many prayers, and so many masses said for my sister's health," she exclaimed. Raising her arms in despair, she cried, "How can we trust in God's mercy?" After saying these words, she collapsed in a chair. Another clergyman, Father Andrés Martínez, took her hand and asked María de Peralta if she realized what she had just said. She denied vehemently having said those words and called the priest a "faggot liar." Five months later, on May 5, Peralta faced the Holy Office. She explained that because she had not eaten well for more than a month, she had been "out of herself," and so, she had not realized what she was saying. She went on to claim that her heart and entrails had trembled when the people at her sister's deathbed told her that she had blasphemed God. On October 1, her lawyer, Don Hernando de Portugal, stated that Peralta had been sick with melancholy when she blasphemed. Inquisitor Alonso Hernández de Bonilla apparently found this a sound explanation, but his colleague, Inquisitor Alonso Granero Dávalos, believed that Peralta deserved to be severely punished. Two months later, Peralta was ordered to pay two thousand gold ducats. As the widow of lawyer and Inquistion functionary Hortuño de Ibarra, María de Peralta had enough leverage to appeal to the Consejo de la Suprema y General Inquisición (Council of the Supreme and General Inquisition) in Madrid where the arguments of her attorney were heard with more benevolence. Thus, six months later, the Holy Tribunal of Mexico was ordered to give María de Peralta her money back.[29]

If Peralta's attorney justified her actions by emphasizing her sadness and dolefulness,[30] other women sought forgiveness by claiming that their unacceptable speech resulted from involuntary outbursts of a sick heart. On September 7, 1657, schoolmaster Joseph de Tapia went before Inquisitor Bernardo de la Higuera y Amarilla at the Holy Office to denounce his tenant, a twenty-three-year-old Spanish woman, Mariana de Espinosa. The night before, Tapia and his wife, Doña María de Luna, had been roused from their sleep by Espinosa's alarmed maid. She asked the couple to help her mistress because Espinosa's lover, Don Francisco de Albistur, had beaten her. When the couple arrived in the room, Albistur was still there, and Mariana was screaming and lying on the floor. When Tapia asked her what had happened, Espinosa shot back that he and his wife were not Christians because they had not come to her aid when she needed them. Renouncing God and all his saints, she told them to leave. She then tried to hang herself with a rope. Doña María took the rope away, but Mariana grabbed Albistur's sword and tried to kill herself. "She was so desperate and choleric," stated Tapia, "that she seemed to be out of herself." They held on to her and asked her to calm down and be quiet, but Mariana said that she would not settle down even if the Holy Virgin asked her. She hit a table several times with her head. When Albistur had left and her anger finally subsided, Espinosa told Tapia and his wife that she was upset because Albistur wanted to take her to live outside of Mexico City. Tapia reprimanded Espinosa for what she had said earlier, and he told her to denounce herself to the Holy Office. Tearfully, she expressed great remorse for having said disparates. The schoolmaster and his wife stayed with her until daybreak, when they took her to her sister's house.

Espinosa was imprisoned by the Holy Office, and she had her first hearing on October 1, 1657. According to her testimony, she had "a bad friendship" with Albistur, and because he believed she was seeing another man, he had tried to force her to leave the city with him. Espinosa resisted and screamed for help. When the schoolmaster and his wife arrived, she renounced God and said other blasphemies that she could not remember because she had been full of wrath on account of her mal de corazón. During the trial, her sister assured the inquisitor that Mariana de Espinosa had suffered from this condition for several years, and the jailer and his wife declared that Espinosa frequently suffered "pains of the heart," which made her wave her arms about furiously, scream, and lose her appetite. On September 6, 1658, the day she was sentenced after a lengthy trial, Espinosa had another "attack." Finally, on September 24, Inquisitor Pedro Medina Rico took pity on Mariana de Espinosa, and considering her cardiac problems, he sentenced her to serve in a hospital in Mexico City for one year.[31]

Although apparently physiological, Mariana de Espinosa's "attacks" hardly resembled a coronary malady. Instead of becoming weak or paralyzed, Espinosa was incredibly energetic and furious during each episode. She did not experience the death of part of the heart muscle, interruption of blood flow, or brain damage. Clearly, like María de Peralta's melancholy, Espinosa's affliction was a way of explaining her mercurial behavior by locating the source of her uncontrollable anger in her heart. Hers was a "disease of the soul" that allowed her to advance an excuse for blaspheming God's name during a quarrel with her lover.³² Luckily for Espinosa, the inquisitor apparently did not find her failure to observe the moral gender conventions demanding virginity in an unmarried woman to be an aggravating circumstance. As will be seen, however, this was not always the case.

Unholy Comparisons

Yet another layer in the dialectical relationship between female blasphemy and sexual reputation was added when women engaged in derogatory utterances to forcefully assert their good name in front of an audience in order to counteract malicious rumors. Being the most precious possession in an honor-based society, a good name was also quite fragile and vulnerable. This vulnerability, as Peter J. Wilson has noted, "stems from the fact that [a good name] is held by people other than the person who is said to possess it, and that it has no tangible substance, it consists entirely of words."³³ By threatening to destroy a person's social standing and reputation through defamatory stories, gossip constituted a powerful tool to create moral conformity.³⁴ This was particularly true for women in groups at risk, such as widows, *solteras* (unmarried women who were not virgins), and *amancebadas* (unmarried women in consensual unions), who often were the subject of gossip. Fearing social estrangement, these women resorted to blasphemy in angry and often futile attempts to assert their good name by comparing their virtue and cleanliness to that of celestial beings. Unfortunately, by blaspheming, they compromised the very reputation they sought to uphold.

Consider the case of Mariana de los Reyes, a Spanish soltera, who had been the amancebada of Melchor de los Reyes for seven years, living in his house in Mexico City alongside his wife, Leonor García. On October 21, 1619, Sebastián Jiménez, a twenty-two-year-old tailor, reported to the Holy Office a discussion he had overheard between Melchor and Mariana. According to Jiménez, Melchor had flown into a jealous rage and accused Mariana of giving her body promiscuously to blacks, mulattoes, and white men. He told her that she was "as vile as the door of the [Church of the] Macarena" in Seville, thus probably intimating that she was "open" to all kinds of people. Mariana reacted by calling Melchor a *bellaco* (rogue) and a liar, and she said was as *honrada* (virtuous) as Saint Catherine. Mariana went so far as to say she deserved to be adored like God himself. Asked by the Holy Office to judge the gravity of the crime, the calificadores agreed that by comparing herself to Saint Catherine, Mariana de los Reyes slanderously blasphemed the saints; to have added that she deserved to be adored like

God, however, was nothing less than heretical blasphemy. Clearly, the incident was deemed important enough to warrant an arrest, but the documents do not indicate whether the Inquisition proceeded against Mariana.[35]

If Mariana resorted to unholy comparisons to assert her own virtuousness, other women used this form of blasphemy to assert the good reputation of their daughters. On November 11, 1564, for example, Father Francisco Gudies denounced María de Bustamante, a forty-year-old Spanish woman who lived in Mexico City. He claimed that she had told a man that her daughter was "as pure and virgin as Saint Catherine or Saint John the Baptist." A month before, customers in the store that María de Bustamante owned had overheard her making the same sinful remarks. Bustamante's blasphemy was deemed scandalous by her denouncer not just because of the unholy comparison itself, but because everybody knew that neither of her two daughters was a virgin.

Father Gudies asserted that he had seen Francisca de Bustamante kissing a man on the mouth, and her sister, Isabel, was the amancebada of Rodrigo de Guzmán. Rodrigo Hurtado, a man who was deeply in love with Isabel, also denounced the couple, probably out of jealousy. While serving their sentence in prison, Isabel and Rodrigo de Guzmán decided to marry because Isabel was pregnant. Only a few days before the wedding, witnesses claimed that María de Bustamante had again sinfully—and inaccurately—compared her daughter to the saints.

In her depositions, Bustamante identified Rodrigo de Hurtado and some other witnesses as her denouncers, claiming that they were her *enemigos capitales* (capital enemies), who had reported her out of animosity. Hurtado, in particular, had once been sent to prison by Bustamante for having broken into her house. She claimed to be a woman *muy templada en su hablar* (someone who controlled her speech), especially when it came to swearing. All these defenses notwithstanding, María de Bustamante was sentenced on March 21, 1565, to hear mass in the cathedral while holding a candle, to buy oil for the church lamps, and to pay two gold pesos for the prosecutor, plus the costs of trial.[36]

A similar case involving the defense of a daughter's honor was recorded in Cholula in 1586 against Elvira Gutiérrez, a forty-year-old woman born in Jeréz de la Frontera in Spain. In contrast to María de Bustamante, however, Elvira Gutiérrez lived in a small rural town, which increased the pressure for conformity and accentuated perceived transgressions of social mores. While searching unsuccessfully for her husband who had vanished, Gutiérrez, with her daughter, Juana Márquez, had arrived in Cholula in 1582. Her cousin, Pedro de Trujillo, lived in the town and invited her to stay at his home. Around 1584, another cousin, Diego de Trujillo, told Gutiérrez that he wanted to marry Juana, who was by then about nineteen years old. Since Diego de Trujillo was a blood relative, Gutiérrez objected to the marriage. She also suspected that Trujillo was not really interested in marrying but simply hoped to cohabit with the girl. Gutiérrez told Diego to ask for Pedro de Trujillo's opinion on this matter, but Diego refused. He continued to visit Gutiérrez with some frequency until they had a fight, and she asked Pedro to tell Diego not to come anymore.

Suddenly, Elvira's daughter was the subject of rumors in the town. Some said that Pedro de Trujillo had forbidden Diego to come to his house because Pedro himself had "bad intentions" toward Juana Márquez. Others believed that Gutiérrez's daughter was pregnant with Diego's child, and he had refused to marry her.

Things escalated in 1586 when Elvira Gutiérrez and her daughter were invited to Easter dinner at the house of Francisco de Valencia, a close friend of Diego de Trujillo. After eating, Juan de León, Valencia's father-in-law and also a friend of Diego, told Gutiérrez that he wanted to play a game with her daughter. He took a tape and measured different parts of Juana Márquez's body. When finished, León hit his forehead with his hand and exclaimed, "I swear to God (voto a Dios) and the Holy Sacrament that this child is as much a virgin (doncella) as that little [one-year-old] grand-daughter of mine!" thus implying sardonically that Gutiérrez's daughter was indeed pregnant. Deeply outraged by the "game," Elvira Gutiérrez beat her breast and shouted angrily that it was intolerable that the daughter of an honest woman should be treated in that way. She then said that her daughter was "as much a virgin as the Holy Mother." Two months later, Juan de León and two of his daughters snatched Gutiérrez while she was walking on the street. While the women restrained her, León threatened her with a dagger and insulted her. Gutiérrez reported León's behavior to the local authorities. While he was in prison, León wrote to the comisario of the Holy Office in Puebla, Melchor Márquez de Amarilla, denouncing Elvira Gutiérrez for blasphemy.

Warned by a neighbor about this, Gutiérrez sought advice from a Franciscan priest, Pedro de Miranda. Several people, León among them, had already denounced Gutiérrez to Miranda, but the priest had not passed those reports on to the Holy Office. He told Elvira not to worry about what she had said because she had clearly done it to praise her daughter's honra (virtue). Preaching from his pulpit in Cholula, Miranda also tried to ease the tension that Gutiérrez´s accusation against León had created by declaring that it was "inconceivable that in a town with such a small number of Spaniards, people would go about blaspheming and testifying against each other."[37] Yet, when the Inquisition comisario started gathering information about this case, using the monastery of Cholula as his headquarters, Miranda urged Gutiérrez to denounce herself in order to avoid a severe punishment. Elvira accused herself on March 21, 1586. The following day, Márquez de Amarilla sent the information he had gathered to the Inquisition. Two months later, Prosecutor Lobo Guerrero requested that Gutiérrez be brought to Mexico City and imprisoned in the headquarters of Holy Office.[38] This is the last thing we know about Elvira Gutiérrez and her tribulations with her neighbors in Cholula. Her case clearly illustrates the extent to which gossip in colonial Mexico constituted both a way of enforcing moral standards and a preferred and anonymous idiom of defamation, aggression, and character assassination.[39]

Another facet of the tense relationship between gossip and blasphemous comparisons was offered by the case of Leonor Arias, a widow in the town of Compostela (in today's state of Jalisco). In this instance, however, blasphemy was used not to challenge gossip but to disavow responsibility for damaging another woman's reputation. In April 1563, Bishop of Guadalajara Pedro de Ayala sent Father Diego de Álvarez to Compostela in order to gather information against Leonor Arias, who had sent a letter to the bishop denouncing herself. During the investigation, the alcalde mayor of Compostela told Álvarez that about a year earlier, Arias had come to visit his wife, Catalina Rodríguez. They engaged in a conversation that revolved around what Álvarez characterized as *cosas de mujeres* (women's concerns), and what Catalina herself would later describe as "things of little importance." According to Álvarez, these dismissive characterizations were deceptive. He had learned that a third woman had also been present, and she blamed Arias for having been the author of *parlería* (gossip) that had ruined the reputation of a married woman in the town. Outraged by the accusation and seeking to deny it, Arias exclaimed that she was as *limpia* (pure and innocent) as the Virgin Mary. According to another witness, Leandro Mejía, Arias confessed this blasphemy to the vicar, Father Angulo, who asked for a bribe of thousand pesos to keep from denouncing her to the Holy Office. Mejía recommended that Arias instead denounce herself to the vicar of Guacatlán, but she decided to write directly to the bishop, who then dispatched Álvarez to look into the matter. Between April 19 and April 23, 1563, Álvarez collected depositions from several witnesses. After spending time in prison, Leonor Arias was

finally sentenced to attend a mass in Compostela while barefoot, to fast on
Saturdays, pray the rosary of the Virgin for a year, and to pay twenty gold
pesos. Seven years later, the provisor of the archbishopric of Guadalajara
charged Arias with the same crime, stating that Diego de Álvarez had not
had the authority to sentence her. The provisor of Nueva Galicia dismissed
the case, however, and ordered the prosecutor not to bother Leonor Arias
again.[40]

Fighting defamation clearly constituted a powerful motive for women
to engage in blasphemy. When targeted by gossip, women resorted to the
highest female symbols of purity, virtue, and cleanliness in the Christian
pantheon to impugn malicious speech. Paradoxically, as we have seen, wom-
en were also active agents in the production of rumors aimed at the regula-
tion of sexual propriety. Indeed, as several historians have shown, in these
still largely oral societies, women played a key role by withholding or circulating information that could affect an individual's social standing.[41] "Telling stories and judging morals," observed Laura Gowing, "made women
the brokers of oral reputation."[42] Thus, as Mary Beth Norton has pointed
out, in preserving community moral standards, female gossipers reinforced
their own reputation at the expense of the people they were defaming.[43] In
this context, women's blasphemous comparisons and gossip could represent
antagonistic forms of asserting honor and defilement that were based on the
Christian ideals of female honesty and gendered morality.

Recogimientos: "Is This Perchance a Symbol of Hell?"

Nonconforming women used blasphemy to fight the informal means of enforcing female morality and also the institutional mechanisms created to
guarantee women's virtue through confinement. Besides convents, *beate-
rios* (a community of lay holy women), and orphanages, the *recogimientos*
(shelters) were the most important institutions for protecting, guarding, and
rehabilitating women who had led "scandalous" lives. In accordance with
the moralists' conviction that seclusion was a remedy for moral corruption
and public disorder, colonial authorities early in the sixteenth century established these shelters for women in order to offer refuge to the virtuous and
punishment and correction to the "fallen." Some recogimientos admitted
only women of the first type, but many others, founded by lay people and
ecclesiastical authorities, sheltered both. Women of all classes and ages voluntarily sought protection in these institutions but were then forbidden to
leave. *Mujeres depositadas* ("deposited women") were left in recogimientos

by their families or were sent there by the colonial courts for correction. In any case, women in the recogimientos had to endure close supervision and were expected to follow an exacting religious regimen. Resistance, however, was not uncommon. Indeed, in an effort to be released from their forced confinement, some women made extraordinary efforts by any means available to draw the attention of the Holy Tribunal.[44]

Consider, for instance, the case of Ana López. In 1590, her husband, León de Candía, deposited her in the recogimiento of Santa Mónica in Mexico City. Candía, a carpenter by trade, had decided to go to work in the Philippines, so Ana was to be confined in order to protect her husband's honor while he was away. This practice was rather common in New Spain, and since its founding in 1582, Santa Mónica had specialized in sheltering married women. The shelter was a mechanism to supervise women in the absence of men, a substitute for the control the husband wielded over the wife.[45] Married to Candía when she was only eleven years old, López had followed her husband from Veracruz, to Puebla, and then to Mexico City. She was only nineteen when he left for the Philippines. Life inside Santa Mónica was hard, however, and Ana López escaped after a year of imprisonment. Unfortunately, she was caught by Alguacil Pedro de Burgos. López, threatening to hang herself in despair, begged him not to take her back. Seeing that Burgos was not moved by her pleas, López renounced God, the Holy Virgin, and the saints, and claimed to give herself in body and soul to the devil. The alguacil dragged her back to Santa Mónica, and when they reached the main door, López exclaimed in front of the female rector of the house that it was not a *cosa de santa* (holy place), but a *putería secreta* (secret whorehouse). Burgos then denounced Ana López to the Holy Office. Facing Inquisitor Santos García, López confessed to uttering those blasphemies, but she explained that she had been "drunk with anger" because of being forced to return to Santa Mónica. She also confessed to having said, "I renounce you," while looking at a Christ figure on a crucifix. The prosecutor charged that such an act was an "infernal audacity" and, to López's dismay, the Holy Office sentenced her to another year of confinement in the recogimiento. She heard her sentence delivered on March 6, 1591, with a gag in her mouth and a white candle in her hand.[46]

A more dramatic example of the female use of blasphemy to resist the harsh conditions endured by women in the recogimientos is provided by a case involving a young woman named Juana de Medina, alias Juana de Güemes, in San Miguel de Belén, a recogimiento in Mexico City. Founded in 1683 by Father Domingo Pérez de Barcia, with the authorization of

Mexican Archbishop Francisco Aguiar y Seijas and Viceroy Tomás Antonio Manrique de la Cerda y Aragón, Belén was the most important institution of its kind in New Spain. The recogimiento accepted poor women of all social backgrounds, submitting them to a severe regimen of austerity, work, and religious discipline that often provoked bitter resistance from the residents. Inside the walls, the *prepósita* (rector), Doña Catalina Rendón, and her assistant enforced order. Among the other personnel were two women who made sure that silence was observed; two more who informed Father Domingo Pérez de Barcia, now the resident priest, of any irregularity; two porters; one woman bell ringer; and two sextons. Belén was by far the largest and most densely populated women's shelter in New Spain. In 1684, more than fifty women resided within its walls, and that number tripled by the end of the century.[47]

Like many other women, Juana de Medina entered San Miguel de Belén voluntarily, looking for shelter and protection. Only later did she discover she could not leave. On Christmas Eve 1688, Medina had fought with her husband, Manuel Antonio de Minaya, because he wanted to move out of her uncle's house where they were living. Juana refused to go, and when Minaya angrily left late at night, Juana went to Belén to ask Father Domingo to give her shelter. He let her in, and Medina sent somebody to pick up her clothes. Minaya refused to give the garments to the messenger, and he declared that there was no reason for the couple to be apart. The following day, he went to talk with Juana, but she refused to see him. Some time later, Minaya wrote to Archbishop Francisco Aguiar, asking him to intervene. Aguiar ordered Father Domingo to return Juana to her husband. However, just before Medina was to be released from Belén, it came out that Minaya had killed a man many years before, and he was tried and exiled to the Philippines.

Unfortunately for Medina, Minaya took measures to make sure she would not leave the shelter during his absence. On January 30, 1689, realizing that Juana's mother was trying to get her released, Minaya wrote to Father Domingo begging him to keep Medina in the recogimiento. When Minaya departed for the Philippines in April, Medina was not allowed to leave Belén. Moreover, Father Domingo and Father Lázaro Fernández forbade Medina to see or communicate with her mother or any other relative. In despair, Juana de Medina tried to kill herself by repeatedly stabbing her throat with scissors. The prepósita stopped her and called Father Lázaro. Seeing the blood, the callous priest told Medina that if she really wanted to kill herself, it would be better to use a knife. He told her that she was going to die in Belén and would never see her mother again. Full of anger, Medina renounced God and screamed that Christ was a cuckold because he let so many sacrileges happen in the recogimiento and did not help her to get released. Scandalized, the prepósita put a woolen gag in Juana de Medina's mouth, but the distraught woman still managed to say that the Virgin was a whore. The episode ended when Father Lázaro slapped her in the face.

Greatly outraged, Father Domingo denounced Juana de Medina to the Holy Office on May 21, 1689. Besides complaining about Medina's blasphemies, he explained she had told him that she had assaulted holy images, whipped a crucifix, and thrown consecrated hosts into "filthy places." He did not know if these things had actually happened, for Medina might have just be lying to get out of Belén, even though the "house rules" were that married women could not leave except to rejoin their husbands.

Three months later, on August 25, 1689, a calificador was sent to San Miguel de Belén to meet with Juana de Medina. He had been instructed to give her a benign sentence, consisting of fasting and praying the rosary. He was then to absolve her because she had apparently blasphemed without "contumacy or perversity," and only out of despair and as a strategy to get released from the institution. The Holy Office told the calificador to admonish the prepósita to treat the women of Belén with the prudence, gentleness, and charity necessary to comfort them and to avoid excessive punishments. However, when the calificador arrived at the recogimiento, he realized that Juana de Medina's blasphemy was only part of the whole picture, and he decided not to absolve her until the inquisitors learned more.

Juana de Medina's story had taken on a new twist in July, when she had attempted to escape across the roof terrace. She was caught and locked in a dark room inside the recogimiento. After two days in this prison, she shouted through the window to people on the street, asking them to denounce her to the Holy Office because she had renounced God. Father Lázaro then sealed off the window, and Medina could see light only when they brought her food. Some women told her that Father Domingo said she would be imprisoned for a year and a half on orders of the Inquisition. This was a lie, but it undoubtedly made Medina desperate. Putting her rosary on the bed, she invoked the devil three times, or so she later claimed, asking him to get her out of San Miguel de Belén. The first time she did it, a shiver ran down her spine, and she thought that the walls were collapsing and the roof was falling in. Then she fell sick. A doctor was called and a Father Sosa heard her confession. She told him that she had renounced God, had had anal intercourse with the devil, and had spit the consecrated host out of her mouth. She wanted to be denounced to the Holy Office and be removed from the recogimiento, but still Sosa did not denounce her. News of her new crimes reached the Inquisition after Father Antonio Núñez agreed to write down Juana's self-denunciation on August 26. The Holy Tribunal then ordered a thorough investigation of the meetings Medina had had with the devil. To avoid further scandals in Belén, she was ordered to be transferred to her mother's house pending the trial. Between September and November 1689, Juana de Medina, Father Lázaro, the prepósita, and other women were interrogated. The records stop, however, soon after that. We do not know the denouement of Juana's trial, but it is certain that she was back in the recogimiento the following year, for she wrote a letter on January 7 asking Inquisitor Juan Gómez de Mier to take pity on her and allow her to leave San Miguel de Belén. Confined to the shelter to protect her husband's honor in his absence, Medina probably stayed a prisoner for years before Minaya returned and finally removed her from this "house of virtue."[48]

The tribunal's reluctance to intervene in Juana's favor may have arisen from the need to avoid establishing a precedent that would allow the women housed in recogimientos to regard blasphemy as a way to get released. The difficulties that San Miguel de Belén faced at that time may have also been a factor. Protesting the institution's harsh discipline, other women refused to comply with the "house rules" in various ways and even attempted to escape. One woman even killed herself by jumping from the second floor to the patio, and another took off her clothes in the chapel in the hope of being expelled. Still other women expressed their frustration in stanzas that circulated in Mexico City:

> She who enters this house
> Should put order in her life,
> For her own will brought her in,
> But only God's will take her out.[49]

Relatives, such as Juana de Medina's mother, sent letters to the viceroy and the archbishop describing the situation inside the institution, but no response was given. "Is this perchance a symbol of hell, and we . . . [mere] portraits of people condemned in life?" asked Medina in one of her letters to the Inquisition, comparing the sighs, curses, and laments heard in the corridors of the recogimiento to the expressions of those enduring the eternal torments of hell.[50]

San Miguel de Belén was surely an extreme case, but the rigid disciplinary norms and harsh living conditions that characterized it could also be found in other houses for both "vicious" and "virtuous" women, such as the

Hospital de la Misericordia, where women from the lower echelons, such as *castas* (mixed-blood), were more likely to be found. In 1692, Father Tomás del Castillo denounced several mulattas who resided in this recogimiento, stating that a María de la Natividad had uttered that God would not redeem her if he was not able to get her released. Two other women named Guadalupe and Francisca had openly claimed that they were not afraid of God or the prepósita. As in Medina's case, the Inquisition admonished the women severely and considered the incidents closed.[51] Secular and ecclesiastical authorities were convinced about the importance of the recogimientos for controlling and supervising women, and the Inquisition was unwilling to debilitate the power of the custodians by offering women interned in these correctional institutions a way out.

As Elizabeth Perry has pointed out, gendered beliefs about the necessity of secluding women would later provide a smooth transition when time came for the creation of prisons for intractable women.[52] Indeed, by the eighteenth century, many recogimientos were accepting women sentenced to imprisonment on criminal charges. Others transformed themselves into prisons during the second half of the eighteenth century, including Santa María Magdalena in Mexico City. Gradually, the state took over these establishments. That reflected an evolution of the perception of female willfulness, from its being seen as a sin to being characterized as delinquency and criminality. As a result of this process, women, such as Juana de Medina, who were unjustly held in forced confinement in order to guard the gendered moral standards of the time, found it more difficult to draw the attention of the tribunal through the use of blasphemy, "meetings" with the devil, and sacrilege.

Conclusion

In her classic *Language and Woman's Place* (1976), Robin Lakoff described what she named, following Gregory Bateson, the woman's double-bind: If a woman uses a powerful speech style, characterized by interruption, challenging, disputes, and uses of expletives (that is, a style normally reserved for men), both men and women ostracize her for being unfeminine. However, if she chooses instead euphemisms, superpolite forms, and generally speaks "like a lady," she is not taken seriously. Instead, "she is a bit of fluff."[53] Women in New Spain faced a similar dilemma. When being defamed or unjustly confined, women resorted to blasphemy in order to make forceful statements to fight back. However, by subverting the gendered moral expectations that demanded that pious women demonstrate verbal restraint, they compromised their status as Christian women.

By failing to control her "unruly member," a woman would fall short of the ideals of female Christianity and also of the social expectations for women. In contrast to their male counterparts, female blasphemers were seen as engaging in acts that implied not merely irreverence but also gender subversion. As Laura Gowing has pointed out in a different context, the problem was not that women were judged more harshly, but that their culpability could not be compared to that of men.[54] Men and women were seen as fundamentally different in terms of intelligence, responsibility, and function within the social body, so their crimes carried different meanings and social consequences. Following a long biblical tradition, early modern Christian writers, moralists, and inquisitors considered female verbal restraint to be a crucial element for the enactment of the ideals of domesticity, charity, and virtuousness that women were expected to follow in a well-ordered society. As with the infamous sexual double standard, this gendered speech morality could not be enforced without the active support and participation of women, who, by supervising and denouncing other women, effectively reinforced the prevailing moral inequalities.

Something similar occurred when women faced the Inquisition as defendants. Female blasphemers often felt compelled to use, and thus confirm, the misogynist stereotypes that depicted them as weak human beings, incapable of controlling their tongues and passions. Blasphemy was thus a risky strategy to use when a woman sought a strong voice in order to fight defamation or resist confinement. Beyond the honor concerns of Spanish women, however, for some men and women in colonial Mexico, blasphemy represented a dramatic means to fight and resist mistreatment and to meet a most basic need under the harsh conditions they endured as slaves: survival.

5

"To Lose One's Soul"

Blasphemy and Slavery

> . . . any Christian [would be] in great danger of renouncing God
> and his just faith.
> —Slave Nicolás Bazán at the Holy Office (1661)

On April 28, 1598, Juan Bautista, slave of Regidor Cristóbal Jiménez, denounced himself to the Puebla's Inquisition Comisario Melchor Márquez de Amarilla. In his testimony, Juan recounted the events of the previous day: Around four in the afternoon, having worked at an unacceptably slow pace that day in the regidor's textile mill, his master beat him severely and applied hot pitch to Juan's wounds. He continued the beating while two other men firmly held Juan down, and in an attempt to appease Jiménez, Bautista begged him to stop, "for the sake of the love of God and Holy Mary." His torturer replied, "I beat you for the sake of God and Holy Mary!" He then forced a firebrand into the slave's mouth. Facing such horrifying abuse, Juan shouted, "Reniego de Dios!" (I renounce God) twice, but the regidor continued to beat him. The next day, *volviendo en sí* (coming to his senses), Juan asked the Inquisition official for mercy. The slave insisted he was a Christian and begged for a transfer to another location so that his soul would not be damned.[1]

More than sixty years later, in 1661, the black slave Nicolás Bazán told Inquisitor Francisco Estrada about the brutal work regime in the Coyoacán textile mill belonging to his master, Melchor Díaz de Posadas. As an example of Díaz de Posadas's cruelty, Bazán described the *gargantón*, an instrument that was a combination of collar and handcuffs used to immobilize the slaves for days at a time. The suffering it inflicted was so rigorous, Nicolás assured the inquisitor, that "any Christian [would be] in great danger of renouncing

God and his just faith"—something he had actually done, according to other witnesses. On his knees, he implored Inquisitor Estrada not to send him back to the textile mill, lest the cruel punishment that was awaiting him lead him to despair and "lose his soul." He concluded that in Coyoácan, the suffering of "Christians redeemed by Christ's blood at the hands of fellow Christians" was so painful that "not even among Turks and Moors was a comparable martyrdom endured."[2]

The cases of Juan Bautista and Nicolás Bazán are good examples of the circumstances under which slaves were held accountable for blasphemy in sixteenth- and seventeenth-century colonial Mexico. Black slaves, the victims of cruelty and mistreatment, renounced God to provoke the intervention of the Inquisition as a strategy to gain at least temporary freedom from the brutal working conditions they endured. Sometimes slaves even succeeded in using their religious transgression to obtain a transfer to another location and a new master. In some instances, they deployed an ingenious rhetoric that transformed the masters' "legitimate" punishment of slaves into torture, chastisement into martyrdom, and the slaves' own blasphemies into painful reactions of persecuted Christians. Moreover, by claiming to "lose their souls" at the hands of the owners of their bodies, black slaves also undertook an inversion of the colonial discourse that justified slavery by predicating the Christian salvation of African souls on the servitude of their bodies.

The paradoxical nature of this "salvational" servitude garnered little criticism until the mid-sixteenth century, when Spanish theologians and jurists began to pay some attention to the Portuguese slave trade. Even then, the isolated protests were mostly directed at the process by which slaves were acquired, not at the legitimacy of slavery itself. As Francisco de Vitoria wrote in 1546, it was better for Africans "to be slaves among Christians than free in their own lands." In Mexico, Archbishop Alonso de Montúfar, challenging that position in a famous letter written to the Spanish Crown in 1560, argued that the benefits of Christianization did not offset the terrible injustices that Africans endured, and he asked the king to terminate the slave trade. Similarly, in his *Arte de Contratos*, jurist Bartolomé de Albornoz forcefully denounced the widespread conviction that "the freedom of the soul should be paid by the servitude of the body." These protests notwithstanding, Madrid did not modify its royal policy and solidly embraced the doctrine of salvation as the main argument for the enslavement of African pagans.[3]

As both property and human beings, Afro-Mexican slaves learned quickly that they could be Christians and still remain in bondage. This could not
have been clearer than when being punished. Whereas slaves begged their
owners to stop the beating for the sake of a god that demanded charity and
fraternity from believers, masters, insisting in a hierarchical society with
slaves at the bottom, claimed that the same god sanctioned that slaves' bodies should answer for all their crimes. Indeed, some masters justified their
cruelty by saying, "I beat you for the sake of God and Holy Mary." Corporal punishment was the currency in which black slaves, mulattoes, and
other "low-caste" people had to pay for their transgressions. Spaniards, in
contrast, normally received monetary fines as punishment for similar mis-
deeds.[4]

In *Slavery and Social Death*, Orlando Patterson offers a poignant analysis of the painful dialectics of inclusion and exclusion endured by slaves in
societies that embraced the Christian doctrine of salvation: "The slave, in
the city of the Christian God, was declared an insider, an integral part of the
brotherhood of man in the service of God; but the slave, in the city of man,
remained the archetypical outsider, the eternal enemy within, in a formalized
state of marginality."[5] In light of this conspicuous contradiction between the
treatment given to the marginalized and that given to the socially included,
it can be argued that Afro-Mexicans' blaspheming was both a rejection of
the Christian moral order that legitimized slavery and an attempt to claim
a Christian identity in order to survive a violent regime. With slaves in this
state of secular excommunication, slaveholders drew their authority from
their control of symbolic instruments, such as the "symbolic whip" of religion. Patterson contends that this control persuaded slaves that "the master
was the only mediator between the living community to which he belonged
and the living death that his slave experienced."[6]

Several blasphemy trials, however, show that Afro-Mexicans were sometimes able to turn this "symbolic whip" against their own masters, to hold
them accountable for the possible condemnation of the slaves' souls. Stemming from unbearable affliction in the city of man, blasphemy extended
a bridge to the city of God, where with the help of the Inquisition, slaves
could occasionally find leverage against their masters. In general, however,
the Mexican Holy Office was very lenient toward violent slaveholders, often
condemning slaves to severe beatings for alleged religious transgressions.
The Inquisition's biased attitude undoubtedly stemmed in part from the fact
that the Holy Office, and the Church, in general, were major slave owners.

Additionally, the fear and repudiation of Afro-Mexicans that had existed from the beginning of the colonial enterprise fueled the Holy Tribunal's determination to curb any sign of slave rebellion in New Spain.

Indeed, during the sixteenth and early seventeenth centuries, letters and reports from royal administrators frequently mentioned serious concerns over the presence of too many slaves in the colony and the possibility of slave rebellions.[7] As early as 1537, New Spain experienced the first of several attempted slave rebellions. On the roads of New Galicia, Guanajuato, Pénjamo, San Miguel, and between Puebla and Veracruz and along the Pacific Coast, bands of runaway slaves robbed and killed Indians and Spaniards. In the mountains near Orizaba, a Congolese chief, Yanga, established an almost impenetrable stronghold, from which his band raided neighboring towns and haciendas with impunity for more than thirty years until 1609. By the second decade of the seventeenth century, the importation of slaves, now in the hands of Portuguese traders, reached its highpoint, further fueling the fear of an urban slave uprising. After an aborted rebellion in 1608 in Mexico City, the colonists faced a new threat in 1611 when an angry crowd of 1,500 blacks belonging to the Cofradía de Nuestra Señora filed past the palaces of the viceroy and the Inquisition, carrying the corpse of a female slave who had been flogged to death by her master. The rebellion was quickly repressed, with thirty-six blacks, seven women included, publicly hanged in the city's main plaza and their heads placed on pikes. Numerous minor revolts occurred in the following years in northern New Spain's ranching regions and in the vicinity of Veracruz. Mexico City itself experienced a new scare in 1665 when the Inquisition, an important instrument of colonial vigilance, detected signs of unrest among the capital's Afro-Mexicans. The alleged conspiracy never materialized, but the ensuing patrols by the Spanish infantry and militia were clear proof of the racial tension in the colony.[8]

Black-white relations were not always abrasive, but it is clear that Afro-Mexicans tended to arouse in Spaniards feelings of fear rather than sympathy or compassion. The obvious difficulty of fulfilling both the need for civil security and economic expectations produced stern legal measures to control the increasing black population and forestall slave revolts. This only made the conditions under which slaves lived even harsher, which sometimes led to new rebellions that, in turn, confirmed the need for vigorous suppression. In this circular process of fear, repression, and backlash, colonial authorities tended to tolerate the slaveholders' physical brutality. Indeed, the lash, the stocks, the pillory, the use of gags and leg irons, and the practices of branding, burning, and even mutilating slaves were evidence of the de facto power held by the slaveholders in New Spain. Although colonial authorities assumed that violence was key to creating and maintaining this dominance relationship, how far a master could go in his disciplinary actions was not clear. Where was the line between "legitimate punishment" and sadistic mistreatment? In colonial Mexico, slaves struggled constantly to set limits to the master's brutality through both institutional and noninstitutional avenues.

Under Spanish law, mistreated slaves could ask for protection from the civil courts, but in practice, few slaves benefited from this legal protection during the first two centuries of Spanish control of the New World.[9] For most bondsmen, work slowdowns, running away, banditry, occasional outbursts of rioting, violence, and blasphemy were recurrent strategies for resisting abusive masters. Of these types of social contention, however, only blasphemy gave slaves access to the Mexican Holy Office, where they could make use of the moral leverage they enjoyed as members of the Christian community.

This strategy of verbal resistance was well known in Spain, especially in centers with high concentrations of slaves, such as Seville. Hoping to spare masters the economic loss incurred when their slaves were imprisoned (and fed and clothed at the slaveholder's expense), the Catholic kings had issued a decree in 1502 allowing the master of a blasphemer to punish the transgressor by publicly administering fifty lashes.[10] Soon, however, the Holy Tribunal insisted on its jurisdiction to try the blasphemers, diluting this "relief" for the slaveholder.[11] As New Spain continued to face the threat of slave revolts, the Inquisition's interest in repressing blasphemy at times worked to the detriment of the masters themselves. When a slave blasphemer forced the Holy Office to intervene, that action not only undermined the disciplinary authority of the slaveholder but also transformed that authority, by apt manipulation, from a coercive colonial institution into a protective shield for the slave. Nevertheless, the stakes were always high when slaves resorted to the Inquisition.

The Meanings of Blasphemy Among Afro-Mexican Slaves

Throughout the colonial period, blasphemy was the most common crime for which Afro-Mexicans faced the Inquisition. In contrast to Spaniards, who frequently resorted to blasphemy as a strategy of masculine self-fashioning, a means of establishing one's autonomy after humiliating defeats in gambling games, and a verbal resource to make strong statements in honor disputes, Afro-Mexicans generally used blasphemous speech as a strategy of resistance and survival under unbearable working and living conditions as bondsmen. Indeed, although some of the defendants were free blacks, most seem to have been slaves, which suggests a direct relationship between slavery and the uttering of "sinful" expletives. Most of the Inquisition's trials of slaves charged with blasphemy occurred between 1596 and 1669. Although it is not always possible to determine a defendant's background from the existing records for that period, it appears that most Afro-Mexican slaves were creole (acculturated) black slaves (20) or mulatto slaves (21); only 3 were *ladinos* (Hispanicized Africans), and one a *bozal* (non-acculturated African).[12] The accused was usually a young male slave. Women counterparts faced the Inquisition less frequently (18 cases).[13] Most of the defendants lived in the urban areas of Mexico City (35) and Puebla (18), with one case each from Veracruz, Jalapa, and Celaya. Four cases came from rural Coyoacán, 2 from Amilpas, and one each from Cholula, Tlalnepantla, the mines of Zacatecas, and Misquiguala. Although many of the slaves were employed as domestic servants, 21 of the defendants worked in obrajes (mills or workshops) in Mexico City, Puebla, and Coyoacán.[14] In both urban and rural settings, blasphemy resulted from excessive punishment meted out by masters in response to their bondsmen's putatively delinquent behavior. Failure to finish work assigned, pilfering, and flight constituted the most common delinquencies that slaveholders and overseers cited for punishing their slaves. A frequent practice was to tie the recalcitrant to a ladder (a procedure known as the Ley de Bayona), or hang him in the air by both hands, from which vantage a slave would have to face his master's anger. Slaves subjected to such abuse blurted out blasphemies, including rejecting God, in an attempt to stop the physical punishment. Early modern writers on the criminal law of the Catholic Church and theologians (such as Domingo de Soto and Francisco de Suárez) considered these outbursts to be a clear sign of faithlessness, which warranted prosecution by the Inquisition.[15]

For a Christian to renounce God was, Spanish moralists felt, an unbearable expression of ingratitude.[16] Indeed, through the Son, the Father had set men and women free from the slavery of sin, hence making of them, as one modern scholar of Philippine colonization has remarked, "recipients of a gift so enormous as to defy equal return."[17] Having received divine liberation from sin, Christians agreed to a new slavery for, as Saint Paul wrote to the Romans, true freedom exists only through enslavement to God.[18] Yet, for those who were *truly* in bondage, renouncing God entailed more than a rejection of otherworldly indebtedness. It also implied a denial of the Christian ideology that justified their subjection as slaves with the promise of future redemption in the afterlife,[19] and a rejection of the God who failed as a "true master" in his duty to protect his slave from unbearable abuse.[20]

"What is the purpose of believing in God if he doesn't help or favor me in these tribulations?" asked Gerónimo, the slave of Juan de Isla, in 1611. The overseer of the Cholula obraje in which Gerónimo worked slapped him in the face for this pronouncement, and Gerónimo then knelt facing an altar and roared: "May the devil take with him our Lord and our Lady! I renounce God and all his saints because I've been taken to this obraje."[21] A parallel case occurred in 1616 (probably in Mexico City). Cruelly battered by her master, a slave, Isabel, asked in despair, "Oh, my Jesus, why did you allow this to happen? . . . You're not God!"[22] Even inquisitors acknowledged that slaves might have renounced God because of his perceived failure to preserve them from the masters' brutality. For instance, when Isabel denounced herself in 1576 for having said, "I am beaten without being guilty of anything! I renounce God! I don't believe in God!" she was asked by Inquisitor Bonilla: "Did you say that blasphemy out of anger against God because he allowed you to be treated in this way?"[23]

As the pain and exasperation of slaves grew under the whip of their masters, rejection of a god who did not exhibit concern about his believers' tribulations acquired increasingly dramatic proportions. A descriptive approach to slaves' verbal repertoire while being beaten shows a clear tendency to couple the renunciation of God and the Christian community (symbolized by the baptismal Chrism)[24] with the rejection of the slaves' own parents, especially a mother and her nurturing milk. In Mexico City in 1601, a slave named Francisco cried out eight times: "I renounce the [baptismal] Chrism I received and the milk I suckled!" In 1617, Pedro, slave of Mexico City merchant Amado Pinto, renounced the father who "made" him, the mother who bore him, and the Holy Mother.[25] In Cholula in 1611, Ambrosio Gutiérrez four times renounced the mother who bore him after he was slapped in the face by the overseer of the obraje. Most noteworthy of all, however, was the case of Felipa, slave of Valeriano de Negrón in Mexico City. She was sentenced to two hundred lashes after she confessed in 1607 to having renounced "God our Lord and his saints," as well as "the mother who bore her and the father who engendered her, and the milk she suckled and the swaddling clothes (pañales) in which she was wrapped when newly born."[26] Under the dubious protection of a god who allowed his people to be beaten, it seems evident that Afro-Mexicans repudiated having entered this world as Christians and slaves or, more strikingly, to have been born at all if birth meant being a slave.

Blasphemy was not a mere expression of anger stemming from the pain or despair experienced by Afro-Mexican bondsmen. It often had another purpose, "more subtle and material," which Jean-Pierre Tardieu has defined as "moral bribery," and the Mexican inquisitors understood as *forzar un pacto* (forcing a pact).[27] Indeed, facing the imminence of physical punishment, Afro-Mexicans threatened their masters with renouncing God. For the slaveholder, this created an impasse: If he decided to proceed with the punishment, he was morally responsible for the resulting blasphemies. Yet, if he dropped the whip, he confirmed the efficacy of this strategy and risked that other slaves would repeat it. Although some masters suspended punishment and took their slave to the Holy Office without delay, most reacted with increased anger to the dilemma set before them. On June 3, 1598, at Juan Ortíz's sombrero obraje in Tlalnepantla, one of the slaves, Antón, faced with being chastised, threatened to renounce God. Antón was severely whipped, Ortíz explained, "so this would not set a precedent among slaves as a way to avoid punishment."[28] Similarly, in 1598, Gabriel de Castro, owner of an obraje in Puebla, yelled at his slave: "Dog! Do you think you can escape punishment in this way? I'll kill you for this!"[29] In the eyes of the inquisitors, a slave's "conditional" utterance involved premeditation and was thus considered especially reprehensible as a sign of *malicia y afectación* (trickery and deceit) on the part of the slave.[30]

In their attempt to thwart the use of this strategy by their slaves, masters often used a wide array of instruments to impose silence on them, including gags, candles, firebrands, sticks, cords, hot oil, and the master's own feet, fists, and fingers. The incredible brutality displayed against the slave's mouth seems to suggest, as Ranajit Guha has argued in a different context, that masters attempted to control the spoken word and to produce "a significant absence" of speech. In other words, masters forced a prescriptive silence on the slave by brutally marking his body as an example and warning to other bondsmen.[31] Exhibiting the cruel traces of their masters' fury, Afro-Mexicans appeared at their hearings with swollen cheeks, broken or missing teeth, black eyes, burned skin, and bleeding wounds. Sometimes, slaves were in such bad physical condition that the Holy Tribunal ordered a *cirujano* (surgeon) to examine them.[32] In such cases, it was not unusual that the inquisitors spared a slave physical punishment because the accused had already been beaten to the extreme.[33]

The slaveholders frequently crowned their extreme physical chastisement with verbal abuse. The term most commonly used was "dog," which masters often employed as a prelude to a severe beating. To use an animal rubric as an imprecation indicates, as Edmund Leach has argued, that the animal category itself is "credited with potency," that it is, in some way, taboo and sacred. Dogs were "potent," because as pets and domesticated animals, they occupied an intermediate category between "human" and "not human."[34] This social limbo inhabited by dogs was similar to the status of social excommunication, or "social death," which according to Orlando Patterson slaves experienced as nonpersons in the master's world. Indeed, incorporated at the margins of society, slaves were "neither human nor inhuman, neither man nor beast, neither dead nor alive, the enemy within who was neither a member nor true alien."[35] Francisco del Rosal, a sixteenth-century Spanish scholar, clearly saw the similarity between these two states. He explained that slaves were called dogs because, like domesticated canids, they were part of the family, though they constituted the vilest members of it.[36]

Yet, however marginalized slaves were in their master's society, they were expected to honor the Christian god as any other "member" of the slaveholder's family. This explains why slaveholders expressed strong feelings of betrayal and outrage when the slave renounced God, leading them to characterize the blasphemer as being not only a "dog" but also a "heretical Other": "Dog, you're a Christian! Do you know what you just said?" "What did you just say, dog, enemy of God?" "Dog of the devil!" "Lutheran dog!" "Rabbi dog!" The use of the rubric "dog," the most faithful of animals, to insult and debase slaves implies that slaves were perceived to have symbolically "changed loyalties," hence, the resulting indignation. Tellingly, slaves were often obliged to confirm their membership in the Christian community by renouncing the anti-God par excellence, the devil: "Dog! It is the devil you should renounce!"[37]

Although fewer slave women than men faced the Inquisition on blasphemy charges, being a woman did not seem to alter the circumstances surrounding the crime committed or how female transgressors were punished. Indeed, in contrast to free women, blaspheming women slaves were less likely to be perceived as having breached the gender conventions of submission and honor. However, they were viewed as having potentially disrupted the balance of power in the master-slave relationship. Notably, most cases involving slave women took place in an urban domestic environment. Scholars of slavery have noted the milder character of urban slavery when compared to the exacting, dangerous living and working conditions prevailing in sugar mills, textile workshops, and mines. Urban slaveholders were likely to view their maids, valets, coachmen, and cooks "as status symbols rather than an economic necessity."[38] Many urban slaves were undoubtedly treated better because of the closer proximity to and familiarity with their owners, but some were exposed to the erratic behavior of masters. This was particularly true for domestic slave women, whose emotional and physical intimacy with their mistresses transformed them into a source of ambivalent emotions: affection and suspicion, compassion and jealousy. In the patriarchal colonial society, women slaveholders were rarely the ultimate authority in the home, but they were directly responsible for running the household, and it is likely that even the most lenient of mistresses would resort to the whip to maintain order among her female servants. Both mistresses and bondswomen were socialized to consider themselves inferior to men, but women slaveholders enjoyed unusual power over their slaves, and many indulged in excessive and unwarranted acts of violence. Female slaves frequently complained of being beaten for *cosas que no importaban nada* (trivial reasons) and subjected to the mala vida at the hands of their mistresses.[39]

Cruelty could indeed reach hideous proportions. In about 1625, Damiana Osorio decided to brand the seven-month-old child of her unruly slave, Isabel de la Cruz, to humiliate the powerless mother.[40] As expected, many female domestic slaves fled, but they were frequently recaptured and even more harshly punished.[41] Slaves and slaveholding women might share the experience of being dominated by master and husband, but because domestic servants relieved female slaveholders of domestic chores, it is unlikely that bonds of solidarity grew between them. As Elizabeth Fox-Genovese put it succinctly, "the privileged roles and identities of slaveholding women depended upon the oppression of slave women, and the slave women knew it."[42]

Despite the Inquisition's condemnation of blasphemy, Afro-Mexican slaves seem to have transmitted it as a strategy to prevent being physically harmed by their owners. For instance, in Jalapa in 1599, Joaquín de Santa Ana told his master, Don Carlos de Sámano, that he blasphemed because a fellow slave, whom he had met in a prison in Tlaxcala, told Joaquín that he could stop punishment by renouncing God. Doña Luisa de Valdés, the wife of Don Carlos, testified to the comisario of the Holy Office that until her slave was taught to blaspheme, he did not do it. Indeed, in the nearly fourteen years she had owned Joaquín, he had run away and committed robbery several times, but she had never heard him "go against the [Catholic] religion."[43]

In a 1658 case, a mulatta, Gertrudis de Escobar, allegedly assured the sadistic nun for whom she was working—just before Gertrudis's own relatives sold her into slavery—that she had learned to renounce from a slave called "Scorpion," who was whipped on the streets of Mexico City for having renounced God. As might be expected, prosecutor Andrés de Zabalza was livid at hearing that a rite of public punishment designed to squelch blasphemy would produce its repetition.[44] Public retribution for blasphemy was supposed to demonstrate the outrageousness of the crime as well as the fearful power of the justice that punished the blasphemers. Nevertheless, however spectacular the public punishment might have been, the possibility always existed that the audience could subvert the original message, transforming the intended pedagogy of repression into one of resistance. Yet, slaves did not need to attend these events "to learn to curse." Renouncing God, as an utterance often stemming from the experience of unbearable agony, must have been a routine aspect of life in slavery. In this sense, renouncing God bore a "legacy of voices," a polyphony in each utterance. By repeating this kind of speech, black slaves transmitted and reenacted a specific practice of resistance.[45] Contrary to what inquisitors wanted to believe, it was not the particular blasphemer on trial who was "the origin" of the condemned expletives. Rather, they arose from a shared and long history of mistreatment and exploitation.

Denunciation

Renouncing God did not immediately provide Afro-Mexican bondsmen respite from the master's cruel hand. Like any other crime, blasphemy had first to be reported in order to be prosecuted. In this sense, the social alchemy that allowed slave blasphemers "to do things with words," as philosopher John L. Austin famously put it, rested not on the slaves but on their audience, who in denouncing the blasphemers endowed the forbidden expletives with the necessary social force to warrant the Holy Office's intervention.[46] The chance of being brought before the Inquisition improved, of course, if, beyond appealing to the master's Christian conscience, the slave drew the attention of a wider audience. This strategy represented a double-edged sword, however, because by renouncing God publicly, slaves committed the ancillary sin of "scandal."[47] What censors most feared was the negative pedagogy that renouncing could have on the "faithful ears" of the audience. In 1660, for instance, Nicolás Ramos, slave of Francisco López in Mexico City, was given a severe sentence because, by renouncing publicly, he had not only sinned as a Catholic but had also committed a scandalous act.[48] Despite harsh punishments, many slaves found it necessary to renounce God publicly in order to increase the likelihood of securing a denunciation to the Holy Office.

Surprisingly, the masters themselves, or their relatives, friends, or employees, made the report in thirty-seven of the cases involving slaves who expressed reniegos. This is striking because it was the slaveholder's responsibility to take the offender to the Holy Office and to pay all costs for transportation and incarceration. A trial could result in the owner having to sell the slave, and because potential buyers had to be notified of the offensive conduct—whether drunkenness, thievery, a tendency to run away or blaspheme, or judgments brought by the Audiencia or Inquisition—the price the bondman would bring could depreciate dramatically.[49] For example, in 1658, when young male slaves cost between three hundred and five hundred pesos, Mexico City silversmith Juan de Padilla paid 158 pesos to cover the year his slave, Juan de la Cruz, spent in prison.[50] Similarly, in 1656, Juan de Campos, owner of a Coyoacán textile mill, paid seventy-three pesos to cover the eleven-month imprisonment of his slave, Marcos Bautista.[51] Nicolás de la Cruz's imprisonment for five months cost forty-six pesos in 1658, and Gerónimo Morón had to pay forty-eight pesos in 1662 for the 166 days his slave, Antonio, spent in prison.[52] These amounts covered food and clothing, occasional medical attention, cutting hair and beards, and the procurement of some tobacco. Since most of the denunciations came from the masters themselves, even though they stood to lose the most by bringing their slaves before the Holy Office, there had to be tremendous pressure on the slaveholder to denounce the blasphemer.

Neighbors and other witnesses undoubtedly exerted substantial influence over a master's decision, since these bystanders would be greatly concerned that if the blasphemer were not punished, it would endanger the entire Christian community. Sometimes the reactions of the witnessing bystanders themselves were reported to the Holy Office, which was particularly interested in the effects of blasphemous speech on those who had heard it. In 1602 in Puebla, for example, Francisca de Vargas stated that she cried and le temblaron las carnes (her innards trembled) when she overheard Pedro Juárez, her neighbor's slave, renouncing God.[53] And in 1609, workers in a Mexico City obraje crossed themselves out of fear when a slave, Diego, blasphemed.[54] In contrast to these rather passive reactions, in Mexico City in 1571, outraged neighbors of Pedro de Munguía repeatedly struck his slave, Tomás de Contreras, across his mouth and cheeks to silence him.[55]

From the Inquisition's records, it is also apparent that some bystanders were horrified and indignant at the sound of a cracking whip and
a slave's cries of pain, and those people blamed the masters themselves
for slaves' sinful utterances. On August 22, 1669, drawn by the screams
of a slave belonging to Francisco de Urriola, owner of a warehouse on El
Relox street in Mexico City, a group of women complained that the wretched bondsman had been *forced to blaspheme* by his torturers when they
poured hot sugar on his skin.[56] Almost seventy years earlier, on May 16,
1598, Comisario Melchor Márquez de Amarilla had reported to the Inquisition that the continuous mistreatment inflicted by Gabriel de Castro on the
slaves in his Puebla obraje scandalized the neighborhood, "for God was daily
blasphemed."[57] Reporting on a black slave who renounced in an obraje in
Puebla, in 1632, Comisario Antonio Cervantes expressed a similar opinion.
He stated that although slaves frequently blasphemed to escape punishment
in that mill, this was often caused by the masters' cruel treatment of them.[58]
Given the great anxiety and distress caused by sinful outcries of Afro-Mexicans, it is understandable that masters would feel strongly obliged to denounce their slaves: Failure to do so meant risking a reprimand from the
inquisitors themselves.

In some instances, slaveholders took steps to keep a slave from going to
trial. Masters prevented their slaves from denouncing themselves—probably by means of threats and close surveillance. Undoubtedly, urban slaves,
particularly domestic servants who enjoyed relatively greater physical mobility, were more likely to circumvent the vigilance of their masters in order to denounce themselves to a comisario in their hometowns or at the
Inquisition's headquarters in Mexico City. This was, however, not always
the case.[59] For instance, Pascual Francisco, a black slave in the Hospital del
Amor de Dios in Mexico City, euphemistically stated to the Inquisition in
July 1606, one month after he had blasphemed, that he had not denounced
himself earlier because his master had been keeping him "very busy."[60]

For those living in the countryside, reaching the Holy Office could pose a
challenge. Antón de Cartagena from Tlalnepantla could not denounce himself until 1598, two years after blaspheming. Even then, his self-denunciation occurred only because as he was on his way to Mass, escorted by the
overseers of the textile mill where he worked, he had shouted to Alguacil
Ochoa to take him to the Inquisition.[61] A more dramatic example occurred
in Puebla in 1603, when a black ladino slave, Baltazar, denounced himself
before Comisario Alonso Hernández de Santiago. On April 22, at about
three in the afternoon, Regidor Alonso Gómez, an officer of Puebla's town

council, had tied Baltazar, his slave, to a ladder in the mill and was beating him. Knowing that a black woman had recently been whipped to death in the same place, and as the overseer was about to pour hot pork fat on his skin, Baltazar renounced God and all his saints. Several slaves heard him blaspheme, but the overseer ordered them not to denounce Baltazar, and he told them that if they were later summoned by the Holy Office, they should declare that Baltazar had been drunk.

Seven days later, Baltazar managed to denounce himself to the comisario, but Gómez, refusing to take his slave to the Holy Office, asserted that he himself would mete out punishment "according to the law." Irritated, the inquisitors told the regidor to "stay out of this business and do not meddle with the jurisdiction of the Inquisition," and they threatened to try him for conspiracy against the Holy Tribunal. Baltazar was brought to Puebla's public jail, but later, he was returned to his master. The Holy Office banned Alonso Gómez from selling the slave and ordered him to imprison Baltazar in the workshop until the matter was settled—something, the slaveholder knew, could take a very long time.[62]

Afro-Mexicans on Trial

Blasphemy trials could be lengthy. After receiving the denunciation of the slave's crime, the Inquisition investigated the charges in detail, by summoning witnesses from all social classes to give an account of the exact words used and the circumstances under which the slave blasphemed, as well as to offer opinions about the transgressor as a Christian. Witnesses were also asked if the accused had been sober and *en su juicio* (of sound mind) when he renounced God, and if the slave was in the *costumbre de renegar* (habit of blaspheming). Before an arrest took place, the calificadores were called in to determine whether the case warranted prosecution. If sufficient evidence was gathered, an arrest order was issued at the request of the fiscal. Brought to jail in Mexico City by the alguacil mayor or the master himself, the slave would then spend months (sometimes more than a year) in prison before a verdict was announced. In seven of the cases, the slaveholder was allowed to keep the slave at his service pending the trial, but that practice may have been more common than that number would indicate.[63]

During the first meeting with the prisoner, the inquisitors elicited information concerning age, marital status, genealogy, and *discurso de la vida* (personal history). Often a slave was ignorant of those details. Some defendants tried to summarize their genealogy, as Marcos Bautista did in

1656, when he explained that he was descended "from good, not from bad, people."[64] The inquisitors would also ask if a defendant had been tried previously by the Holy Office and was a baptized and confirmed Christian who received Holy Communion on the days designated by the Church. Then, to test the defendant's basic knowledge of Christian doctrine and rituals, he or she would be asked to make the sign of the cross and repeat the "four prayers" (Pater Noster, Ave Maria, Salve Regina, and the Credo) and the Ten Commandments.

Customary procedure dictated that neither the names of the denouncer nor the charges be disclosed to the defendant. When the defendant was asked if he or she knew the reason for the trial, the slave sometimes confessed to crimes of which the inquisitors were unaware. Aside from those who had denounced themselves, most slaves claimed to know the charges and promptly offered their own version of the events. Relating as many lurid details as possible, the defendants would depict the horrific conditions under which they had blasphemed. Given that intent was the most important aspect in assigning responsibility for this crime, slaves had to prove beyond doubt that they had not truly intended to renounce God. In order to present their blasphemies as a product of their master's brutality, they attempted to convince the Holy Tribunal that they had been victims of unjustifiable cruelties practiced on their bodies.

In an effort to limit their responsibility and present themselves as pious Christians before the tribunal, slaves resorted to several different strategies of self-presentation. First, they would stress that they have asked their masters, as fellow Christians, to stop the punishment either for the sake of Christ, the Holy Sacrament, or the Holy Virgin. Then, the slaves would explain that *faltándole el vigor* (lacking the strength) to withstand the beating, "forced by the unbearable pain" or *oprimido* (overwhelmed) by the severe punishment, they were compelled to renounce God in order to end their suffering.

Like Spanish men (see chapter 2), slaves often used the passive voice to disclaim responsibility for the sinful utterances. Couching their confessions in a variety of exculpatory expressions, slaves attempted to establish before the Holy Tribunal that being under great duress, they had not been in control of their faculties by using such phrases as *no supe lo que se dijo* (I didn't know what was said), *estaba fuera de mí* (I was out of control), or *estaba fuera de mi juicio natural* (I was out of my mind). Having lost command over themselves, they had learned what they had said only from witnesses to the brutal event. The slaves would claim that when they came back to their senses, they had shown remorse and regret.[65] In addition, Afro-Mexicans drew a distinction between renouncing from the *mouth*—a sort of automatic reaction to intolerable pain—and renouncing from the *heart*, where true intention apparently resided. In 1621, Diego, the young slave of the barber Manuel Roberto, declared that because he was a baptized Christian, he had renounced from his mouth not from his heart.[66] Slaves often claimed that they had renounced *only once*, having repented immediately by uttering a particular formula, "May Jesus be with me!" or asking forgiveness in front of an altar or recanting the sinful utterance. The number of renouncements was important, for the Inquisition held that repetition was a sign of contumacy and thus warranted a harsher punishment.[67] In a final statement, some defendants kneeled and begged for mercy and promised not to blaspheme again *aunque le quiten la vida* (even if it meant death) or if they were *hagan pedazos* (shred to pieces). Slaves often requested that they be sold to another master in order to avoid blaspheming in the future. The tribunal usually admonished slaves to offer a full confession, but since they had nothing more to say, the first hearing would end, and the accused would be returned to prison.

During the second hearing, the defendant was admonished once again to confess fully. Since slaves rarely added anything to their previous statements, the inquisitors would immediately ask the fiscal to proceed with a formal accusation. In turn, he would stress that when the defendant claimed a Christian identity, it only aggravated things, because it was unacceptable for a Christian to blaspheme his own God. Using the testimony of the witnesses, the fiscal summarized the events and almost invariably emphasized that the beating during which the blasphemy had occurred was moderate, well deserved, and *sin género de crueldad* (not cruel in nature). The fiscal's position mirrored that of the slaveholders, who often declared that they had punished their slaves mercifully and "in the name of God."[68] If slaves blasphemed God under these circumstances, the prosecutor would argue, it was only because of their bad disposition.

In 1659, in the case against Gertrudis de Escobar, the prosecutor Andrés de Zabalza stated that "neither instrument, oppression, nor rigors of punishment could inspire such a terrible and audacious vomiting, but only her evil and perverse nature and her crude and corrupt inclinations."[69] To regard blasphemy as a consequence of the "bad nature" of the slave transgressors implicitly required a complete disavowal of the violent history of slavery in the colonial New World.[70] In conclusion, the fiscal would assert that the defendant had committed other offenses, and he would then charge the slave with perjury, alleging that the prisoner had falsely stated that she or he had no further crimes to declare. In replying to the charges, the slave generally adhered to previous statements and denied having committed other crimes. The tribunal would then appoint an abogado for the slave and terminate the hearing.

In the third session, the inquisitors again demanded that the defendant fully declare all crimes. As they prepared to appear before the Holy Tribunal, the abogado often advised the defendant to make a final attempt to establish innocence by appealing to and even manipulating Spanish prejudices against people of African blood: Afro-Mexicans often begged for the Inquisition's "accustomed mercy," claiming to be "wretched" and "ignorant" blacks, with "little judgment" and understanding.[71] Although uncommon, some bonds-women also claimed to have spoken "as a woman without judgment," a simultaneous appeal to both gender and racial prejudices.[72]

At some point after the final hearing, the inquisitors voted and pronounced the sentence in the slave's presence, usually at the Holy Office or in an auto-da-fé, a theater of punishment in which Afro-Mexicans were routinely included as penitents.[73] Penance varied from case to case, but the tribunal generally condemned the offenders to public abjuration de levi, whipping (usually between one hundred and two hundred lashes), public disgrace (being paraded on the streets), and spiritual penance (attending Mass and undergoing a course of religious instruction). Temporary incarceration or working for one or two years in obrajes, which often functioned as labor prisons, were also possible penalties, though less common.[74]

Although it is difficult to establish a clear correspondence between crimes and punishments, it seems that inquisitors reserved lighter penances for slaves who promptly confessed, immediately repented, showed signs of submission, and promised not to blaspheme again. Apparently, a particularly effective way for a slave to avoid punishment was to express profound contrition and vow not to renounce God anew, even if the master were beating him to death. Inquisitors found this act of repentance especially satisfactory because it was an expression of both the defendant's acceptance of the slaveholder's right to torment and discipline the slave's body and a self-depiction of the slave as a law-abiding, obedient, and faithful Christian. This would have been a dramatic statement for the defendant to make because both inquisitors and slaves knew that the possibility of dying at the master's hands was, indeed, very real.[75] In general, the slaves who resorted to this strategy at the Holy Office received only a severe reprimand.[76]

It seems that the Consejo de la Suprema y General Inquisición (Council of the Inquisition, known as the Suprema), frequently considered the sentences meted out by the inquisitors in Mexico City to be overly harsh. Due to the institutional subordination of colonial tribunals to the Suprema, the Mexican Inquisition regularly sent all *relaciones de causas* (summaries of cases) to Madrid. This practice allowed the Suprema to supervise the trials and consider the fairness of the sentences imposed. A letter from the Suprema to the Mexican inquisitors in 1610 shows that Madrid frequently found the decisions against Afro-Mexicans to be excessive: "Generally, these sentences seem too rigorous considering that [the slaves] blasphemed on account of the rigor of the punishment." Showing greater tolerance than its counterpart in New Spain, the Suprema instructed the Mexican inquisitors to warn masters who treated their slaves cruelly "to not give [the slaves] occasion to blaspheme against God, Our Lord, but to treat them well."[77] As a result of this injunction, between 1611 and 1640, the Holy Office seems to have been less severe, with its sentences being limited to a strong admonition and twelve to fifty lashes. In the 1650s, however, punishments returned the previous harsh levels.[78]

The Suprema's greater leniency, especially in slave cases originally adjudicated by the Mexican Inquisition, may be rooted in the distinct social environments faced by each tribunal. As Colin Palmer and Solange Alberro have emphasized, tensions deriving from the pre-1650 numerical inferiority of Spaniards to blacks,[79] the constant fear of rebellion, and the Spaniards' need for self-preservation worked powerfully against any kind of liberalism in the slave system in New Spain.[80]

Decline

The Holy Office clearly enjoyed a reputation among slaves as a possible way out of the severe conditions in which they lived. In the absence of effective civil courts where a slave might lodge a complaint for mistreatment, Afro-Mexicans saw the Inquisition as an avenue to alleviate their miserable condition.[81] Most slaves who came before the tribunal obtained only momentary respite. What abused slaves may have truly longed for was the possibility of changing masters. Spanish law and its colonial variants required brutally treated slaves to be sold, but that provision was rarely respected. Even when the Inquisition ordered a change of masters, which it did in several cases of extreme cruelty, the action was clearly "more a mild punishment of the master than a 'right' of the slave."[82] Still, this alternative gave slaves some chance of gaining a better life through the intervention of the Holy Office.

By the mid-seventeenth century, the tribunal's reputation as a possible way of changing masters was so clearly established among slaves that inquisitors felt it necessary to admonish the slave Juan de Morga in 1650 that "the Holy Office never takes away the slaves from their masters, nor forces [the owners] to sell them, because its only business is to deal with cases related to the Catholic faith."[83] Nevertheless, the court did not always adhere to that rhetoric. Juan de Morga's fate was a case in point. The inquisitors ordered a thorough investigation of Morga's allegations that his master, Diego de Arratia, was inflicting cruelties on the slaves in his Zacatecas mines, and if it were found to be true, they would order Morga to be sold "since the salvation of this mulatto [was] in danger."[84]

However, as the seventeenth century neared its end, slaves found it ever more difficult to draw the attention of the Holy Office, for the tribunal increasingly refused to work as an institutional avenue to free slaves from their master's authority or to spend its time and resources in these often burdensome trials. The weary prosecutor Andrés de Zabalza, in a letter written to the Holy Office in 1663, offered a good example of this change of attitude. Complaining about the way Mexican bondsmen precipitated the intervention of the Inquisition by renouncing God, he stated that slaves simply "intend to evade their master's service and escape his dominion . . . [and as a result,] they have represented a lot of work for this Holy Office, which is continually overburdened with these kinds of cases."[85]

Moreover, some late seventeenth-century cases indicate that the Inquisition was increasingly willing to castigate slaves at the place of their supposed infraction, instead of transferring the defendants to Mexico City. This trend can be seen in the increasing number of petitions to reduce time and distance between crime and punishment. On September 3, 1631, the Inquisition comisario in Puebla, Don Antonio de Cervantes Carvajal, denounced Francisco Sánchez, a mulatto awaiting punishment in the public jail for several crimes. In an attempt to escape punishment by the secular authorities, Sánchez had renounced God and his saints several times, in the hope that he would be removed from prison and taken before the Holy Office. Cervantes asked for permission to proceed against Sánchez, but he also reminded Inquisitor Francisco Bazán de Albornoz that in a recent similar case, he had ordered the culprit "to be given forty lashes in front of those who heard him, and it caused such a good effect that his master will not sell him for any money, because he made such an immense change from bad to good."[86] In the same way, Joseph Ramírez de Arellano, writing from a sugar mill near Pantitlán, requested in 1663 that slaves be punished at the place of the infraction so that the punishment might serve as a lesson to others: "Punishment is better imprinted for the purposes of amendment when they see it in front of their eyes than when they hear about it."[87] Although this request made economic sense, the Inquisition insisted on maintaining its expensive centralist tradition and ordered the accused to be transferred to Mexico City.[88] It seems, however, that the Holy Office gradually honored this type of petition. In 1670, for example, inquisitors condemned the mulatto Miguel de la Cruz to be whipped in the same Puebla obraje where he had renounced God.[89] If this new tendency in punishment affected those slaves who lived in the urban obrajes, it probably had devastating effects for slaves working in sugar mills and mines in rural areas where conditions were even harsher. The distant voices of these unfortunates were rarely heard at the Holy Office, for they were beyond the Inquisition's range.[90] The increasing indifference of the Holy Office to the slaves' blasphemy made it only more difficult for bondsmen to use their time-tested strategy to escape, even temporarily, the living hell to which they were consigned by their often sadistic masters.

Conclusions

Blasphemy among black slaves brought into sharp relief the contradictions Afro-Mexicans experienced living "under the yoke of the Christian faith." Redeemed like their masters through bondage to God, slaves were also enmeshed in a social order in which they had a place only in a state of physical bondage. Equality was a spiritual matter, and no master ever thought of abdicating his authority because the slave was a fellow Christian. And yet, it was no small matter to have recognized that the *instrumentum vocale* (tool with a voice), as Romans called the slave, was also a Christian.[91] Endowed with a soul to be saved, bondsmen were often able to draw the attention of the Holy Office in order to obtain the protection that judicial courts rarely conceded them. Such relief occurred, however, only to the extent that slaves could place the responsibility for the crime on their masters and establish their own strong Christian faith. Claiming to possess a Christian soul, black slaves engaged in a careful exercise of impression management to put on a successful performance in the recurring drama at the Holy Office. In a way, they used Christian religion as a "language of contention," with Christianity being "common ground" shared with the inquisitors, on which slaves could establish their innocence and hold their masters—the true "bad" Christians and God's enemies—responsible for provoking their blasphemies and endangering the salvation of the slaves' souls.[92]

The "common ground" shared by slaves and inquisitors was, of course, only metaphorical. While the Holy Office, as all colonial authorities did, utilized Christianity as a means to exact conformity and submission from bondsmen based on the promise of future redemption, Afro-Mexicans sought leverage against their masters by sharing their masters' faith. As Herman L. Bennett has pointed out, this was possible because "in constituting Africans . . . as subjects with defined Christian obligations, the tribunal bestowed rights that individuals manifested in the narratives that they created for the inquisitors."[93] In this sense, slaves used their "integration" into the Christian community to fight the abuses deriving from their marginality in a slaveholder society. It is true, however, that the slaves who faced the Inquisition on charges of blasphemy struggled to influence the Holy Office in their favor but never challenged slavery per se. As the historian of slavery Eugene D. Genovese has asserted in a different context, for the great majority of Afro-Mexican blasphemers "the practical question . . . was not whether slavery itself was a proper relation but how to survive it with the greatest degree of self-determination."[94]

As an act of defiance, renouncing God resembled those acts of "blind fury," which James Scott associates with individuals who are not only subjected to indignities to which they cannot respond but also atomized by the process of domination. Since in these conditions there is not a rich "hidden transcript"—"a critique of power spoken behind the back of the dominant"—we might expect that defiance would assume an improvised or unstructured form.[95] I have argued, however, that far from being an improvised utterance, renouncing God and the Catholic pantheon was a socially patterned verbal act of resistance that carried within itself a legacy of usage, and in this sense, it constituted a form of oral tradition among Afro-Mexican slaves. In the end, by using and appropriating the Christian moral standards and injunctions of their oppressors to further their own interests, slaves also evidenced and often subverted the painful politics of inclusion and exclusion that permeated their daily lives.

6

Conclusion

In 1569, Dominican Domingo de Soto posed this rhetorical question to the pious readers of his influential treatise on blasphemy: "If you
reprimand a man for blaspheming the name of God, what do you think will
be his response?" The Dominican answered his own question by quoting
from a popular proverb: That man will tell you that *quien bien jura, bien
cree* (a good blasphemer is a strong believer).[1] As expected, Fray Domingo
decried the adage as blasphemous, but the proverb's popularity simply confirmed what both ecclesiastical authorities and transgressors knew all too
well: The world of blasphemy is not too far from that of belief. How could it
be otherwise at a time in which religion dominated every single aspect of
life, from birth to grave; in which work, time, and leisure were regulated
by a Christian calendar; and in which plagues, earthquakes, and riots were
seen as punishments of God for past offenses? Even the encounter with
new peoples across the Atlantic, who had been "mysteriously" kept from
eternal salvation, failed to shake the widespread conviction that Christianity applied to all humankind. Rather, the "discovery" of the New World
triggered a messianic missionary zeal among the well educated, and even
the greediest of soldiers saw themselves as divine instruments for the
expansion of the Christian faith. Clearly, as Lucien Febvre demonstrated,
a religious skeptic would have no ground to stand on in a world entirely dominated by religion and ruled by an omnipotent and omniscient
God.[2]

Although blasphemy hardly evinced a genuine religious skepticism in
the inhabitants of colonial Mexico, it clearly constituted both a dangerous
subversion of the colonial discourse used to justify the Spanish presence
in Mexico and a revelation of the social tensions in the colony. As on the
European continent during the wars of religion, in New Spain, blasphe-

my was conceived as being a crime committed by the "Other," in this case the indigenous peoples.[3] As we have seen, however, the image of Indians as blasphemers did not survive for long after the initial conquest, and Franciscan and Dominican friars were soon leveling the charge against the colonizers, who not only blasphemed the God they were supposed to honor but also forced the Indians to reject the Supreme Divinity by dint of their excesses and brutality.

This early association of blasphemy with violence was later to re-emerge in racial and gender conflicts articulated by defendants before the Holy Office. Afro-Mexican slaves blamed their blaspheming on their masters' cruelty, and Spanish men blamed it on their "intractable" wives. In turn, some "intractable" women blasphemed to resist the violence of compulsory confinement. And yet, blasphemy was itself a language of violence because it both constituted a dangerous assault against God and was speech endowed with social force performed before an audience, in compliance with or defiance of social scripts of domination articulated in terms of class, race, and gender.

Despite the inquisitorial and moral treatises that attempted to establish the boundaries of blasphemous speech and to describe its attenuating or aggravating contexts and circumstances, blasphemy proved to be a mutable concept in colonial Mexico. This was because the distinction between blasphemy and other crimes, such as sacrilege and heresy, was not always clear, and those who claimed to be the sole agents authorized to punish blasphemy typically depended on the competence of common citizens to interpret and report this verbal crime. However, at what point did a reported disparate or disonancia become a blasphemy? Was there a verbal repertoire that could be marked as blasphemous regardless of the context and intentions of the speaker? Or was blasphemous speech an issue of constant negotiation between utterers, denouncers, and repressors? As we have seen, colonial authorities understood blasphemy to be both unrelated to the context of utterance (as was the case with the "five heinous utterances"), and yet it was fully contextual when it came to judging a speaker's intentions and the status of ambiguous expressions (as with "may so-and-so regret it"). This ambivalence arose because blasphemy was always produced in particular circumstances and specific social contexts, but it also broke out of those contexts when the blasphemy was repeated before, and reported to, other audiences.[4]

Indeed, denouncers often expressed their fear of reenacting blasphemous speech when reporting it. As Valentin Voloshinov pointed out in a different context, witnesses could report blasphemous speech in "thematic terms," that is, answering questions about the manner in which the transgressor spoke and the subject of his utterances. However, when it came to "what" the blasphemer had said, the exact words needed to be reported.[5] Understanding the anxieties surrounding blasphemy as a sin, confessors did not always require penitents to repeat the sinful words in the confessional.[6] However, before the Holy Office, denouncers and witnesses were expected to report on the exact words heard (in addition to giving information about the blasphemer's reputation as a Christian and about the circumstances in which the verbal exchange took place). The possibility of reenacting blasphemy, by recirculating the sinful words in their reports, also haunted the repressive authorities. Moralists and authors of inquisitorial manuals cited blasphemous speech at length in their treatises, and inquisitors often repeated the condemned speech in rites of punishment. With this, however, came anxiety over the possibility that the faithful, rather than being deterred, might be encouraged to sin by blaspheming.[7]

Insofar as every act of blasphemy entailed the possibility of its reproduction, colonial authorities associated blasphemous speech with a rhetoric of "sacred contagion." As Mary Douglas has pointed out, the notion of contagion is essentially a theory of transmission, and the fear of infection is predicated upon the conviction that the transgressor has, in Freud's words, "the dangerous property of tempting others to follow his example."[8] In colonial Mexico, the authorities' anxieties over the possibility of sinful mimicry were encapsulated in the notion of "scandal," which both moralists and inquisitors understood as a theory of moral pollution. Defined by Aquinas as "the cause for another's spiritual downfall," the theological notion of scandal was employed by inquisitors to extend the blasphemers' responsibility beyond the words they had uttered and thus hold them accountable for defiling the Christian social body.[9] As we have seen, from the early days of conquest, the idea of scandal was interwoven with the patriarchal ideals of Christian behavior. Indeed, in a society ruled by the Spanish king as a supreme patriarch and administered and policed by viceroys, archbishops, and priests as metaphorical fathers, Spanish men were supposed to follow the example that those dominant figures set by becoming, in turn, models of Christianity for their own subalterns. Since this chain of pious imitation was subverted when sinful mimicry endangered the salvation of others, men were expected to strive for moral excellence by controlling their own tongues and those of the individuals under their authority. In this sense, the rhetoric of contagion soon became connected to patriarchal discourses of domesticity that tended to equate virtuosity with silence and Christian servitude and obedience with verbal restraint.

Although moralists and inquisitors were very concerned about the "transmission" of blasphemous speech through imitation and reenactment, they tended to isolate the speaker as the originator of blasphemy. Like contemporary censors of hate speech, inquisitors charged the speaker with the crime in question without paying attention to the *"legacies of usage* that constrain and enable that speaker's speech," that is, to the ways in which a particular verbal repertoire had been used and put in circulation in the past (my italics).[10] Why did the transgressors' utterances tend to fall within a highly stereotypical catalog of words? What, for example, made slaves "renounce" the Christian god instead of attacking him in other ways? Why did women resort to "unholy comparisons" during arguments? As we have seen, the answer to all these questions cannot be found in the isolated speaker for, paraphrasing Judith Butler, "[blasphemous speech] . . . neither began nor ended with the speaking subject."[11] Like the speakers of hate speech analyzed by Butler, blasphemers rarely spoke in a voice that was entirely singular, for they tended to "cite" others. Indeed, as was particularly clear in the case of slaves, there was a "legacy of voices" in each blasphemous utterance. To be sure, there were cases in which blasphemers departed completely from stereotypical repertoires, but it is unlikely they were entirely original. The tendency to resort to a stereotypical repertoire indicates that blasphemy was not constrained by the utterer or by the specific circumstances surrounding it.

Clearly, the blasphemers' repertoire was socially patterned along the race, class, and gender divides existing in colonial Mexico, and so were defendants' discourses of exculpation and intentionality. Since engaging in blasphemy affected their reputation as pious Christians and endangered the society as a whole, defendants who faced the Inquisition needed to provide a convincing explanation for their transgressions, particularly in relation to their intentions and the specific circumstances in which they blasphemed. In theory, the accused were defended by appointed attorneys, the abogados, but these minor officials of the court could do no more than advise the defendants to confess and ask for mercy. As Stephen Haliczer has emphasized, abogados often found themselves in an ambiguous, even dangerous, position before the court. Wanting the approval and respect of the Holy Tribunal, these officials hesitated to offer a vigorous defense that would place their jobs at risk and possibly even raise the suspicion that they were protectors of heretics and blasphemers.[12] As the influential sixteenth-century canonist Francisco Peña emphasized, the main role of the abogado was "to press the defendant to confess and repent, and request penance for the crime committed."[13] Nevertheless, abogados offered the defendants coaching when it came to asking for forgiveness, according to what was deemed plausible in terms of the defendants' location within the social divisions.

Long before the invention of psychoanalysis, male blasphemers brought before the Mexican Inquisition talked about "slips of the tongue" (as when the accused would claim, "*se me fue la lengua*"). These defendants resorted to a variety of expressions to establish that they had not been in control of their speech because they had been drunk, enraged, in pain, or in distress: "I was *out* of myself," "I was *out* of my mind (*juicio natural*)," or "I didn't realize what was said" (*no supe lo que se dijo*). Anger, reprehensible in a man, was intolerable in a woman. Although women occasionally claimed to have blasphemed out of anger, to excuse it, they normally drew upon a richer vocabulary of emotions and a wider collection of accepted "female conditions," such as melancholy, sadness, and heartsickness. For their part, slaves claimed to have lost command over themselves under their masters' whip and to have renounced from the *mouth* not from the *heart*, where, in their opinion, true intention resided. In contrast to Spanish men who used social stereotypes of virility to assert themselves before an audience, both slaves and free women had to resort to social stereotypes to *exculpate* themselves. While women drew upon misogynist discourse that described them as incapable of controlling their own speech, slaves resorted to Spanish prejudices that depicted Afro-Mexicans as people with diminished mental capacity. Undoubtedly, by manipulating or relying on stereotypes, individuals obtained some degree of maneuver before the Inquisition, but this strategy of exculpation also confirmed the patriarchal conviction that women and servants were in need of constant surveillance and supervision.

In spite of all these claims of verbal automatism, it is clear that the accused consciously relied on specific repertoires to pitch their expletives to specific social audiences. As the work of ethnographers of language has shown, individuals always speak strategically. Even when insulting or blaspheming, one needs a specific linguistic competence that is finely tuned to affect one's audience.[14] In pursuing their specific goals, however, blasphemers hardly exhibited the blind confidence in the power of language so characteristic of the animistic worldview of early modern societies.[15] To be sure, it is highly possible that, like their contemporaries, they believed in the irresistible power of certain prayers, incantations, and magic formulas; but the available evidence does not suggest that they saw blasphemy as one more way of "word worshipping," or that they believed that verbal formulas could annihilate the distance between wishes and actions by virtue of the "omnipotence of thought," as Freud referred to this mechanism in compulsion neurotics.[16] In fact, paraphrasing Malinowski's comments on magic, one could even say that blasphemous speech hardly evinced a belief in the omnipotence of thought "but rather the clear recognition of the limitations of thought, nay, of its impotence."[17] Indeed, as conscious performers of a verbal art associated with discourses of danger, sin, and salvation, blasphemers understood that beyond their megalomaniac pretension of affecting the Christian divinity, an imprecation derived its social force, its capacity "to do things with words," from the audiences before whom it was performed and, paradoxically, from the very authorities and institutions that sought to repress it.

As the colony entered the eighteenth century, however, a combination of religious, social, and institutional factors increasingly undermined the social efficacy of blasphemous speech. Religiously, the gradual demise of the idea of collective salvation and the ensuing decline of the conviction that disasters were punishments by an angry God for human sins delegitimized the discourse of blasphemous speech as a source of sacred contagion. As recent scholarship on colonial Mexico has shown, this momentous change took place under the enlightened despotism of the Bourbons, when civil and religious authorities sought to promote among the faithful a radically spiritual conception of God who, in contrast to the all-intervening Divinity of the Baroque, rarely manifested himself in the material world. Rejecting collective devotion and corporate Catholicism, the reformers advocated an individual path to salvation through personal merit and responsibility that demanded the cultivation of virtues such as moderation, self-mastery, and decorum. In an effort to distinguish themselves from the poor, who were marred by "moral laxity," members of the elite tended to embrace these repressive ideals, controlled forms of piety, and Christian gravitas.[18] In this way, blasphemy gradually became one more example of verbal incivility "proper" to members of plebeian society, such as slaves, poor Spaniards, and "fallen" women.

The authorities accompanied the promotion of these ascetic ideals with a conscious effort to combat social disarray and the breakdown of morals by policing the population and instilling in the poor and the downtrodden notions of sobriety, civility, and hard work. The main concern of the elite was the maintenance of public propriety. "Scandalous" crimes, which in the past endangered the well-being of colonial society, were now mainly seen as a source of social disorder. Pamela Voekel, in her analysis of a 1784 report on tavern life in Mexico City, offers a good example of this change of attitude by a royal commission composed of the archbishop, a representative of the Inquisition, and an official of "a pulque tax organization." As expected, the report condemned the excessive gambling and drinking in the taverns. In contrast to their predecessors, however, the Bourbon officers decried the practice of "prohibited games," not because gambling could lead the participants to blaspheme the name of God, but because it constituted a source of vice, laziness, poverty, and an obstacle to the development of a productive working class.[19]

As blasphemy lost its capacity to "touch" the Divinity, the authorities' interest in repressing this sin and crime also started to dwindle. By the second half of the eighteenth century, the number of cases of blasphemy had declined sharply. With the exception of a brief campaign against a group of foreign soldiers tried for this crime between 1760 and 1770, the Inquisition seemed to have lost interest in prosecuting this transgression.[20] Researchers have noted a similar combination of negligence and leniency in the other two colonial tribunals of the Inquisition in the New World. In Lima, for example, René Millar Carvacho found only sixteen cases between 1697 and 1820. Most of the culprits were given light sentences, and in several instances, the sentences were never carried out. This was a dramatic change for a tribunal that had tried 126 individuals between 1570 and 1635.[21] Similarly, for the tribunal of Cartagena de Indias (present-day Colombia), Toribio Medina found fewer than ten blasphemy cases during the entire eighteenth century.[22] Across the Atlantic, the combined efforts of the tribunals of Granada, Murcia, Seville, Toledo, Córdoba, Valladolid, Santiago de Compostela, Llerena, Madrid, and Zaragoza yielded only forty-four cases between 1660 and 1737.[23] Clearly, the days in which the Spanish king deemed it crucial to punish this crime in order to secure his kingdom and protect his people were long gone.

Almost four hundred years after Domingo de Soto's remarks on the widespread use of blasphemous speech, T. S. Eliot wrote with nostalgia in 1933: "I am reproaching a world in which blasphemy is impossible." In the modern secular world, first-rate blasphemy had become a rarity, because "no one can possibly blaspheme in any sense except that in which a parrot may be said to curse, unless he profoundly believes in that which he profanes." In the past, blasphemy might have been "a sign of spiritual corruption," he contended, but "it might now be taken rather as a symptom that the soul is still alive."[24] As Gauri Viswanathan has recently argued, "Eliot's yearning for a pre-secular era in which blasphemy constituted a healthy sign of belief" was predicated upon the questionable conviction that belief should be reinscribed in civil society as a necessary component.[25] Indeed, few would now endorse unreservedly the idea that civic virtue can only be maintained through the fear of God. In New Spain, however, there was hardly any other way of imagining the well-being of the colony, and even the staunchest of defilers could barely conceive a world without belief.[26] As the image of an all-powerful, omniscient, and intervening God receded, however, blasphemers increasingly faced the possibility of challenging an empty sky. Perhaps blasphemers gradually became parrots; perhaps parroting others became the only way of blaspheming. After all, as Émile Benveniste incisively wrote about the angry outbursts of modern defilers, "one blasphemes the name of God because the only thing one has of him is his name."[27]

Notes

Abbreviations used in the notes: The Archivo General de la Nación in Mexico City is abbreviated as "A.G.N." The Archivo Histórico del Museo Nacional de Antropología e Historia is abbreviated as "A.H.M.N.A.H." The A.G.N. Ramo Inquisición (the archive's Inquisition Division) is abbreviated "Inq." A.G.N. cases contained in volumes and *expedientes* (case files) appear in this format: "10.9, fols. 1–2." Those contained in boxes and expedientes appear as "box 10.9, fols. 1–2." If no folio numbers are provided, the document is unfoliated.

Introduction

1. A.G.N. Inq. 16.9, fols. 332–372.

2. Following a tradition from Roman legislation under Justinian (483–565 CE), Christian writers and theologians frequently stated that blasphemy caused calamities to be visited upon the Christian community. Failure to prevent or punish this crime was often deemed disastrous. See, for instance, Albertino, *De Agnoscendis Assertionibus*, questio 27, no. 21, 146v: "propter has blasphemias fames, terremotus, et pestilentiae super loca blasphemantium veniant."

3. López de Gómara, *Hispania Victrix*, 156.

4. Reeves, *Influence of Prophecy*, 359–374. On Spanish providentialism, see Elliott, *Old World and the New*, 94; Elliott, *Spain and Its World*, 9.

5. Rodríguez de San Miguel, *Pandectas hispano-megicanas*, 527–532. This kind of punishment was applied only to men. Nobles and clerics were normally exempt because of their social rank and supremacy; slaves were exempt for economic reasons. In 1748, the Spanish Armada discontinued the galleons, and culprits were then sentenced to forced labor in mines or military forts. Charles III reinstated this form of punishment in 1784, when the old ships were put into service again before they were definitively withdrawn around 1808 (García-Molina Riquelme, *El régimen de penas*, 213–220).

6. Weckman, *Medieval Heritage*, 301.

7. Gonzalbo, "Tradición y ruptura," 51; Viqueira, *Propriety and Permissiveness*, 1–3; Borah, *New Spain's Century of Depression*; Boyer, *La gran inundación*.

8. See Greenleaf, *Zumárraga*, 7–14; Villa-Flores, "Inquisition, Spanish America."

9. Alberro, *La actividad del santo oficio*, 233–234.

10. O'Gorman, *La inquisición en México*; Medina, *Inquisición en México*; Lewin, *La inquisición en México*.

11. Alberro, "Negros y mulatos"; Greenleaf, *Mexican Inquisition*; McKnight, "Blasphemy as Resistance"; Palmer, "Religion and Magic"; Palmer, *Slaves of the White God*.

12. Huizinga, *Autumn of the Middle Ages*; Delumeau, *La Peur en Occident*.

13. On blasphemy as an expression of faith, see Sommerville, "Religious Faith," 152–155; Berti, "At the Roots of Unbelief," 555–575; for discussions of blasphemy as rebellion, see Dedieu, "Le modèle religieux"; Dedieu, "Inquisition and Popular Culture"; Belmas, "La montée des blasphèmes"; Flynn, "Betrayals of the Soul"; Flynn, "Blasphemy and the Play"; Cabantous, "Du blasphème au blasphémateur"; Cabantous, *Histoire du blasphème*; Edwards, "Religious Faith."

14. See, inter alia, Levy, *Blasphemy: Verbal Offense*; Levy, *Treason Against God*; and Lawton, *Blasphemy*.

15. The reference is of course to John L. Austin's famous pragmatic analysis of speech acts in *How to Do Things with Words*.

16. See, for instance, Cameron, *Verbal Hygiene*; and Briggs, introduction to *Disorderly Discourse*, 14. For discussions on the new social history of language, see inter alia, Burke, *Art of Conversation*, esp. chap. 1; Burke and Porter, *Social History of Language*, and Burke and Porter, *Language, Self, and Society*.

17. From a translation of Aquinas's *Contra mendacium* by the Rev. H. Browne. Available at http://www.greatestbooks.org/studentlibrary/churchfathers/Augustin/againstlying.htm.

18. Casagrande and Vecchio, *Les péchés de la langue*, 174–176.

19. Aquinas, *Summa*, 2–2, questio 13, articulus 1, 165.

20. Craun, "'Inordinata Locutio,'" 146.

21. Ibid., 152.

22. Later writers, such as Dominican Thomas de Vio Cajetan (1469–1534), even believed that blasphemy differed in magnitude according to the importance of the "object" slandered, that is, God, the Virgin, and finally, the saints. The moralist Nicolás de Avila followed this distinction in *Suma de los mandamientos*, 488: "Aunque la blasfemia se diga contra Dios, o contra los santos, todo pertenece a una especie de blasfemia: mas hase de advertir, que sera mas grave, o menos grave segun las cosas de que se blasfemare."

23. For one of the few attempts to consider idolatry as blasphemy, see Alberghini, *Manuale Qualificatorum*, chap. 16, no. 3, 44. Most Christian writers did not consider attacks on images to be blasphemous, see Machado de Cháves, *Perfecto confessor*, 198.

24. Avila, *Suma de los mandamientos*, 440: "Porque el hereje antes piensa que honra y sirve a Dios, que no que le afrenta." As Jesuit Juan de Alloza pointed out (*Flores summarum*, 40), blasphemy was committed by saying something against God (*in dicendo*), not by believing in something wrong in doctrinal terms (*in credendo*).

25. See, inter alia, Santo Tomas, *Excelencias del Nombre*, chap. 3, par. 1, 22; Castro, *De Iusta Hereticorum Punitione*, bk. 1, chap. 12, 63.

26. Carena, *Tractatus de Officio*, pt. 2, title 7, par. 4, no. 19, 130: "Si quis in ira blasphemet, si tamen id faciat ex habitu, et postquam saepe fuit correptus, tunc etiam de vehementi erit de haeresi suspectus"; Sousa, *Aphorismi Inquisitorum*, bk. 1, chap. 19, nos. 18 and 53.

27. This description of speech as the "sonorous double" of the soul is from James T. Brink's study of blasphemous speech among the Bamana of Mali ("Speech, Play, and Blasphemy," 425). However, for a recent analysis of the complex relationship between speech, self, and intentionality as conceived by inquisitors at the time, see Villa-Flores, "Talking through the Chest."

28. Dalcobia, *Primera parte del symbolo de la vida cristiana*, 42–44v. Establishing that some forms of anger were pious and necessary was also important to account for the presence of anger in the Bible, especially in the Old Testament (Barton, "Zealous Anger," 157).

29. Alberghini, *Manuale Qualificatorum*, chap. 16, no. 11, 46: "Blasphemia item haereticalis est: asserere ex fervore iracundiae, etiam absque errore intellectus: Non est Deus."

30. Carena, *Tractatus*, 127–140.

31. Covarrubias a Leyva, *De Pactis*, bk. 6, par. 7, 54.

32. Aquinas, *Summa*, 2–2, questio 13, articulus 1. See also Casagrande and Vecchio, *Les péchés de la langue*, 174–176; Craun, "'Inordinata Locutio,'" 158.

33. Parker, "On the Tongue," 445. Several biblical passages describe the tongue as one of "the things that defile a man" (Matthew 15:20; Mark 7:21–23).

34. See Erasmo, *La lengua*, 145: "Pues luego diga cada uno a su lengua cada vez que se suelta para hablar, para acusar, para murmurar, para dezir torpedades: '¿A dónde vas lengua? ¿Quieres dañar, o aprovechar?' On the extreme popularity of this little work by Erasmus and its multiple editions in Spain (1533, 1535, 1542, 1544, 1550, 1551), see Bataillon, *Erasmo y España*, 311–313.

35. Mazzio, "Sins of the Tongue," 54.

36. Quoting from the medieval code known as *Las Siete Partidas*, Saavedra Fajardo advised the king to avoid garrulity because "el príncipe es un reloj universal de sus estados, los cuales penden del movimiento de sus palabras; con ellos o gana o pierde el crédito, porque todos procuran conocer por lo que dice su ingenio, su condición e inclinaciones." See Saavedra Fajardo, *Idea de un príncipe político*, 446.

On God's *brevitas* as model of Christian behavior to follow, see Erasmo, *La lengua,* 41.

37. Helmholz, *Spirit,* 272.

38. In their *visitas* to the Audiencia, inspectors were required to ask witnesses if the Audiencia officers had zealously punished blasphemy in the colony (Aguirre Zamorano, *La Audiencia de México,* 57).

39. Helmholz, *Spirit,* 275.

40. Kamen, *Spanish Inquisition,* 261–262. For a detailed discussion of the jurisdictional disputes among the Spanish secular, ecclesiastical, and inquisitorial authorities over the right to try the blasphemers, see Lea, *History of the Inquisition,* 328–335.

41. Quotations from the Bible are taken from The New International Version, available at http://www.biblegateway.com.

42. See, for instance, Azpilcueta, *Manual de confesores,* 116–117; Machado de Cháves, *Perfecto Confessor,* 200; Señeri [Segneri], *El confesor instruido,* 186.

43. *Catholic Encyclopedia,* 595–596.

44. Cabantous, *Histoire du blasphème,* 57–59.

45. Burke, "Insult and Blasphemy," 101. See also Horodowich, "Civic Identity."

46. Rodríguez de San Miguel, *Pandectas hispano-megicanas,* 527–532; *Las Siete Partidas,* 7:28:4. See also García-Molina Riquelme, *El régimen de penas,* 243–257.

47. Comisarios were the Holy Office's representatives in major towns.

48. Machado de Cháves, *Perfecto confessor,* 198–200; Señeri, *El confesor instruido,* 179–195.

49. See the insightful article by Jeanne Favret-Saada, "Rushdie et compagnie."

50. On the use of euphemism as a strategy to mask and "disarm" blasphemous speech, see the remarks of Émile Benveniste, "Le blasphème et l'euphémie," 71–73.

51. For an excellent discussion of the "theory and practice" of denunciation and its crucial relevance for the development of the inquisitorial process, see Dedieu, *L'administration de la foi,* chaps. 6 and 7. In recent years, the study of practices of denunciation has drawn the attention of several scholars "as an important but unstudied point of contact between individual citizens and the state, on the one hand, and between family and fellow citizens, on the other" (Fitzpatrick and Gellately, "Introduction to the Practices of Denunciation," 748).

52. Flynn, "Mimesis of the Last Judgment."

53. Scott, *Domination and the Arts of Resistance,* 57. For a classic discussion of early modern society's rituals of punishment as political spectacles aimed at reactivating the power of authorities, see Foucault, *Discipline and Punish,* 58–60 *passim.*

54. Grosz, *Volatile Bodies,* 120.

55. Harris, "Mentioning the Unmentionable," 185. There is a vast literature that associates blasphemy with the purported magical power of "taboo words," see inter alia, Frazer, *Golden Bough,* 318, 418; Crawley, *Studies of Savages and Sex,* 219–282; Blank, "Curse, Blasphemy."

56. Bourdieu, *Language and Symbolic Power,* 107–108.

Chapter 1. From Defenders of God's Honor to Blasphemers

1. Cortés, *Letters from Mexico,* 85–86. The *Reconquista* refers to the warfare between Christians and Muslims in the Iberian Peninsula from the early eighth century onward. As a war to reconquer lands seized by the Muslims, the papacy transformed the armed conflict into a crusade during the twelfth and thirteenth centuries.

2. Cortés's scene of *translatio imperii* is implicitly drawn from Ecclesiasticus 10:8, which attributes the transfer of empires to sin and injustice, thus intimating that the transfer from Aztec to Spanish dominion was the consequence of the Indians' faults and vices: "Because of unrighteous dealings, injuries, and riches got by deceit, the kingdom is transferred from one people to another." On the medieval theory of *translatio imperii,* see Curtius, *European Literature,* 28–29. See also Góngora, *Studies in Colonial History,* 220–225. The idea of a voluntary transferal of the Aztec empire proved so popular that even Bartolomé de las Casas, a severe critic of Spanish colonialism, accepted Moctezuma's "donation" as "a legitimate political charter." Pagden, *Spanish Imperialism,* 32. The highly questionable scene with Moctezuma and Cortés has been rigorously analyzed by Gesa Mackenthum in her *Metaphors of Dispossession,* esp. 137–138.

3. Although Ferdinand of Aragón seemed to accept this assumption willingly, his successor, Charles V, understood that if the universal claims of those Bulls were seriously questioned, the Castilian Crown would be deprived of any rights and left only with the responsibility to evangelize newly conquered native peoples. During their first two decades in the New World, the Spaniards enjoyed an unchallenged possession of the territory based on the papal decrees. However, in 1511, Dominican Antonio de Montesinos provoked a critical reevaluation of the Spanish rights to lands in the New World by denouncing colonial abuses in Hispaniola. The Crown responded by merely issuing a "protocol of conquest"—the *Requerimiento* (1513)—that left intact the papal donation as the basis of the Spanish presence in America. For a recent critical study of the impact of Montesinos's criticism on Spanish colonialism, see Seed, "'Are These Not Also Men?'"

4. Pagden, *Spanish Imperialism,* 14–15; Seed, *Ceremonies of Possession,* 69–99; Mackenthun, *Metaphors of Dispossession,* 81.

5. Mackenthum, *Metaphors of Dispossession*, 81.

6. John H. Elliott, *Old World and the New*, 94; Elliott, *Spain and Its World*, 9.

7. Cortés, "Ordenanzas militares mandadas pregonar por Hernando Cortés en Tlaxcala, al tiempo de partirse para poner cerco a México," in *Documentos cortesianos*, 1:164–169; the ordinances are discussed in Gardiner, *Constant Captain*, 67–70.

8. Ricard, *Spiritual Conquest*, 16; for the full text of Velázquez's ordinances, see *Documentos cortesianos*, 1:45–57.

9. See, for example, Cortés's respective instructions to Francisco Cortés, Hernando de Saavedra, and Alvaro de Saavedra, in *Documentos cortesianos*, 1:311, 354, 440; *Las Siete Partidas*, 7:28:4:3, 689; on Cortés's familiarity with *Las Siete Partidas*, see Frankl, "Hernán Cortés," and Elliott, "Mental World of Hernán Cortés," 44.

10. López de Gómara, *La conquista de México*, 139.

11. Aquinas, *Summa*, 2–2, questio 13 and questio 94.

12. Díaz del Castillo, *Historia verdadera*, 1:198.

13. Andrés de Tapia reports a similar dialogue in Tenochtitlán, where Cortés told Moctezuma that he would gladly fight for his God against the Indians' idols. Apparently drawing on Tapia, Motolinía would later report this same scene to Charles V, with Cortés heroically exhorting his kinsmen: "Let us now die here for God's honor" (*muramos aquí por la honra de Dios*). Tapia, "Relación de algunas cosas," in *La conquista de Tenochtitlan*, 111; Benavente, "Carta al emperador Carlos V," 313.

14. On *la honra de Dios*, see Chauchadis, *Honneur, morale et société*, 53–54. See also Nirenberg, "Conversion, Sex, and Segregation," 1068–1070. There is a vast literature on the anthropology of honor. See the classic essay by Pitt-Rivers, "Honor," and the more recent contributions in Marie Gautheron, *L'honneur*.

15. Thus, Francisco de Aguilar wrote after describing the magnificence of the Indian temples, "no hubo reino en el mundo donde Dios nuestro Señor fuese tan deservido, y adonde más se ofendiese que en esta tierra, y adonde el demonio fuese más reverenciado y honrado." See his "Relación breve," 204. On the demonization of the Indian deities and the belief that idolatrous Indians were active devil-worshippers, see Cervantes, *The Devil*, 5–38.

16. According to Karl Vossler, in sixteenth- and seventeenth-century Spain, the idea of divine reciprocity constituted "el ideal teocrático de una vida, a la vez espiritual y militar." Indeed, "servir a la gloria de Dios . . . glorifica el sentimiento humano del honor. De la misma manera que se imagina a la Iglesia y al poder divino coronando y santificando el poder temporal y el Estado, se concebía el honor divino engrandeciendo y purificando el poder social" (Vossler, *Algunos caracteres*, 121–122).

17. The following discussion is indebted to Trexler, "Aztec Priests," 469–492.

18. Cortés, *Letters from Mexico*, 36.

19. Ibid. Columbus, Gonzalo Fernández de Oviedo, and others also shared the idea that the Indians possessed a "notable religiosity" that was unfortunately placed on the wrong object, that is, Lucifer (Pagden, *European Encounters*, 17–18 *passim*).

20. Here I paraphrase Trexler, "Aztec Priests," 484.

21. At this time, many of the most important critics of Spanish imperialism belonged to the Escuela de Salamanca (School of Salamanca), an important neo-scholastic movement in theology, logic, and law, which counted among its distinguished members Melchor Cano, Domingo de Soto, Diego de Covarrubias, Bartolomé de Carranza, Martín de Azpilcueta, and Francisco de Vitoria.

22. "Letter to Miguel de Arcos," in Vitoria, *Political Writings*, 331, 332.

23. Ibid., 266–267. Although this conclusion seemed easy to reach, some authors engaged in considerable mental gymnastics to prove the opposite. For example, in 1535, Gonzalo Fernández de Oviedo asserted that the Antilles had once been under the authority of Hesperus, the twelfth king of Spain; 3,193 years later, these lands were finally "restituted" to the Spanish Crown. Not content with advancing that incredible claim, Oviedo further contended that the Christian faith had been brought to the Indies long before Columbus. Its inhabitants had been "mysteriously forgotten" by God, who seeing the unnatural vices and idolatries into which the backsliding Indians had fallen, consented to their extermination from disease. Had these absurd allegations been taken seriously, of course, the Indians would surely have been identified as subjects in revolt and, therefore, enemies (Fernández de Oviedo, *Historia general*, 1:20, 30–31).

24. Vitoria, *Political Writings*, 277–286.

25. Ibid., 265.

26. The connection between blasphemy and Judaism was present throughout the medieval period and during part of the early-modern era (Lawton, *Blasphemy*, 86–92; see also Levy, *Blasphemy*, 53–54, 106, *passim*). Mockery of the sacraments and reenactment of the Crucifixion were among the most common accusations against Jews in medieval Spain (Nirenberg, *Communities of Violence*, 220–221).

27. Vitoria is probably referring to the famous episode in the Old Testament in which Sennacherib, king of Assyria, blasphemes Yahweh in a letter he sends to Hezekiah, king of Judah (2 Kings 19:14–16).

28. Vitoria, "Lecture on the Evangelization," in *Political Writings*, 349–350.

29. The *encomienda* was a grant of Indians awarded by the Crown to a Spaniard (*encomendero*) as laborers and tribute payers.

30. Las Casas, *Devastation of the Indies*, 82. Las Casas's reproach strikingly resembles one of the sermons preached by Juan de Avila (1499–1556) in the cathedral in Seville: "Mas tambien sabes señor quan muchos ay en tu Iglesia, que comprehende a buenos y a malos Christianos, que no solo son medio, para que los infieles te conozcan y te honren, mas para que se enajenen de ti, y se cieguen mas. Y en lugar de la honra que en oyendo el nombre christiano, te avian de dar, te blasfemen muy reziamente: pareciendoles con su engañado juyzio, que no puede ser verdadero Dios, ni señor, quien tiene criados que desta tan mal biven" (Avila, *Obras*, 347).

31. Las Casas, *Del único modo*, 248–255.

32. Later in his debate with Ginés de Sepúlveda, Las Casas referred to St. Paul's admonition. Las Casas was probably also familiar with Tertullian's commentary on Paul's Letter, since he used Tertullian's *De idolatria* in writing his own *Historia apologética*: "Now the blasphemy which must quite be shunned by us in every way is, I take it, this: If any of us lead a heathen into blasphemy with good cause, either by fraud, or by injury, or by contumely, or any other matter of worthy complaint, in which 'the Name' is deservedly impugned, so that the Lord, too, be deservedly angry" (Tertullian, *De idolatria*, 49).

33. Las Casas, *Obras completas*, 7:644–650.

34. Palacios Rubios's *Requerimiento* had its origins in the Maliki, an Islamic juridical school (named after its founder, Malik ben Abbas), which emphasized the need to summon the unbelievers to Islam before declaring war (Lemistre, "Les Origines," 171–177; Seed, *Ceremonies of Possession*, 74–76).

35. Soto, "Controversia," 205–206.

36. Las Casas, *Historia de las Indias*, 1:375. For a discussion of Las Casas's pacific method of conversion, see Bataillon, "La Vera Paz," 181–243.

37. Brading, *First America*, 50.

38. Las Casas, *Historia*, 1:193, 358, 342.

39. Ibid., 1:291.

40. "Ordenanzas hechas para los nuevos descubrimientos, conquistas y pacificaciones," in Konetzke, *Colección de documentos*, 1:471–478.

41. Zavala, *Defense of Human Rights*, 23. Of course, as José Rabasa has recently pointed out, the term "peaceful conquest" was an oxymoron. Moreover, the same legislation that banned the use of violence to convert the Indians also prescribed the native inhabitants' subjection and obedience to Spanish rule (Rabasa, *Writing Violence*, 4–5, 67–72, passim).

42. Hanke, *All Mankind Is One*, 121. Hanke contends that Las Casas influenced the Council of the Indies' president, Juan de Ovando, who ordered the Dominican unpublished papers to be brought from Valladolid to Madrid for use by the Council. In the same year, 1573, a new "Instrument of Obedience and Vassalage" replaced the infamous *Requerimiento*. The 1573 document required the Spaniards to notify the Crown before attacking peoples who had not previously heard of the Christian religion (Seed, *Ceremonies of Possession*, 95–96).

43. In accepting the use of force to quicken the conversion of the heathen, Mendieta was simply following his mentor, Franciscan Fray Toribio de Benavente (Motolinía). In a famous letter to Charles V penned on January 5, 1555, Motolinía accused Las Casas of viciously defaming the nation and the prince at home and abroad. Motolinía praised Cortés and his followers for conquering a land where God was so badly defamed. See Benavente, "Carta al emperador Carlos V," 291–315. Marcel Bataillon discusses Motolinía's animosity against Las Casas and his method

of evangelization in *Estudios sobre Bartolomé de las Casas*, 12, 13, 111, 321–322, 327.

44. Mendieta, *Historia Eclesiástica Indiana*, 4:4, 162; the full text of the decree is in Konetzke, *Colección de Documentos*, 1:272–274. See also Baudot, *Utopía e historia*, 108–114.

45. This biblical passage reads: "Put to death, therefore, whatever belongs to your earthly nature: sexual immorality, impurity, lust, evil desires and greed, which is idolatry." In his widely read *Lingua* (1533), Erasmus also decries these vices as idolatrous and denounces them as blasphemous and slandering acts committed by Christians against the God they profess to revere: "todo aquello que tú tienes en más que los mandamientos de Dios, hazes tu dios y señor. El luxurioso tiene por Dios a la luxuria, el glotón tiene por Dios al vientre; el beodo tiene por Dios al vino. . . . Assí que, christianos, si os erizáys, si os escandalizáys quando oys las blasphemias de los impíos contra Dios, acordaos que la vida de todos aquellos que sirven a la gula, a la luxuria, a la borrachez, a la embidia, a la sobervia, a las riquezas, es toda llena de blasphemia, la qual por tanto es más afrentosa porque la cometen aquellos que confiessan el nombre de Dios verdadero, como se quexa Dios por el propheta Ezechiel, diziendo que su nombre era afeado entre los gentiles por la mala vida del pueblo, que de palabra confessava a Dios, y en las obras lo negava. O quán mal quadra que los que cada día dizen a Dios: 'Sea sanctificado tu nombre,' biviendo mal afeen el nombre santíssimo de Dios." See Erasmo, *La lengua*, 108–109.

46. Quiroga, *La utopía en América*, 191, 193.

47. Poole, "The Declining Image," 11–19.

48. González Obregón, *Proceso Inquisitorial*, 64; *Procesos de indios*, ed. Gonzalez Obregón, 127, 201, 226.

49. Clendinnen, *Ambivalent Conquests*, 76–77.

50. Gonzalbo, "Del tercero al cuarto concilio," 6–8; Llaguno, *La personalidad jurídica*, 60.

51. On the colonists' habit of referring to themselves as "Christians," see Seed, *American Pentimento*, 116–118.

52. Mendieta, *Historia Eclesiástica Indiana*, 1:55–57; 4:166. Phelan, *Millennial Kingdom*, 84–85.

53. Indeed, after a series of decrees against vagrants, issued between 1536 and 1563, Spaniards were finally prohibited from living among Indians in 1600. For a discussion of the policy of the Spanish Crown regarding vagrancy, see Martin, *Los vagabundos*.

54. Phelan, *Kingdom of Quito*, 57–65; Borah, *Justice by Insurance*, 29–33; Ouweneel, *Shadows over Anáhuac*, 130–131.

55. In the 1570s, epidemics reduced the native population catastrophically. From 1593 to 1604, the Crown systematically gathered the remaining Indians, justifying

that step as necessary for preserving social and political order, ensuring religious instruction and municipal control, and accelerating the civilizing process in general. The colonial state ordered the forced relocation (*congregación* or *reducción*) of Indians into large mission villages, in the process, destroying entire ancient Indian towns. Although this policy aimed at revitalizing native life under the control of Spanish corregidores and Indian functionaries, this disastrous resettlement program eventually led to the sequestration of Indian lands and the impoverishment of their former owners. See Mörner, *Race Mixture*, 46; Mörner, *La corona española*, 27; Gibson, "Indian societies," 409–410.

56. Konetzke, *Colección de documentos*, 1:272–274; *Recopilación de leyes*, 1:44–45, 132, 204, 206; Pagden, *Fall of Natural Man*, 183; Baudot, *Utopía e historia*, 106–108.

57. Acosta, *Historia natural*, 219; Pagden, *Fall of Natural Man*, 180, 185.

58. Burkhart, *Slippery Earth*, 36–40; Legros, "Acerca de un diálogo," 221–222. See also Lockhart, *Nahuas after the Conquest*; Tavárez, "Naming the Trinity," 25, 43n25.

59. Rafael, *Contracting Colonialism*, 29.

60. See Queen Isabel's early "Instrucción para el gobernador y los oficiales sobre el gobierno de las Indias" (Alcalá de Henares, March 20, 1503), in Kontezke, *Colección de documentos*, 1:9. In a *carta reservada* (confidential letter) to Charles V, Cortés asked the king to limit the Spaniards' contact with the Indians, arguing, "si a estos tales se les diese libre licencia de se andar por los pueblos de indios, antes por nuestros pecados se convertirían ellos a sus vicios" (*Documentos cortesianos*, 1:286). See also Las Casas, *Historia*, 3:43; Mendieta, *Historia Eclesiástica Indiana*, 4:162; Quiroga, *La utopía*, 191.

61. Ricard, *Spiritual Conquest*, 52; Clendinnen, *Ambivalent Conquests*, 52.

62. On the relationship between blasphemy and anger, see Craun, "'Inordinata Locutio,'" 149, 152; Flynn, "Blasphemy and the Play," 29–56. For a recent discussion of the relationship between Galenism, anger, and blasphemy, see Flynn, "Taming Anger's Daughters," 872–874.

63. Temkin, *Galenism*, 17–19; see also *Apologética Historia*, in Las Casas, *Obras completas*, 6:450; Cervantes de Salazar, *Crónica de la Nueva España*, 1:129; Cárdenas, *Primera parte de los problemas*, bk. 3, chap. 3, 257; Mendieta, *Historia Eclesiástica Indiana*, 4:92, 3:167; Phelan, *Millennial Kingdom*, 57. See also Cañizares-Ezquerra, "New World, New Stars."

64. On the sin of scandal as a cause for another's spiritual downfall, see Aquinas, *Summa*, 2–2, questio 43.

65. The concern with "scandal" as a consequence of the use of force was first voiced by Vitoria in *Political Writings*, 342.

66. López de Gómara, *Hispania Victrix*, 156. The chaplain's remarks echoed Cor-

tés's own admonitions to his faltering soldiers in Cempoala, where he asked them to bear in mind that "never at any time had Spaniards been found wanting." Fernández de Oviedo later transformed that phrase into the pompous imperative, "There should be no fear or cowardliness in a Spaniard." Cortés, *Letters from Mexico*, 63; Fernández de Oviedo, *Historia general*, 4:19.

Chapter 2. "He Who Doesn't Blaspheme Is Not a Man"

1. For a detailed discussion of *las cinco palabras nefandas* (the five heinous words), see Domingo de Soto, *De como se a de evitar*, 62–63, 79–83.

2. "*¡Pese al cuerpo de Dios que no es hombre el que no reniega!*" A.G.N. Inq. 1.10, fol. 57v. Rodrigo Rengel was a captain of Cortés who participated in many expeditions. If we are to believe Bernal Díaz del Castillo, Rengel was stubborn and not terribly bright, but he had a leading role in the war against the Zapotecs. Because Rengel endangered the campaign as a consummate blasphemer, Cortés entrusted him with that dangerous enterprise, hoping his subordinate would perish along the way: "y como el Rangel [sic] era muy porfiado y de su tierra de Cortés, húbole de conceder lo que pedía; y según después supimos, Cortés lo hubo por bueno *enviarle do se muriese, porque era de mala lengua*" (Díaz del Castillo, 2:234; my italics).

3. A.G.N. Inq. 1.10; A.G.N. Inq. 40.21. For an extensive analysis of this famous case, see Greenleaf, *Mexican Inquisition*, 19–26.

4. On the use of the passive voice as a disclaimer of responsibility and a strategy to show the speaker's good will, see Douglas, *In the Active Voice*, 8.

5. Mirrer, "Representing 'Other' Men," 169–186.

6. A.G.N. Inq. 114.5. June 14, 1570.

7. *Epistolario de la Nueva España*, 1:85.

8. Greenleaf, *Zumárraga*, 103; Greenleaf, *Mexican Inquisition*, 11–26; Grunberg, *L'inquisition apostolique*, 162–168.

9. On masculinity as performance, see Mirsky, "Three Arguments"; Hopkins, "Gender Treachery."

10. Huizinga, *Autumn*, 186. On the notion of "speech style" as a heuristic tool for the analysis of the multiple ways in which speech is socially patterned by a community of speakers, see Hymes, "Ways of Speaking," pp. 433–434.

11. On Beltrán's contests, see Menéndez Pidal, *Historia de España*, xxxvi; Córdoba, *Jardín de nobles donzellas*, 219.

12. Burke, *Art of Conversation*, 3.

13. Alberro, *Inquisition et société*, 94.

14. Soto, *De como se a de evitar*, 149: "El jurar es a unos hombres como ornamento de su lenguaje, con el qual piensan que añaden gravedad, y severidad a

su razon." Luque Fajardo, *Fiel desengaño*, 145–146: "El que mas sofisterias dize y haze en la materia, entre ellos, es tenido por mas discreto, y desenfadado y corriente y compañero de polvo y lodo, como dizen, *su mas jurar es mayor valentia*, haziendo bramona, de las blasfemias sus bordonzillos" (my italics). The notion of blasphemy as an "adornment" of male speech is apparently very old. In *Gargantua and Pantagruel*, Rabelais includes this revealing dialogue: "Comment, dit Pornocratès, vous jurez, frère Jean?—Ce n'est, dit le moine, que pour orner mon language. Ce sont couleurs de rhétorique cicéroniane." Quoted in Cabantous, "Du blasphème au blasphémateur," 29.

15. See Santo Tomás, *Excelencias del Nombre*, 39: "De los que mucho juran, y blasfeman, dezimos que tienen una boca de escorpion, la cara la tienen de hombres, pero sus infernales lenguas son de escorpiones para hacer mal." In animalizing the blasphemers, moralists were drawing on a long medieval tradition of using beasts as epithets for degrading others. See Madero, *Manos violentas, palabras vedadas*, 150–155.

16. See Martínez de la Parra, *Luz de verdades católicas*, 155: "Y trae en su lengua todo el infierno, porque assi como el alabar repetidas vezes a Dios es señal de predestinación, y es ya ensayarte para el cielo . . . assi el blasfemar, y maldecir su Santo Nombre es ya marca de condenados, y es ensayarse para el infierno." See also Señeri, *El confesor instruido*, 188–189: "Ay mucha correspondencia entre sus voces sacrilegas, y las maldiciones de los condenados al infierno. De suerte que son como una musica de dos coros: el un coro esta debajo de tierra, el otro esta encima: y de los silvos de aquellos Dragones alla abajo en el fuego aprenden aca arriba estas serpientes disfrazadas de hombres a formar el eco con sus blasfemias."

17. See, for instance, Nicolás de Avila, *Suma de los mandamientos*, 443–444: "Y assi lo suelen hazer los cobardes, no pudiendose vengar de su contrario, toman las armas de mujercillas apocadas, que es la lengua, maldiziendo, como este que blasfemo a nombre de Dios, mostrandose valiente con Dios."

18. Aquinas, *Summa*, 1–2, questio 46, articulus 4.

19. Dalcobia, *Primera parte del symbolo*, 44v: "La ira con consideracion, es obra virtuosa, pero sin ella es escandalo: que el que airadamente se descompone mal mira por el bien comun . . . la justa verdadera ira que el prudente debe tener, ha de ser contra sus pecados." See also Flynn, "Taming Anger's Daughters," 864–865. For an analysis of the medieval roots of the distinction between "good anger" and "bad anger," see Barton, "A Zealous Anger," 157. On wrath as one of the seven cardinal (or capital) sins, see Azpilcueta, *Manual de confesores*, 494. See also Oyola, *Los pecados capitales*. For a discussion of Gregory the Great's role in establishing the canon, see Bloomfield, *Seven Deadly Sins*, 72.

20. Albertino, *De Agnoscendis*, questio 27, no. 3, 143; Carena, *Tractatus*, title 7, par. 6, no. 30, 131.

21. Santo Tomás, *Excelencias del Nombre*, 24–41; Martínez de la Parra, *Luz de verdades*, 161–162, 166–167, 172–174.

22. See Erasmo, *La lengua*, 20: "Puso naturaleza dos baluartes o antepechos de treynta y dos dientes . . . con los cuales a bocados puede ser refrenada quando no obedesciere a la razón." See also Fonseca, *Segunda parte del tratado*, 571–572.

23. Covarrubias y Orozco, *Emblemas morales*, 266.

24. As Carla Mazzio has recently shown, making an association between the tongue and the penis was quite common in the sixteenth and seventeenth centuries ("Sins of the Tongue," 60). The depiction of the tongue as a "flabby little organ" comes from Erasmus, as quoted in ibid., 54. Perhaps this association of masculinity, sexual potency, and speech control prompted Victor Hugo to exclaim, "Le blasphème est le cri des impuissants" (quoted in L'Escop, *La lengua catalana*, 2).

25. Salazar, *Veinte discursos*, 53r–59v. About the foundation and goals of the confraternity of the Holy Name of Jesus in Spain, see Victoria, *Regla de la Sancta Cofradía*; Santo Tomás, *Excelencias del Nombre*, 111–116. See also Flynn, *Sacred Charity*, 123; Nalle, *God in La Mancha*, 161–162; García Ayluardo, "A World of Images," 77–114.

26. Grunberg, *L'inquisition apostolique*, 162.

27. On the Edict of Faith and its annual promulgation, see Haliczer, *Inquisition and Society*, 60–61.

28. A.G.N. Inq. 1.10c, fols. 79–79v.

29. A.G.N. Inq. 1.8, fols. 45–45v. For other cases in which Spanish men were sentenced to make penitential pilgrimages, see A.G.N. Inq. 19b, fols. 49–49v, against Alonso de Espinosa, 1527; A.G.N. Inq. 1.10d, fols. 80–80v, against Francisco Núñez, 1527; A.G.N. 14.2a, fol. 37, against Hernando García Sarmiento, 1527. For similar cases under Juan de Zumárraga, see A.G.N. Inq. 14.6, fols. 82–86, against Juan Pérez Montañez, 1536; A.G.N. Inq. 14.9, fols. 160–161, against Sancho de Bullón, 1537; A.G.N. 14.30, fols. 195–196v, against Juan Gómez de Castillejo, 1538.

30. Sousa, *Aphorismi Inquisitorum* (n.d., 1630), bk. 1, chap. 19, no. 4, 51: "Blasphemia proprie non consistit in factis, ut in deturpatione vel spurcatione imaginum, sed in solis verbis mente, ore, vel scripto prolatis." See also Sanctarelli, *De Haeresi, schismate, Apostasia*, third treatise, chap. 1, no. 4, 586.

31. A.G.N. Inq. 1.7, fols. 9–27.

32. A.G.N. Inq. 1.8, fols. 28–44. Morales was tried in 1538 in Oaxaca for practicing Judaism. He migrated to Guatemala, where in 1558, Bishop Marroquín tried him on the same charge. See Greenleaf, *Mexican Inquisition*, 27.

33. A.G.N. Inq. 14.4, fols. 70–74.

34. A.G.N. Inq. 14.10b, fols. 102–106. See also the trial of Juan Díaz, accused in Mexico City on September 14, 1536, for saying "pese a los ángeles de Dios." A.G.N. Inq. 14.13.

35. A.G.N. Inq. 14.9, fols. 91–97.

36. A.G.N. Inq. 14.8, fols. 88–90. For similar cases in which blasphemers denounced themselves before priests, friars, and ecclesiastical judges, see A.G.N. Inq. 14.15, fols. 120–123v, against Francisco Preciado, 1536; A.G.N. Inq. 14.45, against Francisco de Hoyos, 1538; A.G.N. Inq. 14.34, fols. 204–204v, against Juan de la Peña, 1539; and A.G.N. Inq. 14.17, against Hernando Díaz, 1536.

37. Connell, *Masculinities*, 187.

38. A.G.N. Inq. 17.19, fols. 482–491v.

39. A.G.N. Inq. 19.12, fols. 269–277v.

40. A.G.N. Inq. 16.8, fols. 326–331.

41. A.G.N. Inq. 18.15, fols. 249–165v. For similar cases in which blasphemous remarks accompanied unspecified demands for "payment," see A.G.N. Inq. 15.13, fols. 184–190v; A.G.N. Inq. 18.18, fols. 282–290.

42. On breaking Christ's head, see the trial against Spanish Manuel Fernández in Mexico City in 1540, in A.G.N. Inq. 14.37, fols. 225–228v. On fighting God *a campo raso*, see the trials against Gonzalo Hernández in A.G.N. Inq. 45.9, fols. 149–196. This case is discussed in chap. 3.

43. This same expression was used by Rodrigo Rengel in 1527: "y dijo una grave blasfemia contra Nuestra Señora diciendo que descreía de Dios si aun los retraídos se metiesen en el bientre de Ntra. Señora si de ay no los sacaba y los ahorcaba." A.G.N. Inq. 1.10, fol. 57v.

44. A.G.N. Inq. 146.3, fols. 102–262v.

45. A.G.N. Inq. 578.4, fols. 239–287v.

46. A.G.N. Inq. 585.2, fols. 37–74v.

47. A.G.N. Inq., box 166.5, fols. 1–57.

48. A.G.N. Inq. 473.21, fols. 170–173v.

49. Doña Felipa stated on February 17, 1691, that a man called Felix de la Cruz told him "que no sabia como no se avian desbarrancado en las minas." See A.G.N. Inq. 680.81, fol. 485v.

50. A.G.N. Inq. 680.81, fols. 480–496.

51. Kimmel, *Gendered Society*, 246.

52. The idea that men were forced to blaspheme by their unruly wives was a recurrent topos in Christian literature. See chap. 4.

53. A.G.N. Inq. 21.2, fols. 43–87.

54. A.G.N. Inq. 147.7.

55. "Mala vida" referred to the failure of men to offer protection, support, and guidance that they were legally obliged to provide in exchange for the obedience of their wives and daughters. By neglecting these responsibilities, men legitimized women's resistance. See the classic essay by Richard Boyer, "Las mujeres," 271–303.

56. A.G.N. Inq. 17.11, fols. 212–222.

57. Lavrin, "Women in Colonial Mexico," 264.

58. A.G.N. Inq. 8.2, fols. 119–243.

59. A.G.N. Inq. 612, fol. 433: "Me cago en los cuatro evangelios, y en el angel de tu guarda, y en la sepultura de tu madre, y tu padre esta ardiendo en el infierno metido en un cuerno, y el obispo es un cornudo, que me cago en su mitra, y en su consagracion, mas verdad dice mi mierda que tu angel de la guarda."

60. A.G.N. Inq. 612.2, fols. 273–488v.

61. Connell, *Masculinities*, 213.

62. Boyer, "Juan Vazquez," 169. Given their key role in establishing communications between regions, muleteers also played a crucial role in several rebellions in the colonial period, particularly in the Andes. See Stern, "Age of Andean Insurrection," 46, 49, 57; Mörner and Trelles, "A Test of Causal Interpretations," 49–50.

63. Suárez Argüello, *Camino real y carrera larga*, 217–221.

64. Here I draw heavily on Ouweneel, *Shadows*, 294–297.

65. A.G.N. Inq. 14.25, fols. 176–178.

66. A.G.N. Inq. 14.22, fol. 167: "que el oficio que tiene es de harriero es tal que no podia dexar de dezir alguna cosa contra Ntro. Señor."

67. A.G.N. Inq. 14.38, fols. 236–37v.

68. A.G.N. Inq. 15.2, fols. 6–7.

69. Concerning a particularly successful muleteer, see Super, "Miguel Hernández," 298–310. For the late eighteenth century, see Clara Elena Suárez Arguello's detailed discussion of *dueños de recuas* and other forms of transportation entrepreneurship in *Camino real y carrera larga*, 208–217.

70. A.G.N. Inq. 45.8, fols. 145–148v.

71. A.G.N. Inq. 18.20, fols. 299–313v.

72. Gestas and his fellow thief, Dimas, were captured in Jericho and crucified alongside Christ. A.G.N. Inq. 1362, fols. 122r–128r, included in Company, *Documentos lingüísticos*, 682–686.

73. Hernández Díaz, "Asistencia espiritual," 272–273, 276–277. According to Fernández de Oviedo, sailors at sea frequently invoked the Virgin Mary, and in particular the Virgin of Guadalupe. For stories of Mary's miraculous interventions to prevent shipwrecks, see Fernández de Oviedo, *Historia general*, 5:308, 320, 321. See also Pérez-Mallaína, *Spain's Men of the Sea*, 238. I thank Kris Lane for drawing my attention to this work.

74. Guevara, "De muchos trabajos," in Martínez, *Pasajeros de indias*, 243.

75. A.G.N. Inq. 15.11, fols. 141–158v. See also the case of Pedro Martínez Matacorsos, *contramaestre* (mate) of the ship *San Miguel*. He not only blasphemed God and made impious remarks regarding crucifixes, the Holy Host, and the

saints but also declined to participate in the customary prayers on the ship. The ship's chaplain denounced him on November 5, 1565, and one month later, Matacorsos was sentenced to hear mass while gagged, and to serve a ten-year sentence as a galley slave, during which time, he would have to wear a yellow penitential garment (sanbenito) as a sign of his infamy. A.G.N. Inq. 18.12, fols. 208–226.

76. Pérez-Mallaína, *Spain's Men of the Sea*, 54–60.

77. Leonard, *Books of the Brave*, 146; Pérez-Mallaína, *Spain's Men of the Sea*, 60.

78. A.G.N. Inq. 46.16, fols. 336–394v. Another case involving a French sailor was that of Bartholomé Guillón (possibly spelled Guillaume), who had renounced God when someone hit him on the cheek with an orange. On January 27, 1574, he was sentenced to attend a penitential mass, to be paraded naked to the waist on a donkey, and to receive one hundred lashes. See A.G.N. 47.5, fols. 268–287.

79. "Instrucción para la visita de los navíos." See also *Ordenanças reales*, xliii verso. On the Inquisition's inspections of the ships, see Leonard, *Books of the Brave*, 171–178. See also Hernández Aranda, "Ulúa y las misiones religiosas," 189.

80. Pérez-Mallaína, *Spain's Men of the Sea*, 206.

81. A.G.N. Inq. 146.7, fols. 327–360.

82. Leonard, *Books*, 142.

83. Pablo Montero et al., *Ulúa, puente intercontinental*, 69; Hernández, "Veracrúz frente a Ulúa," 173.

84. A.G.N. Inq. 46.14, fols. 294–335.

85. Pérez-Mallaína, *Spain's Men of the Sea*, 82.

86. A.G.N. Inq., box 166.3, fols. 1–74.

87. A.G.N. Inq. 14.9, fols. 260–267.

88. A.G.N. Inq. 5.15, fols. 317–361v.

89. Hernández Aranda, "Se consolida el virreinato," 132; Montero et al., *Ulúa, puente intercontinental*, 57.

90. A.G.N. Inq. 471.13, fols. 55–60v.

91. A.G.N. 143.32.

92. The *capitana* (flagship) and the *almiranta* (the vice-admiral's ship) accompanied commercial ships to protect them from attack during the two annual trips to America. The capitana led the convoy of fifty or more ships, while the almiranta brought up the rear to protect the slower vessels. See Leonard, *Books of the Brave*, 143; Gibson, *Spain in America*, 102–103.

93. A.G.N. Inq. 144.10, fols. 208–287.

94. Escamilla Gómez, "La formación de la Nueva Veracruz," 72–73, quoted in Montero et al., *Ulúa, puente intercontinental*, 78.

95. Upon his appointment as castellano in 1658, Francisco Castejón under-

took an ambitious construction project to strengthen the fortress. The engineer Marcos Lucio, believing that fortifying the port of Veracruz itself was most important, strongly opposed the project. Although it was never completed, Castejón did construct new barracks for 150 soldiers, as well as improving the church on the island and repairing the fortress. See Pablo Montero et al., *Ulúa, puente intercontinental*, 88–92.

96. A.G.N. Inq. 445.4, fols. 523–583v.

97. The *Ecce Homo* is a representation of Jesus wearing a crown of thorns, as he was shown to the people by Pilate, who said to them, "Here is the man!" (*Ecce Homo*) (John 19:5).

98. A.G.N. Inq. 519.1, fols. 1–208.

99. Parker and Parker, *European Soldiers*, 30.

100. Archer, *Army in Bourbon Mexico*, 254–258.

101. Willis, "Masculinity and Factory Labor," 187.

102. Johnson, "Dangerous Words, Provocative Gestures," 130.

103. Taylor, *Drinking, Homicide*, 82–83.

104. Bourdieu, *Language and Symbolic Power*, 93.

105. On expletives and swear words as powerful speech styles among men, see de Klerk, "Role of Expletives," 146–47, *passim*.

106. Cabantous, *Histoire du blasphème*, 119.

107. Elias, *Civilizing Process*.

Chapter 3. On Divine Persecution

1. A.G.N. Inq. 146.4, fols. 263–280v.

2. Ezcaray, *Vozes del dolor*, 348; Etienvre, *Márgenes literarios*, 43. Literally defined as "well-turning," eutrapelia was the Aristotelian virtue of "turning" to play or other relaxing things without losing oneself in them, with the only purpose of resting before returning to serious matters. Following Aristotle, Aquinas stressed the importance of eutrapelia, by calling it "virtue in play." See *Summa*, 2–2, questio 168, articulus 2. See also Rahner, "Eutrapelia," 188, 194; Miller, *Gods and Games*, 110–111; Ménager, *Le Renaissance et le rire*, 87–89.

3. For a discussion of the position of the Catholic Church regarding games and entertainment in the sixteenth century, see Roulos, "Jeux interdits et réglementés," 637–643.

4. Alcocer, *Tratado del juego*, 7.

5. Palafox, *Luz a los vivos*, 118. In the highly popular Byzantine collection of exempla, *Pratum spirituale* (attributed to St. Sophronious and translated into Spanish in 1578 by J. B. Sanctoro), a player is replaced by another at the gaming table because of his alleged incompetence to both play and blaspheme: "Deja el

juego inabil, dexalo, que yo jugare por ti porque tu no sabes jugar ni jurar" (Sanctoro, *Prado espiritual*, 109). Similarly, Renaissance gambling scholar Gerolamo Cardano was convinced that "a confirmed gambler is a perjurer and a blasphemer," an opinion apparently shared by many at the time (*Liber de Ludo Aleae*, 195).

6. Luque Fajardo, *Fiel desengaño*, 142v; Alcocer, *Tratado del juego*, 8; Covarrubias, *Remedio de jugadores*, 51v; Ezcaray, *Vozes del dolor*, 343–345. Bernardino de Siena first advanced this satanic image in 1423 in his *Sermo 62: De alearum ludo*, chap. 2, quoted in Etienvre, *Márgenes literarios*, 314.

7. *Commentary on Matthew*, Homily 6.6, cited in Rahner, *Man at Play*, 98; Bernardino de Siena, *Opera omnia*, 2:20–34, quoted in Sauzet, "La Réforme," 651.

8. "Porque regularmente ablando, conforme la ordinaria experiencia, no ay incentivo mayor de jugar, que hazer voto o juramento" (Luque Fajardo, *Fiel desengaño*, 147). The cardsharp in this moral dialogue is named "Florino," because of his skill at *las flores*, that is, cheating at cards.

9. Alcocer, *Tratado*, 8–9.

10. Luque Fajardo, *Fiel desengaño*, 2:142–143. See also Etienvre, "Le symbolisme de la carte," 84. Etienvre discusses the metaphor of the deck of cards as a book in *Márgenes literarios*, 100–104, 322–326. The suits in Spanish playing cards represented the social strata: the cups stood for the ecclesiastics; the swords, for the nobility; the coins, for the merchants; and, finally, the batons, for the peasants and hunters.

11. Etienvre, "Le symbolisme," 433–434. The idea of playing cards' satanic origin was widespread in early modern Europe (Aretino, *Le carte parlanti*, 39). In seventeenth-century Tuscany, one Father Giovanni Dragoni was convinced that card games were inventions of the Devil (Cipolla, *Faith, Reason and the Plague*, 17). Similarly, in Protestant countries, cards were called "the Devil's picture book" (Parlett, *Oxford Guide to Card Games*, 11). For one of the strongest and better argued Protestant condemnations of cards, dice, and gambling games in general, see Lambert Danae's *Brieue remonstrance*.

12. Baroque moralists and preachers widely used the rhetorical strategy of *desengaño* (disillusion) to reveal to the faithful the theater of disguises, or *engaños* (tricks), that everyday reality and *las cosas exteriores* (external things) represented. For a discussion of the doctrine of desengaño, see Vives, "Introducción a la sabiduría," 240–242. See also Smith, *Preaching in the Spanish Golden Age*, 135–137; Nelson, "Emblematic Representation," 159. Leonard discusses the influence of the theory of desengaño on Baroque Mexico in his *Baroque Times*, 17, 30, 55, 169.

13. On the place of the *exemplum* in the medieval renewal of preaching, see Bremond et al., *L'exemplum*, 13. On the process of identification on the part of the

audience required by the exemplum, see Scanlon, *Narrative, Authority, and Power*, 35. For a discussion of seventeenth- and eighteenth-century Spanish religious writers' use of exempla, see Ricard, *Estudios de literatura religiosa*, 200–226. For a review of the exemplary narratives circulating in Spain during the Middle Ages, see Lacarra, "Pour un *Thesaurus Exemplorum Hispanicorum*," 191–213.

14. Faya de Saona, *Suma de exemplos*, 125v.

15. Besides Faya de Saona, at least two other Jesuits included this tale in their moral works; see Fiol, *Razones para convencer al pecador*, 93–94; and Martínez de la Parra, *Luz de verdades*, 172–174.

16. Martínez de la Parra, *Luz de verdades*, 173.

17. Avila, *Suma de los mandamientos*, 458.

18. Palafox y Mendoza, *Luz a los vivos*, 118.

19. Covarrubias y Orozco, *Empresas morales*, 101; López, *Declaración magistral*, 11. Cistercian mystic and historian Caesarius of Heisterbach (ca. 1180–1240) first used the image of the devil as a ferocious beast, divinely chained, even though the subject of the analogy was a bear or lion. See his *Dialogue on Miracles*, bk. 5, 52, quoted in Gregg, *Devils, Women, and Jews*, 37.

20. Blasphemy could indeed assume a carnivalized form of prayer during a game. See, for instance, the case of Gaspar de Zalaya (Mexico City), who was denounced to the Holy Office in 1573 for uttering, "Blessed is God's prick (*carajo*) for I won the game!" (Archive of the Archbishopric of Mexico, box 1, 8). Flynn raises a similar point in her "Blasphemy and the Play."

21. Covarrubias, *Remedio de jugadores*, xxxvi–xxxvii.

22. "Gobernación espiritual y temporal," *Colección de documentos de ultramar*, 21:105. See also *Recopilación de leyes*, bk. 8, title 2, law 1. The 1771 *pragmática* listed as unlawful *banca, faraón, baceta, quince, carteta, banca fallida, sacanete, parar, treinta y cuarenta,* and *flor,* among many other card games. See López Cantos, *Juegos, fiestas y diversiones*, 272–273.

23. Archivo General de Indias, Indiferente General 415, bk. 2, fol. 3; Weckman, *Medieval Heritage*, 128–129; Aiton, *Antonio de Mendoza*, 100. Mendoza probably followed the precedent established by King Alphonse X, who in 1314 decided to put an end to the "immorality" accompanying the games by closing the *tafurerías*, or gambling houses (*Los códigos españoles*, 236).

24. *Documentos cortesianos*, 1:49.

25. Orozco y Becerra, *Historia antigua*, 4:296.

26. *Documentos cortesianos*, 2:37, 116, 174; López Cantos, *Juegos, fiestas*, 292.

27. *Colección de documentos de ultramar*, 12:510–511. That same year the Spanish Crown suspended the fines for all those who had gambled during the wars of conquest (*Gobernación espiritual y temporal*, nos. 28 and 29).

28. Weckman, *Medieval Heritage*, 128; López Cantos, "Los juegos de suerte," 204–205.

29. Phelan, *Kingdom of Quito*, 163.

30. Cope, *Limits of Racial Domination*, 41.

31. "El rigor que habemos dicho en el visitar y castigar los jugadores y casas de juego no se entiende con algunas casas de caballeros o personas ciudadanas principales, donde suelen juntarse a jugar, más por vía de entretenimiento y conversación que a juegos recios, pues allí ni se sacan baratos para velas, ni hay otros desórdenes que en las tablajerías corsarias, y donde se juegan juegos prohibidos" (Jerónimo Castillo de Bobadilla, *Política para Corregidores y Señores de vassallos*, 1:377, quoted in Jean-Pierre Etienvre, *Márgenes literarios*, 43). Castillo's reference to the *"tablajerías corsarias"* alludes to the popular comparison of card-sharps with pirates (*corsarios*) and thieves.

32. Ezcaray, *Vozes del dolor*, 346–348.

33. *Recopilación*, bk. 2, title 16, laws 74 and 75; bk. 7, title 2, laws 1–3; Zubillaga, *Historia de la iglesia*, 383; Lorenzana, *Concilios provinciales*, 117–118. As late as 1703, the chief ecclesiastical judge, or *provisor*, of Mexico City issued a new edict forbidding clerics to frequent gambling houses or cockfights on pain of excommunication. See Robles, *Diario de sucesos*, 256.

34. *Colección de documentos de ultramar*, 10:396.

35. The illegal manufacture of gambling cards was not uncommon, but the transgressors risked severe punishment. In 1645, the colonial authorities fined Lucas de Alfaro, Audiencia attorney in Mexico, two thousand ducats for profiting from the sale of illegal packs, which had been printed by an individual named Gaspar de Carrillo and several accomplices. Carrillo and his father-in-law had their possessions seized and were exiled for four years; an Indian accomplice was publicly whipped and also exiled for four years (Fernández Bulete, "Aproximación a la delincuencia").

36. Cuello Martinell, *La renta de los naipes*, 9, 15, 18, 26; Benassar, *Spanish Character*, 165–66; Colomar, "El juego de naipes," 383–384.

37. Escandel Bonet, "Las estructuras económicas," 1088.

38. Weckman, *Medieval Heritage*, 129; López Cantos, *Juegos, fiestas*, 312. Bishop Palafox illustrated the discriminatory attitude when he said that women who play cards would lose not only precious time and money but also their *honra* (good reputation) (*Luz a los vivos*, 28).

39. For a discussion of the conflicting relationship between Fortuna and Providencia in fifteenth-century Spain and the theological implications for understanding thorny issues such as predestination and the existence of evil on earth, see Mendoza Negrillo, *Fortuna y providencia*, esp. chaps. 1, 2, and 7.

40. Hardon, "Chance." Providentialism was also widespread in Protestant countries (Walsham, *Providence in Early Modern England*, 21–22).

41. Thomas, *Religion and the Decline*, 121. See also Céard, "Jeu et divination à la Renaissance," 408–409.

42. Christian, *Local Religion*, 47; Thomas, *Religion and the Decline*, 120–122.

43. Ciruelo, *Tratado de las supersticiones*, 50–51. Ciruelo's distinction between the different kinds of *suertes* is based on Aquinas (*Summa*, 2–2, questio 95, articulus 8).

44. A.G.N. Inq. 14.10, fols. 98–101.

45. A.G.N. Inq. 1.10f, fol. 82.

46. A.G.N. Inq. 14.3, fols. 65–69.

47. A.G.N. 14.2bis, fols. 60–74.

48. A.G.N. Inq. 514.18, fols. 105–50.

49. For Juan Baeza, see A.G.N. 14.46. The denunciation against Diego Moreno was included in the trial of Hernando Botello at the Huachinango mines (A.G.N. Inq. 21.5, fols. 302–337v).

50. A.G.N. 3.5a. In an interesting inversion of these reciprocity relationships, moralists also called blasphemy the *barato del diablo*, intimating that gamesters blasphemed in order to secure Satan's help to win the games. See Santo Tomás, *Excelencias del Nombre*, 30: "Con gran rabia, empezó a blasfemar (que este es el barato que los perdidos dan en el juego al diablo)." On the practice of giving el barato as a talisman in the games, see López Cantos, *Juegos, fiestas, y diversiones*, 274–276.

51. Popular card game in which players bet that their chosen card will be drawn from the deck before that of their opponent.

52. A.G.N. Inq. 560.6, fols. 146–191v.

53. A.G.N. Inq. 45.9, fols. 149–196.

54. Bancroft Library Manuscript 72/57m, box 1, file 7.

55. Like Yrregui, many other gamblers expressed a feeling of betrayal and deep injustice after losing. In 1666, at the mines of Sombrerete, Zacatecas, after losing a bet, an angered Pedro Correa asked, "Does God ignore perchance that I deserve this money [*hacienda*] much more than these cuckolds to whom He has just given it?" (Huntington Library HM35131, vol. 37, pt. 2).

56. "En el juego somos incautos porque en el estudio y beodez de [é]l nos declaramos quales somos" (Covarrubias, *Remedio de jugadores*, xlix). Aquinas also advanced the notion that games are a privileged occasion in which the player's authentic self is revealed (*Commentary to Aristotle's Ethic* 4, 16, 4). See Lauand, "Ludus in the Fundamentals."

57. On gestures as "expression" of the soul's movements, see Schmitt, *La raison des gestes*, 25–26, and Thomas, introduction to *Cultural History of Gestures*, 8–9. On Spanish gravity as the European ideal of bodily control during the Counterreformation, see Burke, *Varieties of Cultural History*, 72–73. See also Cascardis, "The Subject of Control." For Pedro de Covarrubias's remark, see his *Remedio de jugadores*, 51v.

58. See, for example, Bäuml and Bäuml, *Dictionary of Gestures*.

59. Schmitt, "Gestures," 1–2; Le Goff, *Lo maravilloso*, 50, 52. For a fine discussion of the religious and political implications of the binary high/low at the time, see Ginzburg, "High and Low." The religious significance of right and left is discussed in the classic essay by Hertz, "La prééminence de la main droite."

60. "En litigio esta," wrote Nicolás de Avila in 1610, "si esta palabra, *pese a tal*, es blasfemia. [Algunos teólogos dicen] que no lo es, con tanto que falte el animo de dezir, *pese a Dios*: empero otros dizen que sera blasfemia, si dizen estas palabras levantando los ojos al cielo" (*Suma de los mandamientos*, 489–490). In 1536, gamester Alonso Carrión offered a good example of the indexical significance of looking skyward. While gambling, he would utter "all kind of blasphemies," and raising his eyes to the ceiling, he would declare, "I know very well to whom I am speaking (*y bien yo sé a quién digo*)" (A.G.N. Inq. 14.3, fol. 67).

61. Melchor Cano mentions the fig as a gesture of anger in his *Tratado de la victoria de sí mismo*, 49. Origins and extended use of the fig among Spaniards are discussed in Caro, *Días geniales o lúdicos*, 2:104, 233–234, and Rosal, *La razón de algunos refranes*, 136. Pedro Covarrubias registers the use of this gesture against the Godhead: "Y despues que perdio dixo Vos Dios toma para vos endereçando la higa al cielo," (*Remedio de jugadores*, 55v).

62. See the 1572 Mexico City case of Gaspar de los Reyes. After complaining that the Virgin had not interceded on his behalf before Christ, "pusose el dedo entre los dientes y alzo la cabeza hacia el cielo en modo airado." Since Gaspar's grandfather had been burned at the stake in Seville for being a Jew, Gaspar was not only administered one hundred lashes but was also forever banned from New Spain (A.G.N. 52.1, fols. 36v–37r). In canvases and retables depicting Christ's Passion, Jews were often portrayed biting the thumb or giving a fig. See plates IX and X in Schmitt, *La raison des gestes*, 42–43.

63. *Las Siete Partidas*, 1:257.

64. A.G.N. Inq. 5.12, fols. 292–295v.

65. A.G.N. Inq. 18.8, fols. 45–72.

66. Juan de Vargas threw an image of the Agnus Dei on the ground after losing the huge amount of two thousand gold pesos on October 3, 1607. See A.G.N. Inq. 467.59, fols. 272–273.

67. A.G.N. Inq. 15.3, fols. 8–18.

68. The "Remigius" was a highly influential treatise on exorcisms. See Remigio Noydens, *La practica de exorcistas*.

69. For a rich analysis of the discourse of possession as "a language without a subject," see the interesting remarks of Certeau in his *La possession de Loudun*, chap. 3, esp. 63–69. The relation between "automatism" and blasphemy in medieval culture is discussed in Casagrande and Vecchio, *Les péchés de la langue*,

177–178. Jean-Claude Schmitt analyzes demonic possession in the Middle Ages as an extreme case of complete loss of mastery over bodily gestures (*La raison des gestes*, 127–128). For an excellent recent discussion of the ambivalent interpretation of gestures of possession by medieval Europeans who were attempting to discern the nature (divine or demonic) of the invading spirit, see Caciola, "Mystics, Demoniacs."

70. Cervantes, *The Devil*, 123.

71. A.G.N. Inq. 520.25, fols. 402–414v.

72. Vives, "Diálogo 20" (1538), and "Diálogo 21," in *Obras completas*, 2:952–953 and 957–961, respectively; Cardano, *Liber de Ludo Aleae*, 187.

73. For a case in which conversation gambits were controlled by asking a gamester to deal with issues "que fuesen de los tejados para abajo," a phrase that restricted their conversation to the sublunar world, see A.G.N. Inq. 18.8, fols. 97–104. For an example of fines established by the players themselves, see A.G.N. 14.5, fols. 75–81.

74. A.G.N. Inq. 14.5, fols. 75–81.

75. A.G.N. Inq. 14.2bis, fols. 60–74.

76. A.G.N. Inq. 14.5, fols. 75–81; A.G.N. Inq. 14.4, fols. 70–74; A.G.N. Inq. 14.3, fols. 65–69; A.G.N. Inq. 14.10, fols. 98–101.

77. On welshing, see Slater, "Betting." Catherine Bates offers interesting insights on "paying up" gambling debts in her *Play in a Godless World*, 2–3. For a discussion of gambling and self-fashioning among Renaissance courtesans, see Kavanagh, *Enlightenment and the Shadows*, 42.

78. A.G.N. Inq. 17.12, fol. 258.

79. A.G.N. Inq. 45.18, fols. 233–314; A.G.N. Inq. 45.19, fols. 233–314.

80. A.G.N. Inq. 591.4, fols. 437–495v.

81. Martínez de la Parra, *Luz de verdades*, 159, 170: "Que diremos de un desventurado Coyme, que en la casa de juego de que vive, esta oyendo continuas blasfemias? O mil vezes hombre desventurado el que assi come de pecados mortales, el que assi vive de las muertes de tantas almas. El que assi fomenta ladrones, el que assi abriga delinquentes. El que assi desune los Matrimonios, despuebla los oficios, empobrece las casas, turba las familias, excita los lamentos, y lagrimas de las pobres mugeres, pierde la juventud, y daña a toda la Republica con un castillo infernal contra el cielo, que todo eso se ve en las casas de juego, y todos esos pecados carga el Coyme. . . . Ahora condénese si quiere ser fomentador, y tapadera de blasfemos." Only three years before Martínez's 1691 sermon, the archbishop of Mexico leveled a strikingly similar criticism against the popular cockfights, arguing that these ludic events caused the "breakup of marriages, thefts, and disgraces." On his advice, the Crown banned cockfights (Viqueira Albán, *Propriety and Permissiveness*, 6).

82. For a thorough analysis of this famous riot, see Cope, *Limits of Racial Domination*, 125–160.

83. Viqueira Albán, *Propriety and Permissiveness*, 9.

84. Cuello Martinell, *La renta de los naipes*, 57–58, 63, 68.

85. Sutton-Smith, *Ambiguity of Play*, 67. Long ago, Johan Huizinga pointed out the ancient relationship between play and religion (or play and the sacred). His *Homo Ludens* traced the origins of play to the idea of the sacred in primitive religions (18–24). Unfortunately, since Huizinga was profoundly convinced that playing for money was a corruption of play—which he defined as an activity free of economic interest—the Dutch historian did not explore the relationship between gambling and the sacred.

86. See, for example, Bergler's classic study, *The Psychology of Gambling*. He was convinced that gamblers were regressed neurotics, who, seeking masochist gratification, gambled with the purpose of losing. See 30–31 *passim*. For a recent update in the same vein, see Knapp, *Gambling, Game, and Psyche*, 9.

87. Caillois, *Man, Play, and Games*, 46.

88. Geertz, *Interpretation of Cultures*, 433–435.

Chapter 4. Through Eve's Open Mouth

1. This Indian revolt was later known as the War of the Mixton (1541–1542). See Byrne, "Indian Resistance to Spanish Power."

2. Fernández de Oviedo, *Historia general*, 4:360–361. Fernández de Oviedo seems to have based his opinion on Rodríguez, *Relacion del espantable terremoto*, 6.

3. Díaz del Castillo, *Historia verdadera*, 2:414, 481–483; Mendieta, *Historia Eclesiástica Indiana*, 2:37–40. See also López de Gómara, *Historia general*, 1:354–355; Torquemada, *Monarquía indiana*, 3: chap. 35, 355–358.

4. Alberro, "El discurso inquisitorial"; Ortega, *De la santidad a la perversión*; Alberro, "Herejes, brujas y beatas"; Alberro, "La sexualidad manipulada"; Atondo, "Prostitutas, alcahuetes y mancebas"; Behar, "Sex and Sin"; Behar, "Sexual Witchcraft"; Holler, "'More Sins than the Queen of England'"; Curcio-Nagy, "Rosa de Escalante's Private Party"; Jaffary, *False Mystics*; Gunnarsdottir, *Mexican Karismata*, esp. 51–62, 178–83; Rubial García, "Josefa de San Luis Beltrán." However, for a recent discussion of two cases of blasphemy among Afro-Mexican slave women, see McKnight, "Blasphemy as Resistance."

5. Maclean, *Renaissance Notion of Woman*, 15–16; Kelso, *Doctrine for the Lady of the Renaissance*, 11–12.

6. Vives, *De institutione feminae christianae*, 75.

7. Maclean, *Renaissance Notion of Woman*, 31, 35, 41. Among the hysterical illnesses, Maclean cites lovesickness, melancholia, listlessness, and irrational behavior.

On the influence of physiology in women's disorderliness, see Davis, *Society and Culture*, 124–125; Davis, *Fiction in the Archives*, 80. For a general discussion of the theory of humors, see also Owsei Temkin, *Galenism*, 17–19.

8. Erasmo, *La lengua*, 156. Excessive talkativeness was encoded in early modern times not only as a feminine transgression but also as a signifier of effeminacy. "Hombre *palabrimujer* guárdeme Dios de él," runs a popular Spanish saying (Núñez, *Refranes o proverbios en romance*, 53v). See also Parker, "On the Tongue," 447.

9. León, *La perfecta casada*, 207. Since speaking in public represented a usurpation of male authority, Pauline precepts established that women should not be allowed to teach or speak publicly: "Let a woman learn in silence, with all submissiveness. I do not allow a woman to teach or have authority over men, but to remain silent" (1 Tim. 2:11–12). This same attitude was also expressed by Saint Paul in a famous letter to the Corinthians: "Let your wives not speak in church; if they have any questions, let them ask their husbands at home" (1 Cor. 14:34–35).

10. The Christian ideals of seclusion and confinement in colonial Iberoamerica have been widely discussed in recent years. See, inter alia, Pescatello, *Power and Pawn*, 20; Lavrin, "Women in Spanish Colonial Society," 331–332; Arrom, *Women of Mexico City*, 47, 166; Franco, *Plotting Women*, xvii–xviii, 5; Gutiérrez, *When Jesus Came*, 213–214, 235. For the Iberian context, see also Perry, "With Brave Vigilance."

11. Boose, "Scolding Brides," 254. In an unpublished misogynist treatise, Sebastián de Horozco stated, for example, that "la mala mujer es habladora y parlera y desvergonzada y desonesta" ("Tratado de las mujeres buenas y malas [Gran tesoro es la buena mujer y gran pestilencia la mala]," in *El libro de los proverbios glosados*, 2:358). Laura Gowing (in *Domestic Dangers*, 61) also discusses the association of women's unrestrained speech with sexual availability.

12. Boose, "Scolding Brides," 254, 263. On the dangers posed since Genesis by the seductress and by the slandering tongues of women, see Kamenski, *Governing the Tongue*. I thank Julia Boss for bringing this work to my attention.

13. Córdoba, *Jardín de nobles donzellas*, 219.

14. Gregorio el Magno [Gregory the Great], *Los diálogos*, bk. 4, chap. 22, fol. 47; see, in English, *Dialogues*, bk. 4, chap. 18, 235. See also Sanctoro, *Prado espiritual*, bk. 4, chap. 36, fol. 14v.

15. In his commentary to Saint Gregory's story, Dominican Lucas de Santo Tomás warned his pious readers, "Esto de jurar, y maldezir, es como herencia, que passa de padres a hijos; pues si los hijos son blasfemos, y juradores, es porque oyen jurar y blasfemar a los padres" (*Excelencias del Nombre*, 34).

16. Menesses, *Tratado de juramentos*, 306–308.

17. Jesuit Juan Martínez de la Parra clearly voiced these ideas in one of his sermons

at La Profesa in Mexico City: "Peca mortalmente la mujer que deja de obedecer a su marido en cosas graves, justas, o a lo menos no injustas, si lo hace con rebeldía, con terquedad y con desprecio; si le pierde gravemente el respeto o con palabras le responde, o le dice palabras que, aunque no sean injuriosas, sabe ya que *le provocan a echar juramentos, votos y blasfemias.* ¡Oh, qué de pecados se siguen por no ser una mujer humilde y callada! Mujer, ¿quieres mandar? Pues el medio es obedecer" (Martínez de la Parra, *Luz de verdades,* quoted in Tostado Gutiérrez, *El álbum de la mujer,* 2:128–129; my italics).

18. Vives, *De institutione feminae,* 51.

19. "Gran malaventura lleva consigo el hombre que con mujer brava se casa, que no echa tanto fuego de sí el monte Etna como su volcán, como echa veneno la mujer brava por su boca.... La mujer brava es muy peligrosa porque embravece al marido, escandaliza los vecinos, malquista de los deudos y aborrecida de los criados. Lo que desto gana es ser medida a pies, y peinada a manos" (Luján, *Coloquios matrimoniales,* 79). Jesuit Alonso de Herrera calls the *mujeres bravas,* "Portraits of Hell" (*Espejo de la perfecta casada,* 44).

20. Martínez de la Parra, *Luz de verdades,* quoted in Tostado Gutiérrez, *El álbum,* 129–130.

21. Here I follow Candace West and Don H. Zimmerman's conception of gender "not as a set of traits, nor a variable, nor a role, but the product of social doings of some sort." Gender, in this sense, "is the activity of managing situated conduct in light of normative conceptions of attitudes and activities appropriate for one's sex category" ("Doing Gender," 132, 133). A similar performative approach to gender can be found in Judith Butler's classic, *Gender Trouble.*

22. A.G.N. Inq. 473.32, fols. 211–214.

23. A.G.N. Inq. 281.30, fols. 600–603v.

24. A.G.N. Inq. 368.129, fols. 490–491r.

25. A.G.N. Inq. 48.2, fols. 72–106.

26. A.G.N. Inq. 467.92, fols. 409–416. Arganda testified on October 6, 1607, that he had a conversation in Puebla with a carpenter named Antonio Hernández in which both men "trataron de que hera mala henbra Fca. del Castillo porque tenia mala lengua."

27. Davis, *Society and Culture,* 146; Pescatello, *Power and Pawn,* 141.

28. Davis, *Fiction in the Archives,* 79–81.

29. A.G.N. Inq. 48.5, fols. 164–254. See also Greenleaf, *Mexican Inquisition,* 172.

30. Stearns, "'Lord Help Me Walk Humbly,'" 51. On melancholy in the Hispanic context, see Bartra, "Melancolía y cultura," 35–64. For studies on melancholy in New Spain, see Germán Franco Toriz and Francisco Barrenechea in Bartra, *El siglo de oro.* For a discussion on the notion that women could use melancholy to gain intel-

lectual stature as particularly sensible scholars and poets, see Soufas, "The Gendered Context of Melancholy," 171–184.

31. Bancroft Library Manuscript 72/57m, box 2, file 15.

32. Interestingly, Mariana de Espinosa's localization of the heart as the source of her state of mind coincided with the increasing symbolism of the heart as the locus of interiority par excellence in the sixteenth century and even more in the seventeenth. See Le Goff, "Head or Heart?" 20.

33. Wilson, "Filcher of Good Names," 100.

34. On gossip as a key aspect in the maintenance of a group and its morality, see the classic essay by Gluckman, "Gossip and Scandal." Robert Paine criticized Gluckman's interpretation in "What Is Gossip About?" Gluckman answered in his "Psychological, Sociological, and Anthropological Explanations." For a review of the debate and a discussion of gossip from the perspective of symbolic interactionism, see Handelman, "Gossip in Encounters."

35. A.G.N. Inq. 325.1.

36. A.G.N. Inq. 18.10, fols. 116–164v.

37. A.G.N. Inq. 143.8. "Que cosa era que en un pueblo de tan pocos vezinos españoles andubiesen jurando, y atestiguando unos contra otros."

38. A.G.N. Inq. 143.8.

39. Scott, *Domination and the Arts of Resistance*, 142.

40. A.G.N. Inq. 45.1, fols. 3–46.

41. See, for instance, Steve Stern's discussion on the female "politics of gossip" in his *Secret History of Gender*, 142–147. On gossip as "information management" dictated by personal interests, see Paine, "What is Gossip About?" 280–283; Cox, "What Is Hopi Gossip About?" See also Boyer, "People, Places, and Gossip."

42. Gowing, *Domestic Dangers*, 123.

43. Norton, "Gender and Defamation," 5.

44. On *recogimientos*, see Muriel, *Los recogimientos de mujeres*; Lavrin, "In Search of the Colonial Woman," 40; Lavrin, "Women in Spanish Colonial Society," 336–337; Lavrin, "Female Religious," 189; Gonzalbo, *Las mujeres en la Nueva España*, 167–182; Van Deusen, *Between the Sacred and the Worldly*.

45. Arrom, *Women of Mexico City*, 213.

46. A.G.N. 144.2, fols. 21–44v.

47. Gonzalbo, *Las mujeres*, 168; Gonzalo Obregón, *El real colegio*, 38.

48. A.G.N. Inq. 677.6, fols. 228–271; A.G.N. Inq. 520.169, fols. 267v–268v.

49. "La que en esta casa entrare / ponga remedio en su vida / que en su mano está la entrada / y en la de Dios la salida" (quoted in Muriel, *Los recogimientos*, 99). See also Benítez, *Los demonios en el convento*, 114–116, 185–193.

50. A.G.N. Inq. 677.6, fol. 242.

51. A.G.N. Inq. 684, fols. 401–402; quoted in Muriel, *Los recogimientos*, 72.

52. Perry, "With Brave Vigilance," 3–18; see also her broader discussion on female unruliness in *Gender and Disorder.*

53. Lakoff, *Language and Woman's Place,* 61. Gregory Bateson gave this classic definition of a "double-bind" as "a situation in which no matter what a person does, [s]he 'can't win.'" This is the case when the individual simultaneously receives orders that contradict each other, such as "Do not do so and so, or I will punish you," and "If you do not do so and so, I will punish you." There are, of course, more elaborated sadistic orders that Bateson calls "secondary injunctions," such as "Do not see me as the punishing agent" and "Do not submit to my prohibitions" (*Steps to an Ecology of the Mind,* 201–227, 271–278).

54. Laura Gowing, *Domestic Dangers,* 4.

Chapter 5. "To Lose One's Soul"

1. A.G.N. Inq. 165.3.

2. The Huntington Library, HM 31131, vol. 37, pt. 1. For a detailed analysis of this case, see Villa-Flores, "Voices from a Living Hell."

3. For a discussion of the tendency of the Spanish Crown to disclaim any responsibility in the slave trade, see Pagden, *Fall of the Natural Man,* 33; Vitoria's remarks are included in his *Political Writings,* 335; Montúfar's letter is included in *Epistolario de Nueva España,* 9:55; and Albornoz elaborates his position in "De la esclavitud," 232–233. For a detailed discussion of the moral qualms and rationalizations generated by the Atlantic slave trade, see Davis, *Problem of Slavery,* esp. chap. 6.

4. Reflecting the hierarchical order in which the tribunals were embedded, they decreed sentences according to the race, social status, occupation, and even gender of the defendants. As Michael Scardaville points out in "(Hapsburg) Law and (Bourbon) Order," "judicial procedures may have been impartial, [but] the ultimate disposition of offenders often was affected by their position within the social order" (11). For the specific case of black slaves as defendants, see Dusenberry, "Discriminatory Aspects."

5. Patterson, *Slavery and Social Death,* 72.

6. Ibid., 8.

7. During the fusion of the Portuguese and Spanish Crowns (1580–1640), the importation of black slaves to America increased enormously. Between 1595 and 1640, the average annual importation was 2,880 individuals (or 132,600 for the whole period). As might be expected, the mining economies of Mexico and Peru absorbed the bulk of this increase. See Bowser, "Africans in Spanish American Colonial Society," 361. For a detailed discussion of the slave trade to the Indies during these years, based on the study of monopoly contracts granted by the Crown (known as *asientos*), see Tardieu, "Les principales structures administratives"; see also Vila Vilar, *Hispanoamérica y el comercio de esclavos.*

8. On slave resistance and racial tension during this period, see Rout, *The African Experience,* esp. 21–22 and 105; Palmer, *Slaves of the White God,* 119–144; Davison, "Negro Slave Control," 246–250; Love, "Negro Resistance to Spanish Rule," 98–99; Israel, *Race, Class and Politics,* 67–75; Vinson, *Bearing Arms for His Majesty,* 15–16; Cope, *Limits of Racial Domination,* 17–18; Laura A. Lewis, *Hall of Mirrors,* 95–96; Joan Cameron Bristol, "Negotiating Authority in New Spain." For a discussion on Yanga and Veracruz, see Naveda Chávez-Hita, *Esclavos negros,* 125–61; Corro, *Cimarrones en Veracruz;* Aguirre Beltrán, *El negro esclavo,* 179–86; Carrol, *Blacks in Colonial Veracruz,* 90–92; Bernard and Gruzinski, *Histoire du nouveau monde,* 2:247–249.

9. In contrast to the litigious reputation earned by Indians in Spanish America early in the colonial period, slaves seemed to have experienced a true "juridical wake-up" by the second half of the seventeenth century (Aguirre, "Working the System," 205). See also Aguirre, *Agentes de su propia libertad,* 184. For a discussion of Indian uses of the law, see, among others, Borah, "Spanish and Indian Law"; Stern, "Social Significance of Judicial Institutions"; Kellog, *Law and the Transformation.*

10. "Que algunos Esclavos destros ntros reynos dizen en offensa de ntro Señor y de nuestra Señora algunas de las palabras que por la dicha ntra pragmatica suso encorporada estan defendidas: y que las ntras justicias en execucion della los prenden y llevan a la carcel; y alli sus dueños les dan de comer: y ellos se estan holgando, de lo que los dueños de los dichos esclavos sin culpa suya reciben daño" (*Las pragmáticas del Reyno,* fol. 11). On blasphemy by Sevillian slaves, see Dedieu, "Le modèle religieux," 249–250. Ruth Pike discusses the characteristics of Sevillian slaves, by far the "largest slave community in Spain," in her *Aristocrats and Traders,* 170–192.

11. Kamen, *Spanish Inquisition,* 261–162.

12. A similar trend is perceived in Lima, where *bozales* were never tried for blasphemy during the period under study here (Tardieu, *L'église et les noirs,* 1:644). According to writers of the time, such as Jesuit Alonso de Sandoval, the fact that creoles and ladinos had previous contact with the religion and language of their often blasphemous masters made them less valuable among Spaniards because they were thought to offer minimal service and have *mañas* (bad habits) (Sandoval, *Un tratado sobre la esclavitud,* 239). An additional reason for preferring bozales over creole blacks and ladinos concerned the assumption that the latter "were usually much less submissive than those who had been transported from Africa" (Israel, *Race, Class,* 68).

13. For a recent discussion of blasphemy from the perspective of gender, see McKnight, "Blasphemy as Resistance," 229–253.

14. Throughout Spanish domination in Mexico, *obrajes* earned what Charles Gibson called "a sordid reputation." Within their walls "the work was hard, food and living conditions were unsatisfactory, and physical abuse was a commonplace" (Gibson,

Aztecs Under Spanish Rule, 243). See also Villa-Flores, "Voices From a Living Hell"; Proctor, "Afro-Mexican Slave Labor."

15. Carena, *Tractatus de Officio,* title 7, chap. 2, no. 8, 129; Alberghini, *Manuale Qualificatorum,* chap. 16, no. 3, 44; Soto, *De Iustitia et Iure,* bk. 8, questio 2, 753; Covarruvias Leyva, *Relectio,* chap. 7, no. 8, 52v; Suárez, *Operis de virtute,* bk. 1, chap. 6, 295. The expression "reniego de Dios" constituted by far the most common one not only in New Spain but also in Peru, Cartagena de Indias (New Granada), Brazil, and Seville. For Seville, see Dedieu, "Les disciplines du langage," 250. For Peru, see Medina, *Inquisición de Lima,* 32; Castañeda Delgado and Hernández Aparicio, *La Inquisición en Lima,* 286–287; Tardieu, *L'eglise et les noirs au Perou,* 643–660. For Cartagena de Indias, see Medina, *Inquisición de Cartagena de Indias,* 118–19; Álvarez Alonso, *La Inquisición en Cartagena,* 179–180. For Brazil, see Mello e Souza, *El diablo en la tierra de Santa Cruz,* 119 and 122.

16. Soto, *De como se a de evitar,* 82; Ávila, *Suma de los mandamientos,* 493.

17. Rafael, *Contracting Colonialism,* 96.

18. "When you were slaves of sin, you were free in regard to righteousness. . . . But now that you have been set free from sin and have become *slaves of God,* the return you get is sanctification and its end, eternal life" (Romans 6:20–22). For an insightful discussion of Paul's theology of freedom, see Patterson, *Freedom,* chap. 19. Also Combes, *Metaphor of Slavery,* chap. 2; and Harrill, *Manumission of Slaves,* chap. 1. For a discussion of slavery to Christ as a soteriological and positive image for early Christians, see also Martin, *Slavery and Salvation,* 50–65.

19. Alberro, "Negros y mulatos," 140; and Alberro, *Inquisition et societé,* 227.

20. Although after the Council of Trent the Church encouraged the identification of the Christian god with the figure of the father, it is unlikely that slaves found paternal metaphors as compelling as free men did. Indeed, often incapable of making natal claims on a father, they also usually had no economic claims to pass on to their children. Under these circumstances, fathers represented rather weak figures to slaves. Consequently, the Christian god was cast in the image of the earthly master himself, the only once capable of offering an image of power and authority. On the tendency of slaves to see the Christian God as a divine master, see Genovese, *Roll, Jordan, Roll,* 167; Palmer, "Religion and Magic," 318. On the Church's stress on the image of God as a father after the Council of Trent, see Thomas, *Religion and the Decline,* 152. See also Robert, "Porter le nom de Dieu."

21. A.G.N. Inq. 480.3, fol. 83r.

22. A.G.N. Inq. 421.1.

23. A.G.N. Inq. 48.7, fol. 273r.

24. Chrism is a mixture of olive oil and balsam used in rites such as baptisms, confirmations, ordinations, and some blessings of altars and other church fixtures.

25. A.H.M.N.A.H. Col. Antigua 366.1, fol. 11; A.G.N. Inq. 421.1.

26. A.H.M.N.A.H. Col. Antigua 366.4, fol. 231.

27. A.G.N. Inq. 421.1; Jean-Pierre Tardieu, *L'église*, 647.

28. A.G.N. Inq. 147.4.

29. A.G.N. Inq. 147.2.

30. See, for example, the accusation of Commissioner Antonio de Cervantes Carvajal against Juan de Jeréz on September 3, 1631, in Puebla (A.G.N. Inq. 375.5).

31. Guha, *Elementary Aspects of Peasant Insurgency*, 46–47.

32. See, for example, the case of Nicolás de la Cruz in 1658 (A.G.N. Inq. 572.13, fols. 187–214v).

33. This was the case of Juan de Luyba, slave of Francisca de Peralta in 1625 (A.G.N. Inq. 421.1).

34. Leach, "Anthropological Aspects of Language," 24, 45.

35. Patterson, *Slavery and Social Death*, 48.

36. "Llamamos asi a los Esclavos, como igualandolos a los perros, que son la mas vil parte de la familia; y el perro en alguna manera hace familia; aunque la mas baxa parte de ella por ser bruto e irracional" (Rosal, *La razón de algunos refranes*, 81).

37. In a recent article, Alberto Ferreira discusses the medieval and early Christian metaphorical tradition of depicting Jews, Muslims, heretics, and general unbelievers as hostile, ravenous, and wild canines to be shunned by Christians ("Simon Magus," 45–90). See also Madero, *Manos violentas*, 152. "Perro" was apparently a favorite Spanish expletive from the early days of conquest of the New World, for the Laws of Burgos (1512–1513) prohibited Spaniards from calling an Indian "dog," or "address[ing] him by any other name other than his proper name alone" (Gibson, *Spanish Tradition*, 74). In spite of increasing miscegenation, *perro* was still clearly identified as a Spanish insult in eighteenth-century New Spain. See Taylor, *Drinking, Homicide and Rebellion*, 82, 140. According to Cheryl E. Martin's analysis of popular speech in eighteenth-century Parral, Chihuahua, the word *perro* or *perra* as an insult was frequently used in disputes that ended in attacks on personal honor ("Popular Speech," 312). For recent discussions of insults and honor in colonial Latin America, see Johnson, "Dangerous Words," 132–35. See also Lipsett-Rivera, "A Slap in the Face of Honor," 182–184, 187–89, 190–191.

38. Cope, *Limits of Racial Domination*, 96.

39. A.G.N. Inq. 576.5, fol. 563.

40. A.G.N. Inq. 421.1.

41. For examples of domestic slaves who fled their homes, see the cases of Polonia (Mexico City, 1615), Magdalena (Mexico City, 1630), and Maria (Mexico City, 1658), in A.G.N. Inq. 421.1.

42. Fox-Genovese, *Within the Plantation Household*, 34.

43. A.G.N. Inq. 48.6.

44. In the opinion of prosecutor Andrés de Zabalza, Gertrudis had abused "del fin porque este santo offo. castiga a los reos en publico que es para exemplo de los que lo ven y se abstengan por el temor de la pena de cometer otros tales ni algunos otros delitos" (A.G.N. Inq. 446 [unnumbered], fol. 180v).

45. Ducrot, *Le dire,* 171–233.

46. Austin, *How To Do Things with Words.*

47. According to Aquinas, this offense signified "something less rightly done or said, that occasions another's spiritual downfall" (*Summa,* 2–2, questio 43, articulus 1, 521). See also A.G.N. Inq. 6, fols. 491v–492v, for a discussion of the crime of scandal as related to blasphemy.

48. A.G.N. Inq. 578.10, fol. 425.

49. Boyd-Bowman offers examples of such transactions in notarial records. See his "Negro Slaves," 137. See also Naveda Chávez-Hita, *Esclavos negros,* 32; Mellafe, *Negro Slavery,* 84; Aguirre Beltrán, *El negro esclavo,* 45–47.

50. A.G.N. Inq. 441.5, fols. 503–543. My estimate of the slaves' price is based on Palmer, *Slaves of the White,* 34. For a general discussion of the prices placed on black slaves in colonial Mexico, consult Brady, "The Domestic Slave Trade," 288; Boyd-Bowman, "Negro Slaves," 137, for 1540 to 1556; Bowser, "The Free Person of Color," for 1580 to 1650; Carrol, *Blacks in Colonial Veracruz,* 34–35, for 1581 to 1690, and 75–76, for 1675 to 1800; also Valdés, "The Decline of Slavery," 171–174, for 1584 to 1756.

51. A.G.N. Inq. 566.1, fols. 1–30v.

52. A.G.N. Inq. 586.6, fols. 373–410.

53. A.G.N. Inq. 452.6, fol. 98.

54. A.H.M.N.A.H. Col. Antigua 366.5, fol. 240r.

55. A.G.N. Inq. 47.1, fols. 2–42.

56. A.G.N. Inq. 514.4, fols. 12–15.

57. A.G.N. Inq. 147.2.

58. A.G.N. Inq. 375.5.

59. For examples in which domestic slaves succeeded in denouncing themselves, see the cases of Juan (Mexico, 1600), Isabel de la Cruz (Mexico City, 1625), Catalina (Puebla, 1606), Pascuala (Mexico City, 1602), Juana de los Reyes (Mexico City, 1613), in A.G.N. Inq. 471.101, fols. 343–345v; A.G.N. Inq. 421.1; A.G.N. Inq. 279.1,, fols. 1–17; A.G.N. Inq. 421.1; A.G.N. Inq. 421.1, respectively.

60. A.G.N. Inq. 279.10, fols. 114–137v.

61. A.G.N. Inq. 147.4. In a similar case, Francisco, a mulatto slave of Tomás de Baeza, secured a denunciation in 1603. While he accompanied his master through the streets of Mexico City, Francisco told a passerby that he renounced God and was not a baptized Christian (A.G.N. Inq. 271.16).

62. A.G.N. Inq. 271.18. Obstructing the Inquisition constituted a grave offense.

The "impeders of the Holy Office" were heavily fined and, in extreme cases, prosecuted as heretics. In 1635, for instance, Spaniard Francisco de la Torre was fined two thousand gold pesos for obstructing the Tribunal. See Medina, *Inquisición en México,* 194. See also Haliczer, *Inquisition and Society,* 19.

63. See the cases of Joaquín de Santa Ana (Jalapa, 1599), A.G.N. Inq. 145.7, fols. 80–132; Francisco (Mexico City, 1601), A.H.M.N.A.H. Col. Antigua 366.1, fols. 1–27; Sebastián (Mexico City, 1603), A.G.N. 271.14; Pascual Francisco (Mexico City, 1606), A.G.N. Inq. 279.10, fols. 114–137v; Pedro (Mexico City, 1607), A.H.M.N.A.H. Col. Antigua 366.2, fols. 168–190; Felipa (Mexico City, 1607), A.H.M.N.A.H. Col. Antigua 366.4, fols. 191–236; Pedro (Mexico City, 1608), A.G.N. Inq. 483.2, fols. 16–42.

64. A.G.N. Inq. 566. 1, fols. 1–30v.

65. In contrast to Jean-Pierre Tardieu's findings for Peru (*L'église et les noirs,* 656), Afro-Mexicans rarely used drunkenness as an exculpatory argument for their blasphemies. For exceptions, see the cases against Juan Sevilla (Antequera, 1560), A.G.N. Inq. 16.14, fols. 464–472; Domingo (México City, 1572), A.G.N. Inq. 46.5, fols. 23–37; and Juan García (México City, 1616), A.G.N. Inq. 421.1.

66. A.G.N. Inq. 421.1.

67. Albertino, *De Agnoscendis Assertionibus,* questio 28, no. 18, 145v; Sousa, *Aphorismi Inquisitorum,* bk. 1, chap. 19, no. 18, 53.

68. For instance, in his 1602 testimony against his slave Pedro Juárez, the priest of the Cathedral of Tlaxcala claimed before the commissary of Puebla, Bartolomé Marqués de Amarilla, that he had reproached Pedro: "Dog! What reason [did] you have to renounce God and His saints? The punishment I give you is moderate and merciful because you're a baptized Christian and you must mend yourself. . . . Treacherous traitor to God and the Holy Trinity! In the name of God and the Holy Trinity in which I believe and I adore, and as an expression of reverence to them I punish you!" (A.G.N. Inq. 452.6, fol. 94).

69. A.G.N. Inq. 446 (unnumbered), fol. 180.

70. "The slaves were tried for their crimes, while the violence which provoked them was ignored" (Davidson, "Negro Slave," 241). Colin Palmer says essentially the same thing (*Slaves of the White,* 118).

71. See, for instance, A.G.N. Inq. 147.2, vs. Domingo, Puebla, 1598; A.G.N. Inq. 48.6, vs. Joaquín de Santa Ana, Jalapa, 1599; A.H.M.N.A.H. Col. Antigua 366.1, fols. 1–27, vs. Francisco, Mexico City, 1601; A.G.N. Inq. 269.1, vs. Juan (Jhoan), Puebla, 1603.

72. See, for instance, the case of Isabel de Córdova (San Juan de Ulúa, Veracruz, 1606), A.G.N. Inq. 279.5, fols. 39–44v.

73. Medina, *Inquisición en México,* 62, 121, 166, 169, 172, 174, 194, 297, 303; also Cañeque, "Theater of Power," 332–333.

74. For cases in which slaves were sentenced to prison, see Juan Criollo (Mexico

City, 1596), sentenced for 6 months, A.G.N. Inq. 161.5 (unfoliated); Juan Montes (Mexico City, 1596), 6 months, A.G.N. Inq. 145.10, fols. 168–205v; Domingo (Puebla, 1598), 6 months, A.G.N. Inq. 147.2 (unfoliated); Baltazar de los Reyes (Puebla, 1603), 4 months, A.G.N. Inq. 271.18 (unfoliated); Ambrosio (Mexico City, 1603), one year, A.G.N. Inq. 271.17 (unfoliated); Pascual Francisco (Mexico City, 1606), 6 months, A.G.N. Inq. 279.10, fols. 114–137v; Pedro (Mexico City, 1608), 4 months, A.G.N. Inq. 483.2, fols. 16–42; María de la Cruz (Mexico City, 1658), 6 years, A.G.N. Inq. 576.5, fols. 518–570. On *obrajes* as prisons, see Kagan, "The Labor of Prisoners"; Kagan, "Penal Servitude in New Spain," 73–84; also Aguirre Beltrán, "La esclavitud en los obrajes." In Peru, bakeries played a similar role since colonial times, see Hünefeldt, *Paying the Price*, 187–194. See also Aguirre, "Violencia, castigo y control social."

75. Some cases never concluded because the defendant died, possibly as a result of mistreatment in the master's house. For examples, see the cases of Tomás (Thomas) de Contreras (Mexico City, 1572) and Antón de Cartagena (Tlalnepantla, 1598) in, respectively, A.G.N. Inq. 47.1, fols. 2–41; and A.G.N. Inq. 147.4.

76. For examples, consult the cases of Juana (Mexico City, 1629), María (Mexico City, 1630), and Gabriel (Mexico City, 1629), in A.G.N. Inq. 421.1. See also the case of Marcos Bautista (Coyoacán, 1656), in A.G.N. Inq. 566.1.

77. A.G.N. Inq. 502 (unnumbered), fol. 385, quoted in Alberro, "Negros y mulatos," 160.

78. For several instances in which a milder punishment was ordered, see A.G.N. Inq. 421.1.

79. Mexico purchased almost half of all Africans sent to the Americas between 1595 and 1622 (the capital alone had more than 10,000 slaves and 3,500 black freemen, mulattoes, and mestizos). However, Mexico began importing fewer slaves in the 1630s. By the 1670s, the trade had virtually come to a halt in important centers of slave acquisition, such as Jalapa. This trend reflected the general withdrawal of New Spain from participation in the Atlantic slave trade after the dissolution of the Spanish-Portuguese union in 1640 and the consequent declining supply of Africans. As a result of these changes, whites came to outnumber blacks in Mexico after the 1650s. For an estimate of the population of Mexico at the end of the sixteenth century, see Baudot, "La population des villes." For discussions of the decline in the importation of slaves to New Spain, see Carrol, *Blacks in Colonial Veracruz*, 31, 145, 146; Bermúdez Gorrochotegui, *Historia de Jalapa*, 317–319; Aguirre Beltrán, *La población negra*, 265–275; Martin, *Rural Society*, chap. 6; Vila Vilar, *Hispanoamérica y el comercio*, 207; Palmer, *Slaves of the White God*, 6. An important exception to the generalized decrease in slave importation was Córdoba, which augmented its acquisition of Africans at the end of the seventeenth century, see Naveda Chávez-Hita, *Esclavos negros*, 35–37. See also Naveda Chávez-Hita, "Trabajadores esclavos," 163.

80. Palmer, *Slaves of the White God*, 88; Alberro, "Negros y mulatos," 159. On

the Suprema's pattern of greater leniency in relation to the provinces, see Haliczer, *Inquisition and Society*, 90–91.

81. According to Palmer, New Spain had two main methods of offering judicial protection to the slave. The first was preventive and involved unannounced, sporadic visits to workshops and mills to note if the workforce, consisting largely of slaves, was suffering abuse. The second was punitive and was triggered when witnesses or the slaves themselves denounced a slaveholder for mistreatment before the Holy Office or the Audiencia. Unfortunately, protection cases were rare throughout the colonial period. In this context, Afro-Mexicans could secure the intervention of the Holy Office only through criminal deeds, such as blasphemy. See Palmer, *Slaves of the White God*, 90–92. See also Davidson, "Negro Slave," 240–241.

82. Orlando Patterson, *Slavery and Social Death*, 202. Changing of masters was a triumph for slaves, but a small one. As Douglas Cope asserts, "A slave's welfare depended in large part on establishing a rapport with his master," which could reduce the coercive element in social control and translate into "a movement along the spectrum toward paternalism and clientage." See Cope, *Limits of Racial Domination*, 96. For examples of slaves who changed masters, see the cases of Juan (Puebla, 1603), Nicolás de la Cruz (Mexico City, 1658), and Salvador (Mexico City, 1707). In these three instances, the masters were ordered to sell them. See, respectively, A.G.N. Inq. 269.1; A.G.N. Inq. 572.13, fols. 187r–214v; A.G.N. Inq. 544.19, fols. 375–387v.

83. A.G.N. Inq. 253 (unnumbered), fol. 270.

84. A.G.N. Inq. 253, fol. 273.

85. A.G.N. Inq. 502.385, quoted in Solange Alberro, "Negros y mulatos," 158.

86. A.G.N. Inq. 374.4, fol. 40r.

87. Quoted in Alberro, "Negros y mulatos," 159.

88. Even Spaniards took advantage of this tradition of judicial centralism. Knowing they could not be tried in the Philippines, Spanish soldiers who wanted to avoid serving there blasphemed in the hope of being transfered to Mexico (Medina, *Inquisición en las islas Filipinas*, 63).

89. A.G.N. Inq. 666.6, fols. 417–442v.

90. Like its counterpart in Spain, the activity of the Mexican Holy Office was restricted mostly to the capital city and surrounding areas. Elsewhere, the degree of social control it could enforce seems to have been negligible. On the other hand, slaves in urban areas apparently had a higher rate of survival not only in Mexico but also in Iberian America in general (Thornton, *Africa and Africans*, 180). For a rich portrait of the working and living conditions in mines and sugar mills, see Alberro, "Juan de Morga y Gertrudis de Escobar."

91. Bloch, "How and Why Ancient Slavery," 14.

92. I draw here on Roseberry's "Hegemony and the Language of Contention," 355–366.

93. Bennet, *Africans in Colonial Mexico,* 181.

94. Genovese, *Roll, Jordan, Roll,* 125.

95. Scott, *Domination and the Arts of Resistance,* xii. Scott discusses the concept of "blind fury" on page 217.

Chapter 6. Conclusion

1. Soto, *De como se a de evitar,* 207.

2. Febvre, *The Problem of Unbelief,* 335–353.

3. Christin, "Sur la condamnation du blasphème," 45–48.

4. I draw here from Judith Butler's analysis of hate speech in her *Excitable Speech,* 14.

5. Voloshinov, *Marxism and the Philosophy of Language,* 115.

6. See, for instance, Machado de Chaves, *Perfecto confessor,* Doc. 2.2, 199.

7. The sixteenth-century canonist Francisco Peña had already raised this issue in his influential commentary to the widely used inquisitorial manual by Nicolau Eimeric. "Is there anything that wicked men cannot pervert?" he reasoned. "There's no doubt that teaching and terrifying people with the proclamation of sentences, the imposition of *sanbenitos,* and so forth, is a good action" (Eimeric and Peña, *El manual de los inquisidores,* 199).

8. Freud, "Totem and Taboo," 874; Douglas, "Sacred Contagion," 93.

9. Aquinas, *Summa Theologica,* 2–2, questio 43, articulus 1, 521.

10. Butler, *Excitable Speech,* 27.

11. Ibid., 34.

12. Haliczer, *Inquisition and Society,* 74–75.

13. Eimeric and Peña, *Manual de los inquisidores,* 168.

14. Labov, *Language in the Inner City,* 297–353.

15. Delumeau, *Catholicisme entre Luther et Voltaire,* 240–241; Watts, *A Social History of Western Europe,* 166.

16. On incantations and magic in New Spain, see, inter alia, Campos Moreno, *Oraciones, ensalmos y conjuros.* On Freud's "omnipotence of thought," see *Totem and Taboo,* 874.

17. Malinowski, *Coral Gardens and Their Magic,* 2:239.

18. Among the most recent literature on this momentous change, especially in Mexico City, see Viqueira Albán, *Propriety and Permissiveness;* Voekel, *Alone before God,* especially chap. 2; and her article "Peeing in the Palace," 183, 192; Curcio-Nagy, *Great Festivals of Colonial Mexico,* 107–117; Larkin, "Liturgy, Devotion and Reform," 509, 515.

19. Voekel, "Peeing in the Palace," 187–188.

20. Medina, *Inquisición en México,* 291–292.

21. Castañeda Delgado and Hernández Aparicio, *La Inquisición de Lima*, 1:285–286.

22. Medina, *La Inquisición en Cartagena de Indias*, 181–192.

23. Escamilla-Colin, *Crimes et châtiments*, 2:215–230. For the specific case of the tribunal of Toledo, see Dedieu, "Le modèle religieux," 238–239. For the analysis of a similar trend in the tribunals of Cordoba and Mallorca, see Guillemont, *Recherches sur la violence verbale*, 2:287–293.

24. Eliot, *After Strange Gods*, 56–57.

25. Viswanathan, "Blasphemy and Heresy," 408, 412.

26. See also Wooton, "The Fear of God."

27. Benveniste, "Le blasphème et l'euphémie," 72.

Glossary

a campo raso. To face someone in the open.

abogado. An attorney for the defendant before the Inquisition tribunal.

albur. A popular card game in which players bet that their chosen card will be drawn from the deck before those of their opponents.

alcalde. A community official, member of the *cabildo*.

alcalde mayor. The district governor, who was appointed by the Crown and exercised administrative and judicial functions; also, *corregidor*.

alguacil. A constable.

alguacil mayor. A governor's constable.

amancebada. An unmarried woman in consensual union.

arriero. A muleteer.

audiencia. The colonial high court, consisting of a president and judges; also, a court of appeal located in a major city.

ayuntamiento. A town council.

baraja. A deck of cards.

beaterio. A community of *beatas* (lay holy women).

bozal. A non-acculturated African slave.

bujarrón. A sodomite (derogatory term).

cabildo. The annually elected town council; same as the *ayuntamiento*.

cabrón. Literally, a goat; asshole.

calificador. An Inquisition counselor or theological consultant.

castellano. A commander (in charge of fortress of San Juan de Ulúa).

castellanos. A Spanish coin equivalent to approximately 490 *maravedís*.

cofradía. A confraternity.

comisario. A local-level representative of the Inquisition.

contramaestre. A shipmaster's assistant; a petty officer.

converso. A Jew who publicly recants his faith and adopts Christianity.

coroza. A cone-shaped hat worn by sinners as a sign of penance.

coyma. A commission collected from gamblers by *coymes*.

coyme. The owner of a gambling establishment or of a house where gambling takes place.

de levi. The Inquisition's sentence for minor offenses.

de vehementi. The Inquisition's sentence for grievous offenses.

depositada. Literally, "deposited"; a woman placed in the trust of an institution (often a *recogimiento*) or of a respected member of the community.

descreo de Dios. Literally, "I don't believe in God!"; connotes a lack of trust in God (a common blasphemy).

deslenguado, –a. Literally, loose-tongued; foulmouthed.

disonancia. Literally, discord, dissonance; euphemism for a blasphemous utterance.

disparate. Literally, to talk nonsense or make an atrocious remark; a euphemism for a blasphemous utterance.

ducat. A Spanish coin equivalent to approximately 375 *maravedís*.

encomienda. A grant of Indians as tribute payers or a labor force.

encomendero. The holder of an *encomienda*.

entradas. Military campaigns.

envite. Literally, the ante.

estanco de naipes. A playing-card monopoly.

eutrapelia. An honest recreation (Latin).

familiar. A member of the Inquisition police.

fiscal. An Inquisition prosecutor.

gente de razón. Civilized and educated people (the Spanish colonists used the term to distinguish themselves from indigenous peoples).

gente principal. Members of the elite.

impertinencias. Unidentified sinful utterances; a euphemism for blasphemies.

judaizante. A Judaizer (one who adopts Jewish customs or beliefs).

juegos prohibidos. Forbidden games.

juramento. Literally, oath; see *voto a dios*.

ladino. An acculturated African slave.

la honra de Dios. The honor of God.

lombardero. A gunner.

mala vida. Literally, "bad life"; the chronic abuse of a woman by her husband or a male relative.

maestre. A shipmaster.

mala hembra. Literally, a bad female; a bad or evil woman.

maravedí. A Spanish coin; the basic unit of currency.

mestizo. A person of mixed Spanish and Indian ancestry.

morbo de vivir. Literally, "illness of living"; an evil life.

mujer brava. A truculent woman.

mujer temeraria y juradora. Literally, a rash and blaspheming woman; a woman fond of uttering oaths.

nao capitana. A flagship.

Noche Triste. A major defeat inflicted by the Aztecs on the Spaniards on June 30, 1520.

obraje. A primitive factory, dependent on forced labor or a combination of forced and free labor, producing textiles or processing agricultural products.

palabras escandalosas. Scandalous words; a euphemism for blasphemies.

palabras nefandas. Heinous words; a euphemism for blasphemous speech.

pendejos. Literally, pubic hair; also carries the connotation of "idiots" or "assholes."

pese a Dios. Literally, "may God regret it!"; connotes "God be damned!" (a common blasphemy).

pese a tal. Literally, "may so-and-so regret it!"; a euphemism for *pese a Dios*.

peso. A gold coin of the Spanish colonies, equivalent to 8 *reales* of silver or approximately 450 *maravedís*.

por vida de Dios. Literally, "by God's life!" (a common blasphemy).

por vida de tal. Literally, "by the life of so-and-so"; a euphemism for *por vida de Dios*.

prepósita. A rector of a women's shelter.

provisor. An ecclesiastical judge.

puta. A whore.

putería. A whorehouse.

real. A Spanish coin equivalent to approximately 34 *maravedís*.

recogimiento. A shelter (usually for women).

reniego [de Dios]. Literally, an act of renouncing or abjuring God.

repartimiento. A labor system; a form of forced-labor draft imposed on tributary Indians.

república. An administrative and fiscal order under the Crown.

ruin costumbre. A despicable habit or practice.

señor de recua. The master of a mule train.

soltera. An unmarried woman who was not a virgin.

tablajería. A gambling house.

translatio imperii. The transfer of rule or political power from one empire or civilization to another; also, the replacement of one empire by another.

trato o conversación. Human dealings or interactions.

valentón jurador. A bullying blasphemer.

venta. An inn.

visita de navíos. An inspection of ships.

voto a Dios. Literally, "I swear to God!"; connotes "God be damned" (a common blasphemy).

References

Archives and Libraries

Archivo del Arzobispado de México, Mexico City
Archivo General de Indias, Madrid, Spain
    Indiferente General
Archivo General de la Nación, Mexico City
    Ramo Inquisición (Inquisition Division)
Archivo Histórico de Madrid, Madrid, Spain
    Inquisition
Bancroft Library, Berkeley, California
    Mexican Manuscripts (Mexican Inquisition Documents)
Biblioteca Nacional de Madrid, Madrid, Spain
    Sala Manuscritos
Biblioteca Nacional de México, Mexico City
    Cronológico Mexicano
    Fondo Reservado
    Fondo Franciscano
Huntington Library, San Marino, California
    Mexican Inquisition Papers
Instituto Nacional de Antropología e Historia library, Museo de Antro-
    pología, Mexico City
    Colección Antigua
John Carter Brown Library, Providence, Rhode Island
    Spanish Codex Collection
Newberry Library, Chicago, Illinois
    Ayer Collection
    Bonaparte Collection
    Case Collection
Rockefeller Library, Brown University, Providence, Rhode Island
    Medina Collection (microfilm)

Published Primary Sources

Acosta, José de. *Historia natural y moral de las indias.* Ed. Edmundo O'Gorman. Mexico City: Fondo de Cultura Económica, 1962.

Aguilar, Francisco de. "Relación breve de la conquista de la Nueva España." In *La conquista de Tenochtitlan,* ed. Germán Vázquez, 157–206. Madrid: Historia 16, 1988.

Alberghini, Juan. *Manuale Qualificatorum Sanctae Inquisitionis.* Zaragoza: Agustín Vargas, 1671.

Albertino, Arnaldo. *De Agnoscendis Assertionibus Catholicis et Haereticis Tractatus.* Rome: In Aedibus Populi Romani, 1572.

Albornoz, Bartolomé de. "De la esclavitud." In *Biblioteca de autores españoles,* 65:232–233. Madrid: Real Academia Española, 1873.

Alboroto y motín de México el 8 de junio de 1692: Relación de Carlos Sigüenza y Góngora en una carta dirigida al almirante don Andrés de Pez. Ed. Irving A. Leonard. Mexico City: Museo Nacional de Arqueología, Historia y Etnografía, 1932.

Alcocer, Francisco de. *Tratado del juego.* Salamanca: Andrea de Portonariis, 1559.

Alloza, Ioann. *Flores summarum.* Liege, Belgium: Impensis Ioannis de Acosta, 1665.

Aquinas, Thomas. *The Summa Theologica.* 2d rev. ed. Trans. Fathers of the English Dominican Province. 22 vols. London: Burns, Oates and Washbourne, 1912–36.

Aretino, Pietro. *Le carte parlanti.* Palermo: Sellerio, 1992 [1543].

Avila, Juan de. *Obras.* Madrid: Pedro Madrigal, 1588.

Avila, Nicolás de. *Suma de los mandamientos, y maremágnum del segundo, que enseña para el confesionario y persuade para el púlpito.* Alcalá, Spain: Juan Gracian, 1610.

Azpilcueta, Martín de. *Manual de confesores y penitentes.* Salamanca: Andrea de Portonariis, 1556.

Benavente, Toribio de. "Carta al emperador Carlos V." In *Historia de los indios de la Nueva España.* Mexico City: Salvador Chávez Hayhoe, 1941.

Borja, Juan. *Empresas morales.* Brussels: Francisco Feppen, 1680.

Cano, Melchor. *Tratado de la victoria de sí mismo.* Madrid: Imprenta de A. Ramírez, 1780.

Cardano, Gerolamo. *Liber de Ludo Aleae.* Trans. Sydney Henry Gould. Notes by Øysten Ore. In *Cardano, the Gambling Scholar,* by Øystein Ore. Princeton, NJ: Princeton University Press, 1953.

Cárdenas, Juan de. *Primera parte de los problemas y secretos maravillosos de las Indias.* Ed. Xavier Lozoya. Mexico City: Academia Nacional de Medicina, 1980 [Mexico City, 1591].

Carena, Cesare. *Tractatus de Officio Sanctissimae Inquisitionis*. Leiden: Sumpti-bus Laurentii Anisson, 1669.

Caro, Rodrigo. *Días geniales o lúdicos*. 2 vols. Ed. Jean-Pierre Etienvre. Madrid: Espasa-Calpe, 1978.

Castro, Alfonso de. *De Iusta Hereticorum Punitione*. Venice: ad signum Spei, 1549.

Cervantes de Salazar, Francisco. *Crónica de la Nueva España*. 2 vols. Ed. Agustin Millares Carlo. Madrid: Atlas, 1971.

Checa, Jorge, ed. *Barroco esencial*. Madrid: Taurus, 1992.

Ciruelo, Pedro. *Tratado de las supersticiones*. Facsimile of 1628 edition. Mexico City: Universidad Autónoma de Puebla, 1986.

Los códigos españoles concordados y anotados. Vol. 6. Madrid: Imprenta de la Publicidad, 1849.

Colección de documentos inéditos relativos al descubrimiento, conquista y organización de las antiguas posesiones de ultramar. 25 vols. Madrid: Sucesores de Rivadeneyra, 1885–1932.

Colección de documentos inéditos relativos al descubrimiento, conquista y organización de las antiguas posesiones españolas de América y Oceanía. 42 vols. Madrid: Imprenta Española, 1864–84.

Cortés, Hernán. *Letters from Mexico*. Trans. and ed. Anthony Pagden, with an introduction by J. H. Elliott. New Haven, CT: Yale University Press, 1986.

Covarrubias, Pedro de. *Remedio de jugadores*. Salamanca: Juan de Junta, 1543.

Covarrubias y Orozco, Sebastián. *Emblemas morales*. Madrid: Luis Sánchez, 1610.

Covarruvias Leyva, Didacus. *Relectio: De Pactis*. Salamanca, Spain: Excudebat Andreas a Portonariis, 1557.

Dalcobia Cotrim, Luis. *Primera parte del symbolo de la vida cristiana*. Mexico City: Juan Ruiz, 1646.

Danae, Lambert. *Brieue remonstrance sure les jeux de sort, ou de hasard: Et principalement de dez et de cartes, en la quelle le premier inueteur desdits jeux, et maux infinis qui en adviennent, sont declarez*. Geneva: Jacques Bourgeois, 1574.

Díaz del Castillo, Bernal. *Historia verdadera de la conquista de la Nueva España*. 3d ed. 2 vols. Ed. Miguel León-Portilla. Madrid: Historia 16, 1985.

Documentos cortesianos. Ed. José Luis Martínez. 2 vols. Mexico City: Universidad Nacional Autónoma de México and the Fondo de Cultura Económica, 1990–91.

Documentos lingüísticos de la Nueva España: Altiplano central. Ed. Concepción Company. Mexico City: Universidad Nacional Autónoma de México, 1994.

Drexelius, Jeremias. *Orbis Phaëton, hoc est, De vniversis vitiis linguae*. Apud Cornel [Cologne]: Ab Egmond, 1631.

Eimeric, Nicolau, and Francisco Peña. *El manual de los inquisidores.* Trans. Francisco Martín. Barcelona: Muchnik, 1996.

Epistolario de la Nueva España (1505–1518). Ed. Francisco del Paso y Troncoso. 16 vols. Mexico City: José Porrúa e Hijos, 1939.

Erasmo, Desiderio. *La lengua de Erasmo nuevamente romançada por muy elegante estilo.* Trans. Bernardo Pérez de Chinchón. Ed. Dorothy S. Severin. Madrid: Real Academia Española, 1975 [1533].

Ezcaray, Antonio de. *Vozes del dolor.* Seville: Thomas López de Haro, 1691.

Faya de Saona, Alexandro. *Suma de exemplos de virtudes y vicios.* Pt. 2. Lisbon: Giraldo Pérez de la Viña, 1633.

Fernández de Oviedo, Gonzalo. *Historia general y natural de las indias.* B.A.E. Ed. Juan Pérez de Tudela Bueso. 5 vols. Madrid: Ediciones Atlas, 1969.

Fiol, Ignacio. *Razones para convencer al pecador para que salga del pecado y se ponga en gracia de Dios.* Mexico City: Joseph Bernardo de Hogal, 1732 [1683].

Fonseca, Cristóbal. *Segunda parte del tratado del amor de dios.* Valencia, Spain: Juan Chrysostomo Garriz, 1608.

Gage, Thomas. *Nuevo reconocimiento de las islas occidentales.* Mexico City: Secretaría de Educación Pública/Fondo de Cultura Económica, 1982.

"Gobernación espiritual y temporal de las Indias." In *Colección de documentos inéditos . . . de ultramar,* vol. 21. Madrid: Imprenta de Archivos, 1928.

Gregory the Great. *Los diálogos del bienaventurado San Gregorio papa traducidos del latin en la lengua castellana de nuevo corregidos y enmendados.* Seville, 1532.

———. *The Dialogues of St. Gregory the Great.* Ed. Henry James Coleridge. London, 1874.

Guevara, Antonio de. "De muchos trabajos que se pasan en las galeras [1539]." In *Pasajeros de indias: Viajes trasatlánticos en el siglo xvi,* ed. José Luis Martínez, 231–251. Mexico City: Fondo de Cultura Económica, 1999.

Herrera, Alonso de. *Espejo de la perfecta casada.* Granada: Blas Martinez, 1636.

Horozco, Sebastián de. *El libro de los proverbios glosados.* Vol. 1. Ed. Jack Weiner. Kassel, Germany: Reicherberger, 1994.

———. "Tratado de las mujeres buenas y malas [Gran tesoro es la buena mujer y gran pestilencia la mala]." In *El libro de los proverbios glosados* (ca. 1570–1573), ed. Jack Weiner, 2:348–361. Kassel, Germany: Reichenberger, 1994.

Instrucciones y Memorias de los virreyes novohispanos. Vol. 1. Ed. Ernesto de la Torre Villar. Mexico City: Miguel Ángel Porrúa, 1991.

Instrucción para la visita de los navíos en los puertos de Nueva España. Madrid? 1618?

Las Casas, Bartolomé de. *The Devastation of the Indies: A Brief Account.* Trans. Herma Briffault. Baltimore: Johns Hopkins University Press, 1992.

———. *Historia de las Indias*. Ed. Andrés Saint-Lu. 3 vols. Madrid: Biblioteca Ayacucho, 1986.

———. *Obras completas*. Ed. Vidal Abril Castelló et al. Madrid: Alianza Editorial, 1992.

———. *Del único modo de atraer a todos los pueblos a la verdadera religión*. Ed. Agustín Millares Carlo. Mexico City: Fondo de Cultura Económica, 1942.

León, Fray Luis de. *La perfecta casada*. Trans. and ed. John A. Jones and Javier San José Lera. Lewiston, NY: Edwin Mellen Press, 1999.

López, Diego. *Declaración magistral sobre los emblemas de Andrés Alciato*. Najera: Juan de Mongaston, 1615.

López de Gómara, Francisco. *La conquista de México*. Ed. José Luis de Rojas. Madrid: Historia 16, 1986.

———. *Hispania Victrix*. 2 vols. Biblioteca de Autores Españoles. Madrid: Ediciones Atlas, 1946.

Lorenzana, Francisco Antonio de. *Concilios provinciales primero, y segundo, celebrados, en la muy noble, y muy leal ciudad de México*. Mexico City, 1769.

Luján, Pedro de. *Coloquios matrimoniales*. Ed. Asunción Rallo Gruss. Madrid: Anejos del Boletin de la Real Academia Española, 1990.

Luque Fajardo, Francisco. *Fiel desengaño contra la ociosidad y los juegos*. Madrid: Miguel Serrano de Vargas, 1603.

Machado de Cháves, Juan. *Perfecto Confessor, y cura de almas*. Madrid: Viuda de Francisco Martínez, 1692.

Martínez de la Parra, Juan. *Luz de verdades catholicas*. Madrid: Diego Fernández de León, 1692.

Mendieta, Gerónimo de. *Historia Eclesiástica Indiana*. Ed. Joaquín García Icazbalceta. 4 vols. Mexico City: Editorial Salvador Chávez Hayhoe, 1945.

Menesses, Felipe. *Tratado de juramentos*. In *Institución de Fray Domingo de Soto de la orden de Santo Domingo a loor del nombre de Dios, de cómo se a de evitar el abuso de juramentos*, by Domingo de Soto. Antwerp: En casa de la viuda y herederos de Juan Stelfio, 1569.

Núñez, Hernán. *Refranes o proverbios en romance, que coligió, y glosó el comendador Hernán Núñez professor de Retórica y Griego, en la Universidad de Salamanca*. Madrid: Juan de la Cuesta, 1619.

Ordenanças reales para la casa de la Contractacion de Sevilla, y para otras cosas de las Indias. Madrid: En casa de Francisco Sanchez, 1585.

Palafox y Mendoza, Juan de. *Luz a los vivos y escarmiento en los muertos*. Madrid: María de Quiñones, 1661.

Las pragmáticas del Reyno. Valladolid: Juan de Villaquiron, 1540.

Proceso Inquisitorial del cacique de Texcoco Don Carlos Ometochtzin. Ed. Luis González Obregón. Mexico City: Biblioteca Enciclopédica del Estado de México, 1980.

Procesos de indios idólatras y hechiceros. Ed. Luis Gonzalez Obregón. Mexico City: Guerrero Hnos., 1912.

Quiroga, Vasco de. *La utopía en América.* Ed. Paz Serrano Gassent. Madrid: Historia 16, 1992.

Recopilación de leyes de los reynos de las Indias. 4 vols. Facsimile of 1681 original edition. Madrid: Ediciones Cultura Hispánica, 1979.

Remigio Noydens, Benito. *La practica de exorcistas y ministros de la Iglesia, en que con mucha erudición y singular claridad se trata de la instrucción de los exorcistas para lanzar y ahuyentar los demonios y curar espiritualmente todo genero de maleficios y hechizos.* Madrid: Andrés García de la Iglesia, 1678.

Rodríguez, Juan. *Relacion del espantable terremoto que agora nueuamente ha acontescido en las Yndias en vna ciudad llamada Guatimala* [Valladolid: Juan de Villaquiran (?), c. 1542]. Boston: Massachusetts Historical Society, 1940.

Rosal, Francisco del. *La razón de algunos refranes.* Ed. B. Russell Thomson. London: Tamesis Books, 1975.

Saavedra Fajardo, Diego de. *Idea de un príncipe político cristiano.* Monaco [Munich]: en la imprenta de Nicolao Enrico, 1640.

Salazar, Juan de. *Veinte discursos sobre el credo en declaración de nuestra Sancta Fe Catholica.* Alcalá de Henares, Spain: Juan Gracián, 1591.

Sanctarelli, Antonio. *De Haeresi, schismate, Apostasia, sollicitatione in sacramento poenitantie, et de potestate romani pontificis in his delictis puniendis.* Rome: Apud Haeredem Bartholomaei Zannetti, 1625.

Sanctoro, Juan Basilio. *Prado espiritual.* Lisbon: Pedro Casbeeck, 1607 [Zaragoza, 1578].

Sandoval, Alonso de. *Un tratado sobre la esclavitud, 1627.* Trans. Enriqueta Vila Vilar. Madrid: Alianza Editorial, 1987.

Santo Tomás, Lucas de. *Excelencias del Nombre de Jesús y su cofradía contra juradores, blasfemos y maldicientes.* Madrid: Diego Martínez Abad, 1697.

Scarlatini, Ottavio. *Homo et eius partes figuratus.* Augustae Vindelicorum et Dilingae [Augsburg]: Sumptibus Joannis Caspari Bencard, 1680.

Señeri [Segneri], Pablo. *El confesor instruido.* Mexico City: Juan Joseph Guillena Carrascoso, 1695.

Las Siete Partidas del Rey Don Alfonso el Sabio. 3 vols. Madrid: Imprenta Real, 1807.

Soto, Domingo de. "Controversia con el doctor Sepúlveda acerca de los indios." In *Obras escogidas de filósofos.* Biblioteca de Autores Españoles, vol. 65. Madrid: Sucesores de Hernando, 1913.

———. *Institución de Fray Domingo de Soto de la orden de Santo Domingo a loor del nombre de Dios, de cómo se a de evitar el abuso de juramentos.* Antwerp: En casa de la viuda y herederos de Juan Stelfio, 1569.

———. *De Iustitia et Iure*. Madrid: Instituto de Estudios Políticos, 1968 [1556].

Sousa, Antonio de. *Aphorismi Inquisitorum in Quatuor Libros Distributi*. Leiden: Apud Petrum Craesbeeck, 1630.

Suárez, Francisco de. *Operis de virtute et statu religionis tomus primus*. Lugduni: Sumptibus Horatii Cardon, 1613.

Tapia, Andrés de. "Relación de algunas cosas de las que acaecieron al muy ilustre señor Don Hernando Cortés, Marqués del Valle, desde que se determinó ir a descubrir tierra en la tierra firme del mar océano." In *La conquista de Tenochtitlan*, ed. Germán Vázquez, 59–123. Madrid: Historia 16, 1988.

Tertullian. *De idolatria*. Translation and commentary by J. H. Waszink and J.C.H. Van Winden. Leiden and New York: E. J. Brill, 1987.

Tomás de Mercado. *Summa de tratos y contratos*. Seville: Hernando Diaz impressor de libros, 1571.

Torquemada, Juan de. *Monarquía indiana*. 3 vols. Seville: Matthias Clavijo, 1615.

Tostado Gutiérrez, Marcela. *El álbum de la mujer: Antología ilustrada de las mexicanas*. Vol. 2. Mexico City: Instituto Nacional de Antropología e Historia, 1991.

Vasco de Quiroga. *La utopía en América*. Ed. Paz Serrano Gassent. Madrid: Historia 16, 1992.

Victoria, Diego de. *Regla de la Sancta Cofradía del Sagrado Nombre de Dios contra la dañada costumbre de jurar, con un tratado o declaración de ella*. Medina del Campo, Spain: Millis, 1588.

Vitoria, Francisco de. *Political Writings*. Ed. Anthony Pagden and Jeremy Lawrence. Cambridge: Cambridge University Press, 1991.

Vives, Juan Luis. *De institutione feminae christianae*. Trans. C. Fantazzi. Ed. C. Fantazzi and C. Matheeussen. Leiden: Brill, 1998.

———. "Introducción a la sabiduría." In *Biblioteca de Autores Españoles*, vol. 65. Madrid: Imprenta de los sucesores de Hernando, 1913.

———. *Obras completas*. Vol. 2. Trans. Lorenzo Riber. Madrid: Aguilar, 1948.

Secondary Sources

Aguirre, Carlos. *Agentes de su propia libertad: Los esclavos de Lima y la desintegración de la esclavitud, 1821–1854*. Lima: Pontificia Universidad Católica de Perú, 1993.

———. "Violencia, castigo y control social: Esclavos y panaderías en Lima, siglo XIX." *Pasado y Presente* (Lima) 1 (1988): 27–37.

———. "Working the System: Black Slaves and the Courts in Lima, Peru, 1821–1854." In *Crossing Boundaries: Comparative History of Black People in Diaspora*, ed. Darlene Clark Hine and Jacqueline McLeod, 202–222. Bloomington and Indianapolis: Indiana University Press, 1999.

Aguirre Beltrán, Gonzalo. "La esclavitud en los obrajes novoespañoles." In *La heterodoxia recuperada: En torno a Angel Palerm*, ed. Susana Glantz, 249–262. Mexico City: Fondo de Cultura Económica, 1987.

———. *El negro esclavo en Nueva España: La formación colonial, la medicina popular, y otros ensayos*. Mexico City: Fondo de Cultura Económica, 1994.

———. *La población negra de México: Estudio ethnohistórico*, 3d ed. Mexico City: Fondo de Cultura Económica, 1989.

Aguirre Zamorano, Pilar. *La Audiencia de México según los visitadores: Siglos XVI y XVII*. Mexico City: Universidad Nacional Autónoma de México, 1985.

Aiton, Arthur Scott. *Antonio de Mendoza: First Viceroy of New Spain*. Durham, NC: Duke University Press, 1927.

Alberro, Solange. *La actividad del santo oficio de la inquisición en Nueva España, 1571–1700*. Mexico City: Instituto Nacional de Antropología e Historia, 1981.

———. "El discurso inquisitorial sobre los delitos de bigamia, poligamia, y solicitación." In *Seis ensayos sobre el discurso colonial relativo a la comunidad doméstica*, ed. Solange Alberro, 215–226. Mexico City: Departamento de Investigaciones Históricas–Instituto Nacional de Antropología e Historia, 1980.

———. "Herejes, brujas y beatas: Mujeres ante el Tribunal del Santo Oficio de la Inquisición en la Nueva España." In *Presencia y transparencia: La mujer en la historia de México*, ed. Carmen Ramos, 79–94. Mexico City: El Colegio de México, 1987.

———. *Inquisition et societé au Mexique, 1571–1700*. Mexico City: Centre d'études mexicaines et centroamericaines, 1988.

———. "Juan de Morga y Gertrudis de Escobar: Esclavos rebeldes (Nueva España, siglo XVII)." In *Lucha por la supervivencia en la América colonial*, ed. David G. Sweet and Gary B. Nash, trans. David Huerta y Juan José Utrilla, 198–214. Mexico City: Fondo de Cultura Económica, 1987.

———. "Negros y mulatos en los documentos inquisitoriales: Rechazo e integración." In *El trabajo y los trabajadores en la historia de México*, ed. Elsa C. Frost, Michael C. Meyer, and Josefina Zoraida Vázquez, 132–161. Mexico City: El Colegio de México and the University of Arizona Press, 1979.

———. "La sexualidad manipulada en Nueva España: Modalidades de recuperación y de adaptación frente a los tribunales eclesiásticos." In *Familia y Sexualidad en Nueva España*, Seminario de Historia de las Mentalidades, 238–257. Mexico City: Secretaria de Educación Publica and Fondo de Cultura Económica, 1982.

Álvarez Alonso, Fermina. *La Inquisición en Cartagena de Indias durante el siglo xvii*. Madrid: Fundación Universitaria Española, 1999.

Archer, Christon I. *The Army in Bourbon Mexico, 1760–1810*. Albuquerque: University of New Mexico Press, 1977.

Arrom, Silvia M. *The Women of Mexico City, 1790–1857*. Stanford, CA: Stanford University Press, 1985.

Atondo, Ana María. "Prostitutas, alcahuetes y mancebas: Siglo XVI." In *Familia y Sexualidad en Nueva España*, Seminario de Historia de las Mentalidades, 275–284. Mexico City: Secretaría de Educación Pública/Fondo de Cultura Económica, 1982.

Austin, John L. *How To Do Things with Words*. Cambridge, MA: Harvard University Press, 1962.

Barton, Carlin. "All Things Beseem the Victor: Paradoxes of Masculinity in Early Imperial Rome." In *Gender Rhetorics: Postures of Dominance and Submission in History*, ed. Richard C. Trexler, 83–92. Binghamton: State University of New York at Binghamton, 1994.

Barton, Richard E. "'A Zealous Anger' and the Renegotiation of Aristocratic Relationships in Eleventh- and Twelfth-Century France." In *Anger's Past: The Social Uses of an Emotion in the Middle Ages*, ed. Barbara H. Rosenwin. Ithaca, NY: Cornell University Press, 1998.

Bartra, Roger. "Melancolía y cultura: Notas sobre enfermedad, misticismo, cortesía y demonología en la España del Siglo de Oro." In *Historia y grafía* (Universidad Iberoamericana) 8 (1997): 35–64.

———, ed. *El siglo de oro de la melancolía: Textos españoles y novohispanos sobre las enfermedades del alma*. Mexico City: Universidad Iberoamericana, 1998.

Bataillon, Marcel. *Erasmo y España*. Trans. Antonio Alatorre. Mexico City: Fondo de Cultura Económica, 1982.

———. "La Vera Paz: Novela e historia." In *Estudios sobre Bartolomé de Las Casas*, trans. J. Coderch and J. A. Martínez Schrem, 181–243. Barcelona: Península, 1976.

Bates, Catherine. *Play in a Godless World: The Theory and Practice of Play in Shakespeare, Nietzsche and Freud*. London: Open Gate Press, 1999.

Bateson, Gregory. *Steps to an Ecology of the Mind*. New York: Ballantine Books, 1972.

Baudot, Georges. "La population des villes du Mexique en 1595 selon une enquête de l'Inquisition." In *Cahiers du monde hispanique et luso-brésilien* (Caravelle) 37 (1981): 5–18.

———. *Utopía e historia en México: Los primeros cronistas de la civilización mexicana, 1520–1569*. Trans. Vicente González Loscertales. Madrid: Espasa-Calpe, 1983.

Bäuml, Betty J., and Franz H. Bäuml. *A Dictionary of Gestures*. Metuchen, NJ: Scarecrow Press, 1975.

Behar, Ruth. "Sex and Sin, Witchcraft and the Devil in Late-Colonial Mexico." *American Ethnologist* 14 (1987): 34–54.

———. "Sexual Witchcraft, Colonialism, and Women's Powers: Views from the Mexican Inquisition." In *Sexuality and Marriage in Colonial Latin America*, ed. Asunción Lavrin, 178–206. Lincoln: University of Nebraska Press, 1989.

Belmas, Elisabeth. "La montée des blasphèmes à l'age moderne du Moyen Âge au XVIIe siècle." In *Injures et blasphèmes*, ed. Jean Delumeau, 13–33. Paris: Editions Imago, 1989.

Benassar, Bartolomé. *The Spanish Character: Attitudes and Mentalities from the Sixteenth to the Nineteenth Century*. Trans. Benjamin Keen. Berkeley and Los Angeles: University of California Press, 1979.

Benítez, Fernando. *Los demonios en el convento: Sexo y religión en la Nueva España*. Mexico City: Ediciones Era, 1985.

Bennet, Herman L. *Africans in Colonial Mexico: Absolutism, Christianity, and Afro-Creole Consciousness, 1570–1640*. Bloomington: Indiana University Press, 2003.

Benveniste, Émile. "Le blasphème et l'euphémie." In *L'analyse du langage théologique: Le nom de Dieu*, ed. Enrico Castelli, 71–73. Paris: Aubier, 1969.

Bergler, Edmund. *The Psychology of Gambling*. New York: Hill and Wang, 1957.

Bermúdez Gorrochotegui, Gilberto. *Historia de Jalapa: Siglo xvii*. Jalapa, Mexico: Universidad Veracruzana, 1995.

Bernard, Carmen, and Serge Gruzinski. *Histoire du nouveau monde: Les métissages*. Paris: Fayard, 1993.

Berti, Silvia. "At the Roots of Unbelief." *Journal of the History of Ideas* 56:4 (1995): 555–575.

Blank, Sheldon H. "The Curse, Blasphemy, the Spell, and the Oath." *Hebrew Union College Annual* 23 (1950–51): 73–95.

Bloch, Marc. "How and Why Ancient Slavery Came to an End." In *Slavery and Serfdom in the Middle Ages*, ed. Marc Bloch, trans. William R. Beer, 1–32. Berkeley: University of California Press, 1975.

Bloomfield, Morton W. *The Seven Deadly Sins*. East Lansing: Michigan State College Press, 1952.

Boose, Lynda E. "Scolding Brides and Bridling Scolds: Taming the Woman's Unruly Member." In *Materialist Shakespeare*, ed. Ivo Kamps, 239–279. London and New York: Verso, 1995.

Borah, Woodrow. *Justice by Insurance: The General Indian Court of Colonial Mexico and the Legal Aides of the Half-Real*. Berkeley: University of California Press, 1983.

———. *New Spain's Century of Depression*. Berkeley: University of California Press, 1951.

———. "The Spanish and Indian Law: New Spain." In *The Inca and Aztec States, 1400–1800: Anthropology and History*, ed. George A. Collier, Renato I. Rosaldo, and John D. Wirth, 265–288. New York: Academic, 1982.

Bourdieu, Pierre. *Language and Symbolic Power,* ed. John B. Thompson, trans. Gino Raymond and Matthew Adamson. Cambridge, MA: Harvard University Press, 1991.

Bowser, Frederick P. "Africans in Spanish American Colonial Society." In *The Cambridge History of Latin America.* vol. 7, ed. Leslie Bethell, 357–379. Cambridge: Cambridge University Press, 1984.

———. "The Free Person of Color in Mexico City and Lima: Manumission and Opportunity, 1580–1650." In *Race and Slavery in the Western Hemisphere: Quantitative Studies,* ed. Stanley L. Engerman and Eugene D. Genovese, 331–368. Princeton, NJ: Princeton University Press, 1975.

Boyd-Bowman, Peter. "Negro Slaves in Early Colonial Mexico." *The Americas* 26:2 (October 1969): 134–151.

Boyer, Richard. *La gran inundación: Vida y sociedad en la ciudad de México (1629–1638).* Mexico City: Secretaría de Educación Pública, 1975.

———. "Juan Vazquez: Arriero desafortunado (Nueva España, siglo XVII)." In *Lucha por la supervivencia en la América colonial,* ed. David G. Sweet and Gary B. Nash, 165–179. Mexico City: Fondo de Cultura Económica, 1987 [1981].

———. *Lives of the Bigamists: Marriage, Family, and Community in Colonial Mexico.* Albuquerque: University of New Mexico Press, 1995.

———. "Las mujeres, la 'mala vida' y la política del matrimonio." In *Sexualidad y matrimonio en la América hispánica,* ed. Asunción Lavrin, trans. Gustavo Pelcastre, 271–303. Mexico City: Grijalbo, 1991.

———. "People, Places, and Gossip: The Flow of Information in Colonial Mexico." In *La ciudad y el campo en la historia de México: Memoria de la VII Reunión de Historiadores Mexicanos y Norteamericanos,* ed. Richard Sánchez, Eric Van Young, and Gisela von Wobeser, 1:143–150. Mexico City: Universidad Nacional Autónoma de México, 1992.

Brading, David. *The First America: The Spanish Monarchy, Creole Patriots, and the Liberal State, 1492–1867.* Cambridge: Cambridge University Press, 1991.

Brady, Robert L. "The Domestic Slave Trade in Sixteenth-Century Mexico." *The Americas* 24:3 (1968): 281–289.

Bremond, Claude, Jacques Le Goff, and Jean-Claude Schmitt. *L'exemplum.* Turnhout, Belgium: Brepols, 1982.

Briggs, Charles L. Introduction to *Disorderly Discourse: Narrative, Conflict and Inequality,* ed. Charles L. Briggs, 3–40. New York: Oxford University Press, 1996.

Brink, James T. "Speech, Play, and Blasphemy: Managing Power and Shame in Bamana Theater." *Anthropological Linguistics* 24:4 (1982): 423–431.

Bristol, Joan Cameron. "Negotiating Authority in New Spain: Blacks, Mulattos, and Religious Practice in Seventeenth Century Mexico." PhD diss., University of Pennsylvania, 2001.

Burke, Peter. *The Art of Conversation*. Ithaca, NY: Cornell University Press, 1993.

———. "Insult and Blasphemy." In *The Historical Anthropology of Early Modern Italy: Essays in Perception and Communication*, 95–109. Cambridge: Cambridge University Press, 1987.

———. *Varieties of Cultural History*. Ithaca, NY: Cornell University Press, 1997.

Burke, Peter, and Roy Porter, eds. *Language, Self, and Society*. Cambridge, MA: Polity Press, 1991.

———, eds. *The Social History of Language*. Cambridge: Cambridge University Press, 1987.

Burkhart, Louise. *The Slippery Earth: Nahua-Christian Moral Dialogue in Sixteenth-Century Mexico*. Tucson: University of Arizona Press, 1991.

Butler, Judith. *Excitable Speech: A Politics of the Performative*. New York: Routledge, 1997.

———. *Gender Trouble*. New York: Routledge, 1990.

Byrne, Stephen J. "Indian Resistance to Spanish Power in Northern Mexico and the American Southwest, 1540–1600." PhD diss., Florida Atlantic University, 1971.

Cabantous, Alain. "Du blasphème au blasphémateur : Jalons pour une histoire, xvie-xixe siécle." In *Blasphèmes et libertés*, ed. Patrice Dartevelle, Philippe Denis, and Johannes Robyn, 11–31 . Paris: CERF, 1993.

———. *Histoire du blasphème en Occident, xvie-xixe siècle*. Paris: Albin Michel, 1998.

Caciola, Nancy. "Mystics, Demoniacs, and the Physiology of Spirit Possession in Medieval Europe." *Comparative Studies of Society and History* 42:3 (July 2000): 268–306.

Caillois, Roger. *Man, Play, and Games*. Trans. Meyer Barash. New York: The Free Press of Glencoe, 1961.

Cameron, Deborah. *Verbal Hygiene: Politics of Language*. New York: Routledge, 1995.

Campos Moreno, Araceli. *Oraciones, ensalmos y conjuros mágicos del archivo inquisitorial de la Nueva España, 1600–1630*. Mexico City: El Colegio de México, 1999.

Cañeque, Alejandro. "Theater of Power: Writing and Representing the Auto de Fe in Colonial Mexico." *The Americas* 52:3 (January 1996): 321–343.

Cañizares-Ezquerra, Jorge. "New World, New Stars: Patriotic Astrology and the Invention of Indian and Creole Bodies in Colonial Spanish America, 1600–1670." *American Historical Review* 104 (February 1999): 33–68.

Carrasco, David. *Quetzalcóatl and the Irony of Empire: Myths and Prophecies in the Aztec Tradition*. Chicago: University of Chicago Press, 1982.

Carrol, Patrick J. *Blacks in Colonial Veracruz: Race, Ethnicity, and Regional Development*. Austin: University of Texas, 1991.

Casagrande, Carla, and Silvana Vecchio. *Les péchés de la langue*. Preface by Jacques Le Goff. Trans. Phillippe Baillet. Paris: CERF, 1991.

Cascardis, Anthony. "The Subject of Control." In *Culture and Control in Counter-Reformation Spain*, ed. Anne Cruz and Mary Elizabeth Perry, 231–254. Minneapolis: University of Minnesota Press, 1992.

Castañeda Delgado, Paulino, and Pilar Hernández Aparicio. *La Inquisición en Lima*. Vol. 1. Madrid: DEIMOS, 1989.

Céard, Jean. "Jeu et divination à la Renaissance." In *Les Jeux à la Renaissance*, ed. Philippe Ariès et Jean-Claude Margolin, 405–420. Paris: Libraire Philosophique J. Vrin, 1982.

Certeau, Michel de. *La possession de Loudun*. Paris: Gallimard/Juillard, 1980.

Cervantes, Fernando. *The Devil in the New World: The Impact of Diabolism in New Spain*. New Haven, CT: Yale University Press: 1994.

———. "The Devils of Querétaro: Scepticism and Credulity in Late Seventeenth-Century Mexico." *Past and Present* 130 (February 1991): 51–69.

Chauchadis, Claude. *Honneur, morale et société dans l'Espagne de Philippe II*. Paris: CNRS, 1984.

Christian, William A., Jr. *Local Religion in Sixteenth-Century Spain*. Princeton, NJ: Princeton University Press, 1981.

Christin, Oliver. "Sur la condamnation du blasphème, xvie-xiie siècles." *Revue d'histoire de l'Eglise de France* 80 (1994): 43–64.

Cipolla, Carlo M. *Faith, Reason and the Plague in Seventeenth-Century Tuscany*. Trans. Muriel Kittel. New York: Norton, 1979.

Clendinnen, Inga. *Ambivalent Conquests: Maya and Spaniard in Yucatan, 1517–1570*. Cambridge: Cambridge University Press, 1994 [1987].

Colomar, María Antonia. "El juego de naipes en Hispanoamérica: Las pruebas y muestra de naipes conservados en el Archivo General de Indias." *Buenavista de Indias* 7:55–87. Madrid: Ediciones Aldaba, 1992.

Combes, I.A.H. *The Metaphor of Slavery in the Writings of the Early Church*. Sheffield, Eng.: Sheffield Academic Press, 1998.

Company, Concepción. *Documentos lingüísticos de la Nueva España: Altiplano central*. Mexico City: Universidad Nacional Autónoma de México, 1994.

Connell, R. W. *Masculinities*. Berkeley and Los Angeles: University of California Press, 1995.

Cope, Douglas R. *The Limits of Racial Domination: Plebeian Society in Colonial Mexico City, 1660–1720*. Madison: University of Wisconsin Press, 1994.

Córdoba, Fray Martín de. *Jardín de nobles donzellas*. Ed. Harriet Goldbert. Chapel Hill: University of North Carolina Press, 1974.

Corominas, Joan. *Breve diccionario etimológico de la lengua castellana*. 3d rev. ed. Madrid: Gredos, 1996 [1961].

Corro, Octoviano R. *Cimarrones en Veracruz y la fundación de Amapa*. Veracruz: Editorial Citlaltepetl, 1974.

Cox, Bruce A. "What Is Hopi Gossip About? Information Management and Hopi Factions." *Man* (new ser.) 5:1 (March 1970): 88–98.

Craun, Edwin D. "'Inordinata Locutio': Blasphemy in Pastoral Literature, 1200–1500." *Traditio* 39 (1983): 135–162.

Crawley, Ernest. *Studies of Savages and Sex*. London: Methuen and Co. Ltd., 1929.

Cuello Martinell, María Angeles. *La renta de los naipes en Nueva España*. Seville: Escuela de Estudios Hispano-americanos, 1966.

Curcio-Nagy, Linda A. *The Great Festivals of Colonial Mexico City: Performing Power and Identity*. Albuquerque: University of New Mexico Press, 2004.

———. "Rosa de Escalante's Private Party: Popular Female Religiosity in Colonial Mexico City." In *Women in the Inquisition: Spain and the New World*, ed. Mary E. Giles, 254–269. Baltimore: Johns Hopkins University Press, 1999.

Curtius, Robert Ernest. *European Literature and the Latin Middle Ages*. Trans. Willard R. Trask. Princeton, NJ: Princeton University Press, 1953.

Davidson, David M. "Negro Slave Control and Resistance in Colonial Mexico, 1519–1650." *Hispanic American Historical Review* 46 (1966): 235–253.

Davis, David Brion. *The Problem of Slavery in Western Culture*. Ithaca, NY: Cornell University Press, 1966.

Davis, Natalie Zemon. *Fiction in the Archives: Pardon Tales and Their Tellers in Sixteenth-Century France*. Stanford, CA: Stanford University Press, 1987.

———. *Society and Culture in Early Modern France*. Stanford, CA: Stanford University Press, 1991 [1975].

Davison, David M. "Negro Slave Control and Resistance in Colonial Mexico, 1519–1650." *Hispanic American Historical Review* 46 (1966): 235–253.

Dedieu, Jean-Pierre. *L'administration de la foi: L'inquisition de Tolède, XVIe-XVIIIe siècles*. Madrid: Casa de Velázquez, 1989.

———. "The Inquisition and Popular Culture in New Castile." In *Inquisition and Society in Early Modern Europe*, ed. Stephen Haliczer, 129–146. London: Croom Helm, 1987.

———. "Le modèle religieux: Les disciplines du langage et de l'action." In *L'inquisition espagnole*, ed. Bartolomé Benassar, 241–267. Paris: L'Hachette, 1979.

de Klerk, Vivian. "The Role of Expletives in the Construction of Masculinity." In *Language and Masculinity*, ed. Sally Johnson and Ulrike Hanna Meihof, 144–158. London: Blackwell Publishers, 1997.

Delumeau, Jean. *Catholicisme entre Luther et Voltaire*. Paris: Presses Universitaires de France, 1971.

———. *La Peur en Occident, xive-xviiie siècles: Une cité assiégée*. Paris: Fayard, 1988 [1978].

Douglas, Mary. *In the Active Voice*. London: Routledge and Kegan Paul, 1982.

──── . *Risk and Blame: Essays in Cultural History*. London: Routledge, 1992.

──── . "Sacred Contagion." In *Reading Leviticus: A Conversation with Mary Douglas*, ed. John F. A. Sawyer, 86–123. Sheffield, Eng.: Sheffield Academic Press, 1996.

Ducrot, Oswald. *Le dire et le dit*. Paris: Minuit, 1984.

Dusenberry, William H. "Discriminatory Aspects of Legislation in Colonial Mexico." *Journal of Negro History* 33 (1948): 284–302.

Edwards, John. "Religious Faith and Doubt in Late Medieval Spain: Soria *circa* 1450–1500." *Past and Present* 120 (August 1988): 3–25.

Elias, Norbert. *The Civilizing Process*. Vol. 1: *The History of Manners*. Trans. E. Jephcott. Oxford: Basil Blackwell, 1978.

Eliot, T. S. *After Strange Gods: A Primer of Modern Heresy*. New York: Harcourt, Brace and Co., 1934.

Elliott, John H. "The Mental World of Hernán Cortés." *Transactions of the Royal Historical Society*, 5th ser., 17 (1967): 41–58.

──── . *The Old World and the New, 1492–1650*. Cambridge: Cambridge University Press, 1970.

──── . *Spain and Its World*. New Haven, CT: Yale University Press, 1990.

Escamilla-Colin, Michèle. *Crimes et châtiments dans l'Espagne inquisitoriale*. 2 vols. Paris: Berg International, 1992.

Escandel Bonet, Bartolomé. "Las estructuras económicas de la inquisición indiana." In *Historia de la Inquisición en España y América*, ed. Joaquín Pérez Villanueva and Bartolomé Escandell Bonet, 2:1077–1110. Madrid: Biblioteca de Autores Cristianos/Centro de Estudios Inquisitoriales, 1993.

Étienvre, Jean-Pierre. *Márgenes literarios del juego: Una poética del naipe siglos XVI–XVIII*. London: Tamesis Books Ltd., 1990.

──── . "Le symbolisme de la carte à jouer dans l'Espagne des XVIe et XVIIe siècles." In *Les jeux à la renaissance*, ed. Philippe Ariès and Jean-Claude Margolin, 421–444. Paris: Libraire Philosophique J. Vrin, 1982.

Ettingham, Henry, ed. *Noticias del siglo xvii: Relaciones españolas de sucesos naturales y sobrenaturales*. Barcelona: Pubill Libros, 1995.

Favret-Saada, Jeanne. "Rushdie et compagnie: Préalables à une anthropologie du blasphème." *Ethnologie française* 22:3 (1992): 251–266.

Febvre, Lucien. *The Problem of Unbelief in the Sixteenth Century: The Religion of Rabelais*. Trans. Beatrice Gottlieb. Cambridge, MA: Harvard University Press, 1982.

Fernández Bulete, Virgilio. "Aproximación a la delincuencia en el México del siglo xvii." *Vinculo Jurídico* 15 (1993). Journal available at http://www.ciu.reduaz .mx/vinculo/webrvj/rev15–6.htm.

Ferreira, Alberto. "Simon Magus, Dogs, and Simon Peter." In *The Devil, Heresy and Witchcraft in the Middle Ages,* ed. Alberto Ferreiro, 45–90. Leiden: Brill, 1998.

Fitzpatrick, Sheila, and Robert Gellately. "Introduction to the Practices of Denunciation in Modern European History." *Journal of Modern History* 68:4 (1996): 748–777.

Flynn, Maureen. "Betrayals of the Soul in Spanish Blasphemy." In *Religion, Body and Gender in Early Modern Spain,* ed. Alain Saint-Saëns, 30–44. San Francisco: Mellen Research University Press, 1991.

———. "Blasphemy and the Play of Anger in Sixteenth-Century Spain." *Past and Present* 149 (November 1995): 29–56.

———. "Mimesis of the Last Judgment: The Spanish Auto de Fe." *Sixteenth Century Journal* 22:2 (Summer 1991): 281–297.

———. *Sacred Charity: Confraternities and Social Welfare in Spain, 1400–1700.* Ithaca, NY: Cornell University Press, 1989.

———. "Taming Anger's Daughters: New Treatment for Emotional Problems in Renaissance Spain." *Renaissance Quarterly* 51:3 (1998): 864–886.

Foucault, Michel. *Discipline and Punish: The Birth of Prison.* New York: Vintage Books, 1977.

Fox-Genovese, Elizabeth. *Within the Plantation Household: Black and White Women of the Old South.* Chapel Hill: University of North Carolina Press, 1988.

Franco, Jean. *Plotting Women: Gender and Representation in Mexico.* New York: Columbia University Press, 1989.

Frankl, Victor. "Hernán Cortés y la tradición de las siete partidas." *Revista de Historia de América* 53–54 (1962): 9–74.

Frazer, James G. "Tabooed Words." In *The Golden Bough: A Study in Magic and Religion,* vol. 2: *Taboo and the Perils of the Soul,* 3d. ed., 318–418. London: Macmillan, 1955.

Freud, Sigmund. "Totem and Taboo." In *The Basic Writings of Sigmund Freud,* trans. and ed. A. A. Brill, 807–930. New York: Modern Library, 1966.

García Ayluardo, Clara. "A World of Images: Cult, Ritual, and Society in Colonial México City." In *Rituals of Rule, Rituals of Resistance: Public Celebrations and Popular Culture in Mexico,* ed. William H. Beezley, Cheryl English Martin, and William E. French, 77–94. Wilmington, DE: Scholarly Resources, 1994.

García-Molina Riquelme, Antonio M. *El régimen de penas y penitencias en el tribunal de la inquisición de México.* Mexico City: Universidad Nacional Autónoma de México, 1999.

Gardiner, C. Harvey. *The Constant Captain Gonzalo Sandoval.* Carbondale: Southern Illinois University Press, 1961.

Gautheron, Marie, ed. *L'honneur: Image de soi ou don de soi un ideal equivoque.* Paris: Editions Autrement, 1991.

Geertz, Clifford. *The Interpretation of Cultures.* New York: Basic Books, 1973.

Genovese, Eugene D. *Roll, Jordan, Roll: The World the Slaves Made.* New York: Pantheon Books, 1974.

Gibson, Charles. *The Aztecs under Spanish Rule: A History of the Indians of the Valley of Mexico, 1519–1810.* Stanford, CA: Stanford University Press, 1964.

———. "Indian Societies under Spanish Rule." In *The Cambridge History of Latin America,* ed. Leslie Bethell, 2:384–422. Cambridge: Cambridge University Press, 1984.

———. *Spain in America.* New York: Harper and Row, 1966.

———. *The Spanish Tradition in America.* New York: Harper and Row, 1968.

Ginzburg, Carlo. "High and Low: The Theme of Forbidden Knowledge in the Sixteenth and Seventeenth Centuries." *Past and Present* 73 (1976): 28–42.

Gluckman, Max. "Gossip and Scandal." *Current Anthropology* 4 (June 1963): 307–315.

———. "Psychological, Sociological and Anthropological Explanations of Witchraft and Gossip: A Clarification." *Man* (new ser.) 3:1 (March 1968): 20–34.

Góngora, Mario. *Studies in the Colonial History of Spanish America.* Trans. Richard Southern. London: Cambridge University Press, 1975.

Gonzalbo, Pilar. *Las mujeres en la Nueva España: Educación y vida cotidiana.* Mexico City: El Colegio de México, 1987.

———. "Del tercero al cuarto concilio provincial mexicano, 1585–1771." *Historia Mexicana* 35:1 (1986): 5–31.

———. "Tradición y ruptura en la educación femenina del siglo xvi." In *Presencia y transparencia: La mujer en la historia de México,* ed. Carmen Ramos Escandón et al., 33–60. Mexico City: El Colegio de México, 1992.

Gowing, Laura. *Domestic Dangers: Women, Words, and Sex in Early Modern London.* Oxford: Oxford University Press, 1996.

Greenblatt, Stephen J. *Learning to Curse: Essays in Early Modern Culture.* New York: Routledge, 1990.

Greenleaf, Richard. *The Mexican Inquisition of the Sixteenth Century.* Albuquerque: University of New Mexico Press, 1969.

———. *Zumárraga and the Mexican Inquisition, 1536–1543.* Washington, DC: Academy of American Franciscan History, 1961.

Gregg, Joan Young. *Devils, Women, and Jews: Reflections of the Other in Medieval Sermon Stories.* Albany: State University of New York Press, 1997.

Grosz, Elizabeth. *Volatile Bodies: Toward a Corporeal Feminism.* Bloomington and Indianapolis: Indiana University Press, 1994.

Grunberg, Bernard. *L'inquisition apostolique au Mexique.* Paris: L'Harmattan, 1998.

Guha, Ranajit. *Elementary Aspects of Peasant Insurgency in Colonial India*. Oxford: Oxford University Press, 1994 [1983].

Guillemont, Michèle. *Recherches sur la violence verbale en Espagne aux xvie et xviie siècles: Aspects sociaux, culturels et littéraires*. 2 vols. Lille: Atelier national de reproduction des thèses, 1992.

Gunnarsdottir, Ellen. *Mexican Karismata: The Baroque Vocation of Francisca de los Ángeles, 1674–1744*. Lincoln: University of Nebraska Press, 2004.

Gutiérrez, Ramón. *When Jesus Came, the Corn Mothers Went Away: Marriage, Sexuality, and Power in New Mexico, 1500–1846*. Stanford, CA: Stanford University Press, 1991.

Haliczer, Stephen. *Inquisition and Society in the Kingdom of Valencia, 1478–1834*. Berkeley: University of California Press, 1990.

Handelman, Don. "Gossip in Encounters: The Transmission of Information in a Bounded Social Setting." *Man* 8:2 (June 1973): 210–227.

Hanke, Lewis. *All Mankind Is One*. De Kalb: Northern Illinois University Press, 1974.

———. "The 'Requerimiento' and Its Interpreters." *Revista de historia de América* 1 (1938): 25–34.

Hardon, John A. "Chance." In *Modern Catholic Dictionary*. New York: Doubleday, 1980.

Harrill, J. Albert. *The Manumission of Slaves in Early Christianity*. Tübingen: J.C.B. Mohr [Paul Siebeck], 1995.

Harris, R. "Mentioning the Unmentionable." *International Journal of Moral and Social Studies* 2:3 (1987): 175–187.

Helmholz, R. M. *The Spirit of Classic Canon Law*. Athens: University of Georgia Press, 1996.

Hernández Aranda, Judith. "Se consolida el virreinato." In *San Juan de Ulúa, Puerta de la historia*, ed. Pablo Montero, 123–136. Mexico City: Instituto Nacional de Antropología e Historia/Internacional de Contenedores Asociados de Veracruz, 1996.

———. "Ulúa y las misiones religiosas." In *San Juan de Ulúa: Puerta de la historia*, ed. Pablo Montero, 183–196. Mexico City: Instituto Nacional de Antropología e Historia/Internacional de Contenedores Asociados de Veracruz, 1996.

———. "Veracrúz frente a Ulúa." In *San Juan de Ulúa: puerta de la historia*, ed. Pablo Montero, 159–182. Mexico City: Instituto Nacional de Antropología e Historia/Internacional de Contenedores Asociados de Veracruz, 1996.

Hernández Díaz, Concepción. "Asistencia espiritual en las flotas de indias." In *Andalucía, América y el mar: Actas IX Jornadas de Andalucía y América*, ed. Bibiano Torres Ramírez. Seville: Artes Gráficas Rodriand, 1991.

Hertz, Robert. "La prééminence de la main droite: Étude sur la polarité religieuse." In *Sociologie religieuse et folklore*, 84–109. Paris: PUF, 1970.

Holler, Jacqueline. "'More Sins than the Queen of England': Marina de San Miguel before the Mexican Inquisition." In *Women in the Inquisition: Spain and the New World*, ed. Mary E. Giles, 209–228. Baltimore: Johns Hopkins University Press, 1999.

Hopkins, Patrick D. "Gender Treachery: Homophobia, Masculinity, and Threatened Identities." In *Rethinking Masculinity: Philosophical Explorations in Light of Feminism*, ed. Larry May and Robert A. Strikwerda, with the assistance of Patrick D. Hopkins, 95–115. Lanham, MD: Rowman and Littlefield, 1992.

Horodowich, Elizabeth A. "Civic Identity and the Control of Blasphemy in Sixteenth-Century Venice." *Past and Present* 181 (November 2003): 3–33.

Huizinga, Johan. *The Autumn of the Middle Ages*. Trans. Rodney J. Payton and Ulrich Mammitzsch. Chicago: University of Chicago Press, 1996 [1921].

———. *Homo Ludens: A Study of the Play Element in Culture*. Boston: Beacon Press, 1950.

Hünefeldt, Christine. *Paying the Price of Freedom: Family and Labor among Lima's Slaves, 1800–1854*. Berkeley and Los Angeles: University of California Press, 1994.

Hymes, Dell. "Ways of Speaking." In *Explorations in the Ethnography of Speaking*, ed. Richard Bauman and Joel Sherzer, 433–451. Cambridge: Cambridge University Press, 1974.

Israel, Jonathan I. *Race, Class and Politics in Colonial Mexico, 1610–1670*. New York: Oxford University Press, 1975.

Jaffary, Nora E. *False Mystics: Deviant Orthodoxy in Colonial Mexico*. Lincoln: University of Nebraska Press, 2004.

Johnson, Lyman L. "Dangerous Words, Provocative Gestures, and Violent Acts: The Disputed Hierarchies of Plebeian Life in Colonial Buenos Aires." In *The Faces of Honor: Sex, Shame, and Violence in Colonial Latin America*, ed. Lyman L. Johnson and Sonya Lipsett-Rivera, 127–151. Albuquerque: New Mexico University Press, 1998.

Joly, Monique. "Pour une nouvelle approche du discours de la folie et la simplicité d'esprit au siècle d'or." In *Les problèmes de l'exclusion en Espagne (xvie-xviie siècles): Idéologie et discours*, ed. Augustin Redondo, 227–237. Paris: Publications de la Sorbonne, 1983.

Kagan, Samuel. "The Labor of Prisoners in the Obrajes of Coyoacán, 1660–1693." In *El trabajo y los trabajadores en la historia de México*, ed. Elsa Cecilia Frost, Michael C. Meyer, and Josefina Zoraida Vázquez, 201–214. Mexico City: El Colegio de México and University of Arizona Press, 1979.

———. "Penal Servitude in New Spain: The Colonial Textile Industry." PhD diss., City University of New York, 1977.

Kamen, Henry. *The Spanish Inquisition: A Historical Revision*. New Haven, CT: Yale University Press, 1998.

Kamenski, Jane. *Governing the Tongue: The Politics of Speech in Early Modern England*. New York: Oxford University Press, 1997.

Kavanagh, Thomas M. *Enlightenment and the Shadows of Chance: The Novel and Culture of Gambling in Eighteenth-Century France*. Baltimore: Johns Hopkins University Press, 1993.

Kellog, Susan. *Law and the Transformation of Aztec Cutlure, 1500–1700*. Norman: University of Oklahoma Press, 1995.

Kelso, Ruth. *Doctrine for the Lady of the Renaissance*. Urbana: University of Illinois Press, 1978 [1956].

Kimmel, Michael S. *The Gendered Society*. Oxford: Oxford University Press, 2000.

Knapp, Bettina L. *Gambling, Game, and Psyche*. Albany: State University of New York Press, 2000.

Konetzke, Richard. *Colección de documentos para la historia de la formación social de Hispanoamérica, 1493–1810*. Madrid: Consejo Superior de Investigaciones Científicas, 1953.

Labov, William. *Language in the Inner City: Studies in the Black English Vernacular*. Philadelphia: University of Pennsylvania Press, 1972.

Lacarra, María Jesús. "Pour un *Thesaurus Exemplorum Hispanicorum*." In *Les exempla médiévaux: nouvelles perspectives*, ed. Jacques Berlioz and Marie Anne Polo de Beaulieu, 191–213. Paris: Honoré Champion, 1998.

Lafaye, Jacques. *Mesías, cruzadas y utopías: El judeo-cristianismo en las sociedades ibéricas*. Mexico City: Fondo de Cultura Económica, 1984.

———. *Quetzalcóatl and Guadalupe: The Formation of the Mexican National Consciousness, 1531–1813*. Chicago: University of Chicago Press, 1976.

Lakoff, Robin. *Language and Woman's Place*. New York: Harper & Row, 1976.

Larkin, Brian. "Liturgy, Devotion and Reform in Eighteenth-Century Mexico City." *The Americas* 60:4 (April 2004): 439–518.

Lauand, L. Jean. "Ludus in the Fundamentals of Aquinas's World-View." Trans. Alfredo H. Alves. *International Studies on Laws and Education* 2. Departamento de Filosofia e Ciéncias da Educaçao da Faculdade de Educaçao da Universidade de São Paulo/ Harvard Law Association of Brazil. http://www.hottopos.com/harvard2/ludus.htm.

Lavrin, Asunción. "Female Religious." In *Cities and Society in Colonial Latin America*, ed. Louisa Schell Hoberman and Susan Migden Solow, 165–195. Albuquerque: University of New Mexico Press, 1986.

———. "In Search of the Colonial Woman in Mexico: The Seventeenth and Eighteenth Centuries." In *Latin American Women: Historical Perspectives*, ed. Asunción Lavrin, 3–22. Westport, CT: Greenwood Press, 1978.

———. "Women in Colonial Mexico." In *The Oxford History of Mexico*, ed. Michael C. Meyer and William E. Beezley, 245–274. Oxford: Oxford University Press, 2000.

———. "Women in Spanish Colonial Society." In *The Cambridge History of Latin America*, ed. Leslie Bethell, 2:321–355. Cambridge: Cambridge University Press, 1984.

Lawton, David. *Blasphemy*. Philadelphia: University of Pennsylvania Press, 1993.

Lea, Henry Charles. *A History of the Inquisition in Spain*. Vol. 4. London: Macmillan, 1907.

Leach, Edmund. "Anthropological Aspects of Language: Verbal Categories and Verbal Abuse." In *New Directions in the Study of Language*, ed. Eric H. Lenneberg, 23–63. Cambridge, MA: MIT Press, 1964.

Le Goff, Jacques. "Head or Heart? The Political Use of Body Metaphors in the Middle Ages." In *Fragments for a History of the Human Body*, pt. 3, ed. Michel Feher with Ramona Naddaff and Nadia Tazi, 13–27. New York: Zone, 1989.

———. *Lo maravilloso y lo cotidiano en el occidente medieval*. Trans. Alberto L. Bixio. Barcelona: Gedisa, 1986.

Legros, Monique. "Acerca de un diálogo que no lo fue." In Seminario de Historia de las Mentalidades, *Familia y Sexualidad en Nueva España*, 207–237. Mexico City: Secretaría de Educación Pública/Fondo de Cultura Económica, 1982.

Lemistre, Annie. "Les Origines du 'Requerimiento.'" In *Mélanges de la Casa Velázquez* 6 (1970): 171–177.

Leonard, Irving A. *Baroque Times in Old Mexico: Seventeenth-Century Persons, Places, and Practices*. Ann Arbor: University of Michigan Press, 1959.

———. *Books of the Brave*. Cambridge, MA: Harvard University Press, 1949.

———. *Don Carlos de Sigüenza y Góngora: A Mexican Savant of the Seventeenth Century*. Berkeley: University of California Press, 1929.

L'Escop, Juan. *La lengua catalana: Manual contra la blasfemia*. Barcelona: Editorial Políglota, 1931.

Levy, Leonard. *Blasphemy: Verbal Offense against the Sacred from Moses to Salman Rushdie*. New York: Alfred A. Knopf, 1993.

———. *Treason against God: A History of the Offense of Blasphemy*. New York: Schocken Books, 1981.

Lewin, Boleslao. *La Inquisición en México: Impresionantes relatos del siglo xvi*. Puebla: Editorial José A. Cajica, 1968.

Lewis, Laura A. *Hall of Mirrors: Power, Witchcraft, and Caste in Colonial Mexico*. Durham, NC: Duke University Press, 2003.

Lipsett-Rivera, Sonya. "A Slap in the Face of Honor." In *The Faces of Honor: Sex,*

Shame, and Violence in Colonial Latin America, ed. Lyman L. Johnson and Sonya Lipsett-Rivera, 179–200. Albuquerque: University of New Mexico Press, 1998.

Llaguno, J. A. *La personalidad jurídica del indio y el tercer concilio mexicano.* Mexico City: Miguel Ángel Porrúa, 1963.

Lockhart, James. *The Nahuas after the Conquest: A Social and Cultural History of the Indians of Central Mexico; Sixteenth through Eighteenth Centuries.* Stanford, CA: Stanford University Press, 1992.

López Cantos, Angel. "Los juegos de suerte, envite y azar en los conquistadores de América." In *Congreso de Historia del descubrimiento,* 4:197–212. Madrid: Real Academia de la Historia/Confederación Española de Cajas de Ahorros, 1992.

———. *Juegos, fiestas y diversiones en la América española.* Madrid: MAPFRE, 1992.

Love, Edgar F. "Negro Resistance to Spanish Rule." *Journal of Negro History* 52 (1967): 89–103.

Mackenthun, Gesa. *Metaphors of Dispossession: American Beginnings and the Translation of Empire, 1492–1637.* Norman: University of Oklahoma Press, 1997.

Maclean, Ian. *The Renaissance Notion of Woman: A Study in the Fortunes of Scholasticism and Medical Science in European Intellectual Life.* Cambridge: Cambridge University Press, 1980.

Madero, Marta. *Manos violentas, palabras vedadas: La injuria en Castilla y León (siglos xiii-xv).* Madrid: Taurus, 1992.

Malinowski, Bronislaw. *Coral Gardens and Their Magic: A Study of the Methods of Tilling the Soil and of Agricultural Rites in the Trobriand Islands.* Vol. 2. Introduction by Jack Berry. London: George Allen and Unwin, 1965.

Maravall, J. A. "La utopía político-religiosa de los franciscanos en Nueva España." *Estudios americanos* 1:2 (1949): 199–227.

Martin, Cheryl E. *Governance and Society in Colonial Mexico: Chihuahua in the Eighteenth Century.* Stanford, CA: Stanford University Press, 1996.

———. "Popular Speech and Social Order in Northern Mexico, 1650–1830." *Comparative Studies in Society and History* 33:2 (April 1990): 305–324.

———. *Rural Society in Colonial Morelos.* Albuquerque: University of New Mexico Press, 1985.

Martin, Dale B. *Slavery and Salvation: The Metaphor of Slavery in Pauline Christianity.* New Haven, CT: Yale University Press, 1990.

Martin, Norman. *Los vagabundos en la Nueva España: siglo XVI.* Mexico City: Editorial Jus, 1957.

Mauriño Márquez, José Angel. "Las congregaciones hispanoamericanas: Provincia de Tlanochinol, 1604." *Anuario de Estudios Americanos* 47:2 (1990): 27–59.

Mazzio, Carla. "Sins of the Tongue." In *The Body in Parts: Fantasies of Corporeality in Early Modern Europe*, ed. David Hillman and Carla Mazzio, 53–70. Routledge: New York, 1997.

McKnight, Kathryn Joy. "Blasphemy as Resistance: An African Slave Woman before the Mexican Inquisition." In *Women in the Inquisition: Spain and the New World*, ed. Mary E. Giles, 229–253. Baltimore: Johns Hopkins University Press, 1999.

Medina, José Toribio. *Historia del tribunal del Santo Oficio de la Inquisición de Cartagena de Indias*. Santiago, Chile: Imprenta Gutenberg, 1899.

———. *Historia del santo tribunal del santo oficio de la inquisición de Lima (1569–1820)*. Santiago, Chile: Imprenta Gutenberg, 1887.

———. *Historia del tribunal del santo oficio de la inquisición en México*. Mexico City: Ediciones Fuente Cultural, 1905.

———. *Historia del tribunal del santo oficio de la inquisición en México*. Mexico City: CONACULTA, 1991 [1905].

———. *La imprenta en México, 1539–1821*. 8 vols. Santiago, Chile: The Author, 1907–12.

———. *La inquisición en Cartagena de Indias*. Bogota, Colombia: Carlos Valencia Editores, 1978.

———. *El tribunal del santo oficio de la inquisición en las islas filipinas*. Santiago, Chile: Imprenta Elzeviriana, 1899.

Mellafe, Rolando. *Negro Slavery in Latin America*. Trans. J.W.S. Judge. Berkeley: University of California Press, 1975.

Mello e Souza, Laura de. *El diablo en la tierra de Santa Cruz*. Trans. Teresa Rodríguez Martínez. Madrid: Alianza, 1993.

Ménager, Daniel. *Le Renaissance et le rire*. Paris: Presses Universitaires de France, 1995.

Mendoza Negrillo, Juan de Dios. *Fortuna y providencia en la literatura castellana del siglo xv*. Madrid: Anejos del boletín de la Real Academia Española, 1973.

Menéndez Pidal, Ramón, ed. *Historia de España*. Madrid: Espasa-Calpe, 1969.

Miller, David L. *Gods and Games: Toward a Theology of Play*. New York: Harper & Row, 1973.

Mirrer, Louise. "Representing 'Other' Men: Muslims, Jews, and Masculine Ideals in Medieval Castilian Epic and Ballad." In *Medieval Masculinities*, ed. Clare A. Lees, 169–186. Minneapolis: University of Minnesota Press, 1994.

Mirsky, Seth. "Three Arguments for the Elimination of Masculinity." In *Men's Bodies, Men's Gods: Male Identities in a (Post-) Christian Culture*, ed. Björn Krondorfer, 27–42. New York: New York University Press, 1996.

Montero, Pablo, with the collaboration of Minerva Escamilla Gómez, Adriana Gil Maronño, Judith Hernández Aranda, Abel Lara Morales, and Liliana Rivera

Sánchez. *Ulúa, puente intercontinental en el siglo xvii*. Mexico City: Instituto Nacional de Antropología e Historia/Internacional de Contenedores Asociados de Veracruz, 1997.

Mörner, Magnus. *La corona española y los foráneos en los pueblos de indios de América*. Stockholm: Almquist & Wiksell, 1970.

———. *Race Mixture in the History of Latin America*. Boston: Little, Brown and Company, 1967.

Mörner, Magnus, and Efrain Trelles. "A Test of Causal Interpretations of the Túpac Amaru Rebellion." In *Resistance, Rebellion, and Consciousness in the Andean Peasant World, 18th to 20th Centuries*, ed. Steve J. Stern, 94–109. Madison: University of Wisconsin Press, 1987.

Muriel, Josefina. *Los recogimientos de mujeres*. Mexico City: Universidad Nacional Autónoma de México, 1974.

Nalle, Sara T. *God in La Mancha: Religious Reform and the People of Cuenca, 1500–1650*. Baltimore: Johns Hopkins University Press, 1992.

Naveda Chávez-Hita, Adriana. *Esclavos negros en las haciendas azucareras de Córdoba, Veracruz, 1690–1830*. Jalapa, Veracruz: Universidad Veracruzana, 1987.

———. "Trabajadores esclavos en las haciendas azucareras de Córdoba, Veracruz, 1714–1763." In *El trabajo y los trabajadores en la historia de México*, ed. Elsa Cecilia Frost, Michael C. Meyer, and Josefina Zoraida Vázquez, 162–182. Mexico City: El Colegio de México and the University of Arizona Press, 1979.

Nelson, Bradley J. "Emblematic Representation and Guided Culture in Baroque Spain: Juan de Horozco y Covarrubias." In *Culture and the State in Spain, 1550–1850*, ed. Tom Lewis and Francisco J. Sánchez, 157–195. New York: Garland Publishing, 1999.

Nirenberg, David. *Communities of Violence: Persecution of Minorities in the Middle Ages*. Princeton, NJ: Princeton University Press, 1996.

———. "Conversion, Sex, and Segregation: Jews and Christians in Medieval Spain." *American Historical Review* 107:4 (October 2002): 1065–1093.

Norton, Mary Beth. "Gender and Defamation in Seventeenth-Century Maryland." *William and Mary Quarterly*, 3d ser., 44:1 (January 1987): 3–39.

Obregón, Gonzalo. *El real colegio de San Ignacio de México (las Vizcaínas)*. Mexico City: El Colegio de México, 1949.

O'Gorman, Edmundo. *La Inquisición en México*. Mexico City: Secretaría de Educación Pública/CONASUPO, 1981.

Orozco y Becerra, Manuel. *Historia antigua de la conquista de México*. 4 vols. Mexico City: Fondo de Cultura Económica, 1978.

Ortega, Sergio, ed. *De la santidad a la perversión o de por qué no se cumplía la ley de Dios en la sociedad novohispana*. Mexico City: Grijalbo, 1985.

Ouweneel, Arij. *Shadows over Anáhuac: An Ecological Interpretation of Crisis and Development in Central Mexico, 1730–1800.* Albuquerque: University of New Mexico Press, 1996.

Oyola, Eliécer. *Los pecados capitales en la literatura medieval española.* Barcelona: Puvill, 1979.

Padden, R. C. *The Hummingbird and the Hawk: Conquest and Sovereignty in the Valley of Mexico, 1503–1541.* New York: Harper, 1970.

Pagden, Anthony. *European Encounters with the New World: From Renaissance to Romanticism.* New Haven, CT: Yale University Press, 1993.

———. *The Fall of the Natural Man: The American Indian and the Origins of Comparative Ethnology.* Cambridge: Cambridge University Press, 1994 [1982].

———. *Spanish Imperialism and the Political Imagination.* New Haven, CT: Yale University Press, 1990.

Paine, Robert. "What Is Gossip About? An Alternative Hypothesis." *Man,* new ser., 2:2 (June 1967): 278–285.

Palmer, Colin. "Religion and Magic in Mexican Slave Society, 1570–1650." In *Race and Slavery in the Western Hemisphere: Quantitative Studies,* ed. Stanley Engerman and Eugene D. Genovese, 311–328. Princeton, NJ: Princeton University Press, 1975.

———. *Slaves of the White God: Blacks in Mexico, 1570–1650.* Cambridge: Cambridge University Press, 1976.

Parker, Geoffrey, and Angela Parker. *European Soldiers, 1550–1650.* Cambridge: Cambridge University Press, 1977.

Parker, Patricia. "On the Tongue: Cross Gendering, Effeminacy, and the Art of Words." *Style* 23:3 (Fall 1989): 445–465.

Parlett, David. *The Oxford Guide to Card Games.* New York: Oxford University Press, 1990.

Parma Cook, Alexandra, and Noble David Cook. *Good Faith and Truthful Ignorance: A Case of Transatlantic Bigamy.* Durham, NC: Duke University Press, 1991.

Patterson, Orlando. *Freedom.* Vol. 1: *Freedom and the Making of Western Culture.* New York: Basic Books, 1991.

———. *Slavery and Social Death: A Comparative Study.* Cambridge, MA: Harvard University Press, 1982.

Pérez-Mallaína, Pablo E. *Spain's Men of the Sea: Daily Life on the Indies Fleets in the Sixteenth Century.* Trans. Carla Rahn Phillips. Baltimore: Johns Hopkins University Press, 1998.

Perry, Mary Elizabeth. *Gender and Disorder in Early Modern Seville.* Princeton, NJ: Princeton University Press, 1990.

———. "With Brave Vigilance and a Hundred Eyes: The Making of Women's Prisons in Counter-Reformation Spain." *Women and Criminal Justice* 2:1 (1990): 3–18.

Pescatello, Ann M. *Power and Pawn: The Female in Iberian Families, Societies, and Cultures.* Westport, CT: Greenwood Press, 1976.

Phelan, John L. *The Kingdom of Quito in the Seventeenth Century: Bureaucratic Politics in the Spanish Empire.* Madison: University of Wisconsin Press, 1967.

———. *The Millennial Kingdom of the Franciscans in the New World.* Berkeley and Los Angeles: University of California Press, 1956.

Pike, Ruth. *Aristocrats and Traders: Sevillian Society in the Sixteenth Century.* Ithaca: Cornell University Press, 1972.

Pitt-Rivers, Julian. "Honor." In *International Encyclopedia of the Social Sciences,* vol. 6, ed. David L. Sills, 503–511. New York: Macmillan Company and Free Press, 1968.

Poole, Stafford. "The Declining Image of the Indian among Churchmen in Sixteenth-Century New Spain." In *Indian-Religious Relations in Colonial Spanish America,* ed. Susan E. Ramírez, 11–20. Syracuse, NY: Maxwell School of Citizenship and Public Affairs, Syracuse University, 1989.

Proctor, Frank T. "Afro-Mexican Slave Labor in the Obrajes de Paños of New Spain: Seventeenth and Eighteenth Centuries." *The Americas* 60:1 (2003): 33–58.

Quezada, Noemí. "Congregaciones de indios y grupos étnicos: El caso del Valle de Toluca y zonas aledañas." *Revista complutense de Historia de América* 21 (1995): 141–165.

Rabasa, José. *Writing Violence in the Northern Frontier: The Historiography of Sixteenth-Century New Mexico and Florida and the Legacy of Conquest.* Durham, NC: Duke University Press, 2000.

Raboteau, Albert J. *Slave Religion: The "Invisible Institution" in the Antebellum South.* New York: Oxford University Press, 1978.

Rafael, Vicente. *Contracting Colonialism: Translation and Christian Conversion in Tagalog Society under Early Spanish Rule.* Durham, NC: Duke University Press, 1993 [1988].

Rahner, Hugo. "Eutrapelia: A Forgotten Virtue." In *Holy Laughter: Essays on Religion in the Comic Perspective,* ed. M. Conrad Hyers, 185–197. New York: Seabury Press, 1969.

———. *Man at Play.* Trans. B. Battershaw and E. Quinn. New York: Harper and Row, 1968.

Reeves, Marjorie. *The Influence of Prophecy in the Later Middle Ages: A Study in Joachimism.* Oxford: Clarendon Press, 1969.

Reulos, Michel. "Jeux interdits et réglementé." *Les Jeux à la Renaissance,* ed. Philippe Ariès and Jean-Claude Margolin, 635–644. Paris: Libraire Philosophique J. Vrin, 1982.

Ricard, Robert. *Estudios de literatura religiosa española*. Madrid: Gredos, 1964.

———. *The Spiritual Conquest of Mexico: An Essay on the Apostolate and the Evangelizing Methods of the Mendicant Orders in New Spain.* Trans. Lesley Byrd Simpson. Berkeley and Los Angeles: University of California Press, 1966 [1933].

Robert, Odile. "Porter le nom de Dieu." In *Histoire des pères et de la paternité*, ed. Jean Delumeau and Daniel Roche, 131–154. Paris: Larousse, 1990.

Robles, Antonio de. *Diario de sucesos notables (1665–1703)*. Vol. 3. Mexico City: Porrúa, 1946.

Rodríguez de San Miguel, Juan N. *Pandectas hispano-megicanas*. Mexico City: Librería de J. F. Rosa, 1852.

Roncal, Joaquín. "The Negro Race in Mexico." *Hispanic American Historical Review* 24:3 (August 1944): 530–540.

Rosal, Francisco del. *La razón de algunos refranes*, ed. B. Bussell Thomson. London: Tamesis Books Ltd., 1975.

Roseberry, William. "Hegemony and the Language of Contention." In *Everyday Forms of State Formation: Revolution and the Negotiation of Rule in Modern Mexico*, ed. Gilbert M. Joseph and Daniel Nugent, 355–366. Durham, NC: Duke University Press, 1994.

Rosenwein, Barbara H. "Worrying about Emotions in History." *American Historical Review* 107:3 (June 2002): 821–845.

Rout, Leslie B., Jr. *The African Experience in Spanish America, 1502 to the Present Day*. Cambridge: Cambridge University Press, 1976.

Rubial García, Antonio. "Josefa de San Luis Beltrán, la cordera de Dios: Escritura, oralidad y gestualidad de una visionaria del siglo xvii Novohispano." In Asunción Lavrin and Rosalva Loreto, *Monjas y beatas: La escritura femenina en la espiritualidad barroca novohispana, Siglos xvii y xviii*, 161–177. Mexico City: Universidad de las Americas, 2002.

Russell-Wood, A.J.R. "Iberian Expansion and the Issue of Black Slavery." *American Historical Review* 83:1 (February 1978): 16–42.

Sarabia Viejo, María Justina. *El juego de gallos en Nueva España*. Seville: Escuela de Estudios Hispanoamericanos, 1972.

Sauzet, Robert. "La Réforme, le magistrat et le jeu à Strasbourg au xvie siècle." In *Les jeux à la Renaissance*, ed. Philippe Ariès and Jean-Claude Margolin, 649–658. Paris: Librairie Philosophique J. Vrin, 1982.

Scanlon, Larry. *Narrative, Authority, and Power: The Medieval Exemplum and the Chaucerian Tradition*. Cambridge: Cambridge University Press, 1994.

Scardaville, Michael. "(Hapsburg) Law and (Bourbon) Order: State Authority, Popular

Unrest, and the Criminal Justice System in Bourbon Mexico City." In *Reconstructing Criminality in Latin America*, ed. Carlos A. Aguirre and Robert Buffington, 1–17. Wilmington, DE: Scholarly Resources, 2000.

Schmitt, Jean-Claude. "Gestures." *History and Anthropology* 1:1 (1984): 1–23.

———. *La raison des gestes*. Paris: Gallimard, 1990.

Scott, James C. *Domination and the Arts of Resistance: Hidden Transcripts*. New Haven, CT: Yale University Press, 1990.

Seed, Patricia. *American Pentimento: The Invention of Indians and the Pursuit of Riches*. Minneapolis: University of Minnesota Press, 2001.

———. "'Are These Not Also Men?': The Indians' Humanity and Capacity for Spanish Civilization." *Journal of Latin American Studies* 25 (1993): 629–652.

———. *Ceremonies of Possession in Europe's Conquest of the New World, 1492–1640*. Cambridge: Cambridge University Press, 1995.

Slater, T. "Betting." In *The Catholic Encyclopedia*, ed. Charles G. Herberman, 2:595–596. New York: Robert Appleton Co., 1909.

Smith, Hilary Dansey. *Preaching in the Spanish Golden Age: A Study of Some Preachers of the Reign of Philip III*. Oxford: Oxford University Press, 1978.

Sommerville, John C. "Religious Faith, Doubt and Atheism." *Past and Present* 128 (August 1990): 152–155.

Soufas, Teresa S. "The Gendered Context of Melancholy for Spanish Golden Age Women Writers." In *Spanish Women in the Golden Age: Images and Realities*, ed. Magdalena S. Sánchez and Alain Saint-Saëns, 171–184. Westport, CT: Greenwood Press, 1996.

Stearns, Carol Z. "'Lord Help Me Walk Humbly': Anger and Sadness in England and America, 1570–1750." In *Emotion and Social Change: Toward a New Psychohistory*, ed. Carol Z. Stearns and Peter N. Stearns, 39–68. New York: Holmes and Meier, 1988.

Stern, Steve J. "The Age of Andean Insurrection, 1742–1782: A Reappraisal." In *Resistance, Rebellion, and Consciousness in the Andean Peasant World, 18th to 20th Centuries*, ed. Steve J. Stern, 34–93. Madison: University of Wisconsin Press, 1987.

———. *The Secret History of Gender: Women, Men and Power in Late Colonial Mexico*. Chapel Hill: University of North Carolina Press, 1995.

———. "The Social Significance of Judicial Institutions in an Exploitative Society: Huamanga, Peru, 1570–1640." In *The Inca and Aztec States, 1400–1800: Anthropology and History*, ed. George A. Collier, Renato I. Rosaldo, and John D. Wirth, 289–317. New York: Academic Press, 1982.

Suárez Argüello, Clara Elena. *Camino real y carrera larga: La arriería en la Nueva España durante el siglo xviii*. Mexico City: CIESAS, 1997.

Sullivan, John Joseph. "Un diálogo sobre la congregación en Tlaxcala." *Colonial Latin American Review* 8:1 (June 1999): 35–59.

Super, John C. "Miguel Hernández: Master of Mule Trains." In *Struggle and Survival in Colonial America*, ed. David G. Sweet and Gary B. Nash. Berkeley: University of California Press, 1981.

Sutton-Smith, Brian. *The Ambiguity of Play*. Cambridge, MA: Harvard University Press, 1997.

Tardieu, Jean-Pierre. *L'église et les noirs au Perou, xvie et xviie siècles*. Vol. 1. Paris: L'Harmattan, 1993.

———. "Les principales structures administratives espagnoles de la traite des Noirs vers les Indes Occidentales." *Caravelle* 37 (1981): 51–84.

Tavárez, David. "Naming the Trinity: From Ideologies of Translation to Dialectics of Reception in Colonial Nahua Texts, 1547–1771." *Colonial Latin American Review* 9:1 (2000): 21–47.

Taylor, William B. *Drinking, Homicide, and Rebellion in Colonial Mexican Villages*. Stanford, CA: Stanford University Press, 1979.

Temkin, Owsei. *Galenism: Rise and Decline of a Medical Philosophy*. Ithaca, NY: Cornell University Press, 1973.

Thomas, Keith. Introduction to *A Cultural History of Gestures*, ed. Jan Bremmer and Herman Roodenburg. Ithaca, NY: Cornell University Press, 1991.

———. *Religion and the Decline of Magic: Studies in Popular Beliefs in Sixteenth and Seventeenth Century England*. New York: Pantheon Books, 1974.

Thornton, John. *Africa and Africans in the Making of the Atlantic World, 1400–1680*. Cambridge: Cambridge University Press, 1992.

Todorov, Tzvetan. *The Conquest of America: The Question of the Other*. New York: Harper and Row, 1984.

Torre Villar, Ernesto de la. *Las congregaciones de los pueblos de indios: Fase terminal; Aprobaciones y rectificaciones*. Mexico City: Universidad Nacional Autónoma de México, 1995.

Trexler, Richard. "Aztec Priests for Christian Altars: The Theory and Practice of Reverence in New Spain." *Church and Community, 1200–1600: Studies in the History of Florence and New Spain*, ed. Richard Trexler, 175–196. Rome: Edizioni di Storia e Letteratura, 1987.

Valdés, Dennis. "The Decline of Slavery in Mexico." *The Americas* 44:22 (October 1987): 167–194.

Van Deusen, Nancy. *Between the Sacred and the Worldly: The Cultural and Institutional Practice of Recogimiento among Women in Colonial Lima*. Stanford, CA: Stanford University Press, 2001.

Van Young, Eric. *The Other Rebellion: Popular Violence, Ideology, and the Mexican*

Struggle for Independence, 1810–1821. Stanford, CA: Stanford University Press, 2001.

Vila Vilar, Enriqueta. *Hispanoamérica y el comercio de esclavos: Los asientos portugueses*. Seville: Escuela de Estudios Hispanoamericanos, 1977.

Villa-Flores, Javier. "Inquisition, Spanish America." *Iberia and the Americas*, ed. J. Michael Francis, 590–598. Santa Barbara, CA: ABC-CLIO, 2005.

———. "Talking through the Chest: Divination and Ventriloquism among African Slave Women in Seventeenth-Century Mexico." *Colonial Latin American Review* 14:2 (December 2005): 299–321.

———. "Voices from a Living Hell: Slavery, Death, and Salvation in a Mexican Obraje." In *Local Religion in Colonial Mexico*, ed. Martin Nesvig. Albuquerque: University of New Mexico Press, 2005.

Vinson, Ben, III. *Bearing Arms for His Majesty: The Free-Colored Militia in Colonial Mexico*. Stanford, CA: Stanford University Press, 2001.

Viqueira Albán, Juan Pedro. *Propriety and Permissiveness in Bourbon Mexico*. Trans. Sonya Lipsett-Rivera and Sergio Rivera Ayala. Wilmington, DE: Scholarly Resources, 1999.

Viswanathan, Gauri. "Blasphemy and Heresy: The Modernist Challenge." *Comparative Studies in Society and History* 37:2 (1995): 199–213.

Voekel, Pamela. *Alone before God: The Religious Origins of Modernity in Mexico City*. Durham, NC: Duke University Press, 2002.

———. "Peeing in the Palace: Bodily Resistance to Bourbon Reforms in Mexico City." *Journal of Historical Sociology* 5:2 (June 1992): 183–208.

Voloshinov, V. N. *Marxism and the Philosophy of Language*. Trans. Ladislav Matejka and L. R. Titunik. Cambridge, MA: Harvard University Press, 1996.

Vossler, Karl. *Algunos caracteres de la cultura española*. Trans. Carlos Clavería. Madrid: Espasa-Calpe, 1962.

Walsham, Alexandra. *Providence in Early Modern England*. Oxford: Oxford University Press, 1999.

Watts, Sheldon J. *A Social History of Western Europe, 1456–1720: Tensions and Solidarities among Rural People*. London: Hutchinson University Library, 1984.

Weckmann, Luis. *The Medieval Heritage of Mexico*. Trans. Frances M. Lopez-Morillas. New York: Fordham University Press, 1992 [1983].

West, Candace, and Don H. Zimmerman. "Doing Gender." In *The Gendered Society Reader*, ed. Michael S. Kimmel, with Amy Aronson, 131–150. New York: Oxford University Press, 2000.

Willis, Paul. "Masculinity and Factory Labor." In *Culture and Society: Contemporary Debates*, ed. Jeffrey C. Alexander and Steven Seidman, 183–198. Cambridge: Cambridge University Press, 1990.

Wilson, Peter J. "Filcher of Good Names: An Enquiry into Anthropology and Gossip." *Man*, new ser., 9:1 (March 1974): 93–102.

Wooton, David. "The Fear of God in Early Modern Political Theory." *Canadian Historical Association Historical Papers* 17 (1983): 56–79.

Young Gregg, Joan. *Devils, Women, and Jews: Reflections of the Other in Medieval Sermon Stories*. Albany: State University of New York Press, 1997.

Zavala, Silvio. *The Defense of Human Rights in Latin America: Sixteenth to Eighteenth Centuries*. Belgium: UNESCO, 1964.

Zubillaga, Félix. *Historia de la iglesia en la América Española*. Vol. 1. Madrid: Editorial Católica, 1965.

Index

audience, importance: for blasphemy,
7, 8, 36, 39, 40, 74, 75, 76, 90, 96,
137–40, 149, 152–53; for gestures,
94, 96
Audiencia, 12–13, 85, 86, 138, 160n38,
191n81
Augustine, St.: on blasphemy, 9; on
casting lots, 88; on Donatists, 28
Augustinians, 40, 44
Austin, John L., 137, 158n15
Avila, Nicolás de, 82
Ayala, Pedro de, 119
Aymon d'Auxerre, 9
Azpilcueta, Martín de, 163n21
Azpita, Juan de, 52–53

Barbosa, Francisco, 91–92
Bateson, Gregory, 125, 184n53
Bautista, Juan, 127, 128
Bautista, Marcos, 138, 140–41
Bazán, Nicolás, 127–28
Bazán de Albornoz, Francisco, 145
Bennett, Herman L., 147
Benveniste, Émile, 155, 160n50
Betanzos, Domingo de, 37, 38, 39,
46–48, 86
Betanzos, Marcos de, 67–68
Biamonte, Bernardo de, 3–4
Bible passages: Acts 1:26, 88;
Apocalypse 16:9, 27, 82; Colossians
3:5, 30, 165n45; Deuteronomy
9 and 12, 28; Ecclesiasticus
10:8, 161n2; Ezekiel 20:27, 23; 1
Chronicles 24:5, 88; 1 Corinthians
11:1, 35; 1 Corinthians 14:34–35,
181n9; 1 Samuel 2:30, 20, 24,
162n16; 1 Samuel 10:17, 88; 1
Timothy 2:11–12, 181; James 3:2,
41; John 19:5, 173n97; Leviticus
16:8, 88; 24:11, 7; 24:15–16, 13;

Luke 1:9, 88; Mark 7:21–23,
159n33; Matthew 15:20, 159n33;
Nehemiah 11:1, 88; Numbers
26:52–56, 88; Proverbs 16:33, 77,
89; Proverbs 18:21, 44, 81; Romans
2:22–26:, 20, 27, 32; Romans 6:20–
22, 186n18; 2 Kings 19:14–16,
163n27
blasphemy. *See* attitudes toward
blasphemy; motivation for
blasphemy
Bohórquez, Martos de, 54, 77
Boose, Lynda E., 108
Bourdieu, Pierre, 19, 75
Boyer, Richard, 59, 170n55
bozales, 132, 185n12

Cabantous, Alain, 76
Caillois, Roger, 102
Cano, Melchor, 163n21, 178n61
canon law: on blasphemy, 12–14;
on gambling, 78–79, 86–87; on
marriage, 55
Cardano, Gerolamo, 98, 174n5
Carranco, Francisco, 65, 67, 70, 77
Carranza, Bartolomé de, 163n21
Carrillo, Gaspar de, 176n35
Carrión, Alonso de, 89–90, 99, 178n60
Cartagena de Indias, 186n15;
Inquisition at, 154
Casafuerte, Marquées de, 101
Casarrubias, María, 55–56
Castejón, Francisco, 71, 172n95
Castillo de Bobadilla, Jerónimo, 86,
176n31
Castro, Gabriel de, 134, 139
Castro, Pascual de, 68–69
Catherine, St., 116–17
Cerda y Aragón, Tomás Antonio
Manrique de la, 122

136, 137, 141, 144–45, 146–47,
149; to resist confinement in
recogimientos, 120, 121–25, 126,
149; to retrieve self-esteem, 90, 96,
102–3, 131–32. *See also* attitudes
toward blasphemy
Motolinía, Toribio de, 38, 162n13
Moya de Contreras, Pedro, 6, 64
mulattoes, 86, 101, 125, 129, 132, 145,
190n79
muleteers, 18, 38, 40, 58–62, 75,
171n62
Muslims, 4–5, 25–26, 28, 164n34

natural law, 21, 25–26
Nexapa, 51
Norton, Mary Beth, 120
Núñez, Diego, 47–48
Núñez, Pedro, 67–68

Oaxaca, 31, 39, 50, 78, 96, 106;
See Antequera, Guajolotitlán,
Huatulco, Nexapa
obrajes, 65, 66, 134, 135–36, 138, 139;
slaves in, 127–28, 132, 133, 143,
145–46, 185n14
Ometochzin, Carlos, 6, 31
Ortega y Montañez, Juan de, 57
Ovando, Juan de, 164n42

Pagden, Anthony, 161n2, 162n19
Palacios Rubios, Juan López de,
164n34
Palafox, Juan de, 79, 82, 176n38
Palmer, Colin, 144
papacy: Alexander VI, 21; Clement
IV, 14; *Exponi nobis/Omnímoda,*
6; Gregory IX, 13, 41, 108; *Inter
Caetera,* 21; Julius III, 15; Leo X,
13; Pius IV, 44; Pius V, 13–14; and

Spanish colonialism, 21, 25, 28, 29,
161n3
Patterson, Orlando, 129, 135
Paul, St., 31–32; on blasphemy, 20, 27,
29, 30, 164n32; on enslavement to
God, 132, 186n18; on imitation of
Christ, 35; on women, 107, 181n9
Peña, Francisco, 152, 192n7
Peralta, Alonso de, 51, 55, 66, 68, 70
Pérez, Hernán, 61–62
Pérez de Barcia, Domingo, 121–22, 123
Pérez-Mallaína, Pablo E., 63, 68
Pérez Rebolledo, Francisco, 66–67
Perry, Elizabeth, 125
Peru, 25, 186n15; Lima Inquisition,
154, 185n12, 189n65
Peter, St., 3, 57, 93
Philip II, 5, 6, 31
Philip IV, 70
Philippines, 44, 58, 68–69, 71, 122,
191n88
Pius IV, 44
Pius V, 13–14
Porras, Juan de, 89–90, 98–99
Portillo, Esteban de, 92
Portugal: relations with Spain, 5,
184n7, 190n79; sailors from, 63,
65–66; slave trade of, 128
Protestantism, 4, 6, 174n11, 176n40
providentialism: vs. chance, 77, 78, 88,
102–3, 176nn39, 40; and gambling,
18, 76, 77–78, 88–93, 102–3; and
Spanish colonialism, 4–5, 28,
35–36, 148, 153
provisores, 13, 39, 55, 56, 61, 96, 120,
176n33
Puebla, 39, 78, 106, 111, 130, 132, 134,
138, 139–40, 145
Pullo, Gerónimo, 63–64
punishment for blasphemy:

About the Author

Javier Villa-Flores is an assistant professor in the Department of History and the Latin American and Latino Studies Program at the University of Illinois at Chicago. He received his doctorate in Latin American history from the University of California, San Diego, and an undergraduate degree in sociology from the Universidad de Guadalajara in Mexico. In addition to numerous journal articles and book chapters, he is the author of *Carlo Ginzburg: El historiador como teórico*.